Cathkin Peak

Monk's Cowl

Cathedral Peak

The Bell

Mnweni Needles

Mnweni Cutback

Ross Osborn fell here

Amphitheatre Wall

Christensen's body found here

Tugela Falls

Position of Hut

The Gully

Cave

Chain Ladder

DRAGON'S WRATH

Come not between the dragon and his wrath

Shakespeare: *King Lear*

DRAGON'S WRATH

Drakensberg Climbs, Accidents and Rescues

R. O. Pearse
James Byrom

M

ISBN 0 86954 269 9

First edition, first impression 1986

Published by
Macmillan South Africa (Publishers) (Pty) Ltd
P O Box 31487, Braamfontein, 2017
Johannesburg

Associated companies throughout the world

Cover design by Graphicor (Pty) Ltd
Maps by Designaline (Pty) Ltd
Set in 11 on 13 pt Plantin
by Unifoto (Pty) Ltd, Cape Town
Printed and bound by Printpak Books, Cape Town

*Dedicated to all those
in the Natal Mountain Club
who are ready to pledge
life itself in the service of life*

Far down in the valley the wind arose. It whispered softly in the long grass, and the leaves of the aged yellowwood beside the pool stirred and trembled. Then it suddenly leapt across the valley, gathering speed and strength as it climbed the gaunt spurs of the Drakensberg, until it stabbed the summit and roared across the high plains of Lesotho.

And as it came it sang its old immemorial song, ageless, timeless. It sang of the rock-girt peaks and of the snows, of rain-meshed hills and of dreaming valleys. It sang of the clouds as they wrapped themselves around the high peaks in the blue of twilight, and it sang of the silence . . . and the loneliness . . . ; of the emptiness, and of the star-studded night. It sang of the men who came to the high places, who loved with a passionate love the loneliness and the silence and the brooding menace of toppling peaks.

And it sang of the wrath of the Dragon: the Dragon of the Dragon Mountains; the Dragon of the ancient tale told by the old men of the Amangwane as they sat in the kraals of Dukuza and in the far valleys of the Mnweni. The old ones told how the Dragon, in his wrath, claimed a human life each year from those who ventured into his grim lair.

It sang also of the men who were ready to measure themselves as men against the wrath of the Dragon. It sang of the clenched fear of the cragsman poised over the bottomless abyss, and of those who were ready to pledge life itself in the service of life. And it sang of the heart-warming comradeship of the climbers of long ago, some of whose voices are now stilled for ever, but whose stories are told in the pages of this book.

Preface

"Please come and see me when next you are up this way," wrote R. O. Pearse. "I have an idea for a book." I drove from Durban to see him that weekend.

The idea was just a germ when we sat down to talk in the sun on the front lawn of his mountain home. Later, when the sun dipped behind the lofty peaks of Champagne Castle and Cathkin, the chilling shadow of the peaks sent us indoors to continue our discussion beside a crackling fire. Gradually the idea took shape. We would write about the people of the Drakensberg, about those who, for many different reasons, walked and climbed in the mountains, and for just as many reasons created the triumphs, dramas, mysteries and tragedies that are part of the great Drakensberg saga.

Some stories have been written before. Many have not. Many have changed with repeated tellings and have become legends, the truth being known only to the cliffs and crags. Research has thrown new light on some events and those stories have to be rewritten for the record.

But in the tragedies always there is the other facet, stories of selflessness and concern, of compassion, of courage and steadfast determination. There have been times when we have looked up in awe at those rescuers on the peaks and wondered what point of danger was too dangerous, what risk too great, what price too high to attempt to save a life? These things, we feel, are worth recording.

In researching the tragedies of the Drakensberg, I took as my guide a passage from Reg Pearse's *Barrier of Spears*. He wrote: "Why do men climb mountains? Why are they so eager to accept the challenge of the high peaks? When George Mallory, of Everest fame, was asked that question, he replied 'Because they are there'. This is no evasion of the question. Those who have known the silence of high places, the beauty of snow-girt peaks, good fellowship round the camp fire, night bivouacs under the stars, the long tramp home in the evening light after a day on the hills, will know that there is more in that short answer than mere evasion. It *is* because the mountains are there – steadfast, immutable, holding their pools of blue light between banks of drifting cloud, the air sweet with the scent of flowers. They belong to the world of cloud and wind and open skies. The mountains hold peace, and fulfilment, and healing. When men climb mountains they go in search of themselves. They seek mastery over self, mastery over their fears, a greater self-knowledge, a deeper sensitivity to the sheer joy of being alive. They seek a beauty that is not of this world. Their motives are essentially personal. The mountaineer finds a challenge there that is both physical, mental and spiritual. And the fact that death is often at his elbow is but a heightened joy, for danger is the salt of life. When you visit the margins of death you are more conscious of life, and life takes on a sharpness, an intensity, a clarity that you will find nowhere else. Yes, men climb mountains because they *are* there."

I once heard somebody berating a reporter because the newspaper for which he worked had published the details of a tragedy. His reply, too, was not an evasion. "It happened," he said. In the details could be the lesson to prevent another tragedy.

And so I came away from the meeting with my assignment. For more than four years I sought out people and events – while Reg Pearse spent his time writing his book *Joseph Baynes.*

Today the assignment is complete and we have teamed up in a partnership which I have found stimulating and interesting. This book is the result.

J. B.
Westville
Natal

"Great things are done when men and mountains meet," wrote William Blake, and this is a book about mountains and men. The mountains are the Drakensberg, on the western borders of Natal, and the men are simple men, like you and me. But they are men to whom came the supreme challenge of life, the challenge to conquer fear. Some failed. Some succeeded, but most were just ordinary men (and women), who faced the ultimate test, survived, and quietly went their way. Some died. But all have a story to tell, and we believe these stories should be preserved and told. For they are stories of matchless courage and endurance, stories that enhance the stature of humanity and add colour to the richness of life. Some of these stories have been told before, and some, over the years, have gathered inaccuracies. Some are new. We have tried to tell an ungarnished tale. Only you, the reader, can say whether the tale has been worth the telling.

The book is the work of two men who know and love the mountains, myself and James Byrom. When a book is co-authored the reader is always curious to know how the partnership worked. Briefly, the essential research work was undertaken by James, while I did the bulk of the writing. But there was a good deal of overlapping. The one would supplement, and correct, the work of the other. We can only say that it has been a happy partnership and we can only hope that you the reader will have as much pleasure in the reading of it as we had in the writing of it. Occasionally the first personal pronoun is used. Unless otherwise stated it must be assumed in these cases that Reg Pearse is speaking.

From this book it must not be inferred that the Drakensberg is a dangerous place for your ordinary tourist. Practically all the accidents and emergencies that are described in this book took place in the High Berg, where the tourist rarely goes. In the pleasant hills of the Little Berg, where all the hotels and caravan parks are situated, we can recall only a handful of fatal accidents, far fewer, statistically, than in large cities like Johannesburg, Durban or Cape Town. Even on the summit accidents need not happen, providing a few simple precautions are taken. It is part of the object of this book to pinpoint and examine these accidents, find out how they happened, and suggest ways of avoiding them.

R. O. P.
"Emkhizweni"
Winterton

Acknowledgements

It would have been impossible to write a book such as this without the active help of a host of people who were willing to share with us their knowledge and experience. The ready response of these people to our appeals for help has warmed our hearts, and we are deeply grateful to them all. We hope the list which follows is full, but if any have been left out we can only offer our apologies and assure them that they still have our gratitude. Their omission has been completely inadvertent.

First of all are those who have actually figured in some of the epic stories of courage and hardihood we recount in these pages. Of these we are particularly grateful to Doyle Liebenberg, Brian Godbold, Tony Maddison, Peter Newman, Bill Barnes, Mike Kruger, Ephney l'Hoest, Gunter Stein, Mrs Joy Halliday (née Surgeon), Mrs Valerie O'Neill (née Parker), Mrs Gillian Earle (née Bettle), Bob Hining, Harold Corbett, Malcolm Moor, Miles Mattson, Bill Trauseld and Dick Reed. We also thank John Russel-Boulton, Trevor Hornby of the Natal Parks Board, Major Neall Ellis of the SAAF and Mrs Joyce Catlett. Martin Winter, veteran climber and leader of many mountain rescues, even allowed us access to his five priceless diaries, a rare privilege which we deeply appreciate.

The collection and preparation of the various photographs was a mammoth task, and here we have to express our gratitude to Dave Osborne (who went to great trouble to take many of the photographs), John Hone, Arthur Bowland, Roy Gooden, Brian Godbold, Malcolm Pearse, Peter Newman, John McLeod, Mrs Muriel Zonneveld, Mrs J. B. Osborn, Mr and Mrs M. G. E. Schaeffer and Mr Cyril Rennie, PRO of the Royal Natal National Park Hotel, and the hotel management generally. Colour pictures (except two snake pictures) are by author Reg Pearse and his son Malcolm. Black and white scenic pictures are by Malcolm Pearse and Dave Osborne.

Others who helped in the collection of material are Messrs Pagan, Osborne & Grace of Cupar, Scotland, Mrs Leila Barnes, Kenneth Franklin, Mrs Margie Osborne, and Mr C. Adkins. Dr George Hughes and Dr O. Bourquin of the Natal Parks Board, and Johan Marais, former curator of the Transvaal Snake Park, were kind enough to help us with the chapter on snakes and snakebite. We are also grateful for permission to use John Marais' photographs of the Puff-adder and Rinkals, opposite p. 121. Mrs Barbara Versveld gave us invaluable information on the early life of her brother Dick Barry, and Malcolm Pearse helped in ways too numerous to mention.

Mrs Ethel Thomson gave us invaluable information regarding her late husband, George; Dr Graham Hukins also helped with the chapter on snakes, and acted as our consultant on all medical matters; and Mrs Pat Harries gave us details of the lightning tragedy of 21 December 1979, while Bob Beck and Mrs Elodie Wiid (née de la Harpe) gave us similar details of the Mont-aux-Sources lightning tragedy of December 1932.

The Editors of the *Daily News* and *Natal Mercury* allowed us access to the extensive files in their libraries, and from these we have been able to compile the most complete record of Natal Drakensberg rescues. The archives of these newspapers also contain some of the photographs we have been able to reproduce. We are also grateful to the Editors of the *Daily News*, *Natal Mercury*, *Sunday Tribune*, *Sunday Times* and *Natal Witness* for permission to quote from their newspapers.

We are particularly grateful to the men of the SAAF helicopter squadrons based in Durban, and their officers, for advice in all matters connected with air rescue work. Their assistance and advice have been invaluable.

There are many others who have been generous in their help, but whom we can hardly mention by name because, in the final analysis, we found we could not use the information they gave us. We remind all such of the words of the Prophet in Ecclesiastes, that though they have left no name behind, they are not forgotten! We, certainly, are grateful.

The book was written on a small home computer word-processor, and our sincere thanks are due to Baden Hall and Chris Kenward for introducing us to the mysteries of the system and for the loan of certain items of equipment.

We are deeply grateful to our publishers for the meticulous care they have put into the publication of this book, for their advice, and for the understanding and tolerance they have shown to us, the authors, at all times. It has been a pleasure working with them, and we would particularly like to mention Basil van Rooyen, the Editorial Director, and Mrs Marina Pearson, the Publishing Services Manager.

Finally, perhaps most important of all, our wives! Uncomplainingly, they have endured night after night while their husbands were either locked together in conference or hammering away on typewriter or word-processor. They little know how grateful we are for their patience and their forbearance. Eileen and Edith, a warm and very sincere "thank you!"

Contents

Part I

THE EARLY CLIMBERS

Bliss was it in that dawn to be alive,
But to be young was very heaven

Wordsworth: *The Prelude*

The early years in the Natal Drakensberg are shrouded in mystery. We do not even know how, when or by whom the name was bestowed. The first white men to look upon the Drakensberg were almost certainly the Portuguese. On 24 March 1593 a Portuguese vessel, the Santo Alberto, was wrecked on the Transkei coast. The survivors, on their long trek to Lourenço Marques (the present Maputo) decided to travel inland rather than along the usual coastal route. One day in May, when they were somewhere in the midlands of Natal, they reported seeing, away to the west, a great range of snow-covered mountains. These could have been none other than the Drakensberg.

The first record we have of any white men actually visiting the Drakensberg is the Kommissie Trek of 1834. In that year Piet Uys led a party of Cape farmers up to Natal, travelling through the Transkei and using Dr Andrew Smith's 1832 coast route. But on their return they travelled much further inland, through the present Underberg and Himeville areas, crossing the upper reaches of the Umkomaas, the Umzimkulu and the Umzimvubu Rivers. They almost certainly explored the foothills and possibly even climbed to the summit of the Drakensberg.

The first recorded white men to tread the summit of the Drakensberg were the Reverends Arbousset and Daumas, two French missionaries, who, in April 1836, two years after the Kommissie Trek and eighteen months before the Voortrekkers reached the Drakensberg, gazed down in awe at the stupendous, battlemented precipices of the Amphitheatre. Subsequent to that date, as the plains of Natal began to fill up with the advancing Voortrekkers and the new settlers from the British Isles, there must have been many expeditions into the foothills of the Drakensberg of which we have no record; hunting parties with their wagons and their tents who gazed in breathless wonder at this new and exciting world of towering peaks and richly wooded valleys that lay so tantalisingly before them.

Later, officers from the various British regiments quartered at Harrismith, Ladysmith, Estcourt and further south would make weekend trips into the mountains, pitting their courage and their skill in vain attempts to scale the terrifying heights that filled their wondering eyes. We have records of some of these attempts.

In the next two chapters we tell the stories of the first major recorded climbs in the Drakensberg, and of a remarkable summit trek, the second (and longest) summit trek of those days of which we have a record. The third chapter records a Drakensberg first of nearly 50 years ago, remarkable for the light it throws on early climbs, and which, we feel, should not be allowed to lie forgotten in the faded records of the past.

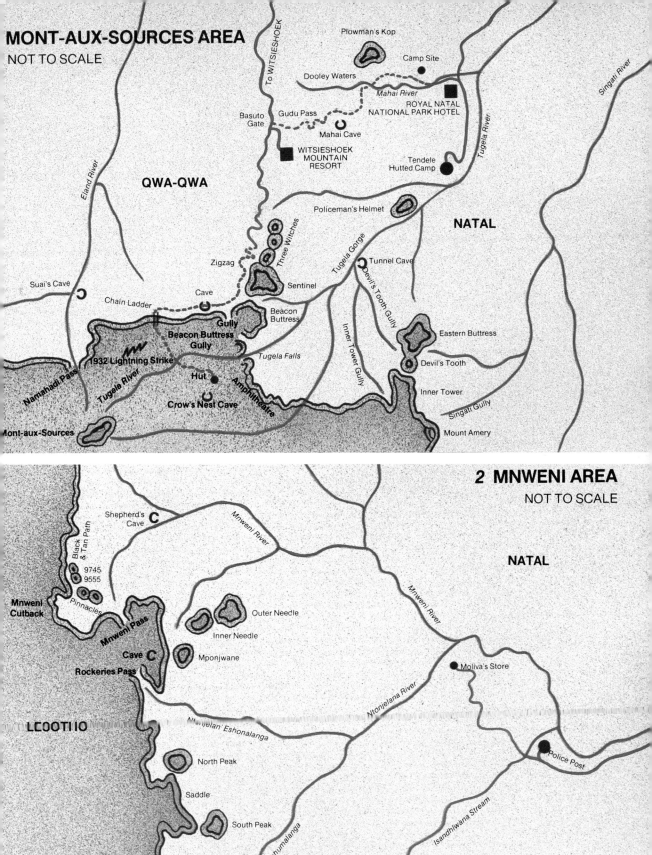

MONT-AUX-SOURCES AREA
NOT TO SCALE

Plowman's Kop

Camp Site

To WITSIESHOEK

Dooley Waters

Mahai River

Singati River

Basuto Gate

Gudu Pass

ROYAL NATAL
NATIONAL PARK HOTEL

Mahai Cave

WITSIESHOEK
MOUNTAIN
RESORT

Tugela River

Tendele
Hutted Camp

Eland River

QWA-QWA

Policeman's Helmet

NATAL

Three Witches

Tugela Gorge

Tunnel Cave

Zigzag

Devil's Tooth Gully

Sentinel

Suai's Cave

Chain Ladder

Cave

Beacon Buttress

Inner Tower Gully

Eastern Buttress

Gully

Beacon Buttress
Gully

Devil's Tooth

1932 Lightning Strike

Tugela Falls

Hut

Namahadi Pass

Tugela River

Inner Tower

Crow's Nest Cave

Amphitheatre

Singati Gully

Mont-aux-Sources

Mount Amery

2 MNWENI AREA
NOT TO SCALE

Shepherd's
Cave

Mnweni River

NATAL

Black
& Tan Path

9745
9555

Mnweni River

Mnweni
Cutback

Pinnacles

Outer Needle

Mnweni Pass

Inner Needle

Cave

Mponjwane

Rockeries Pass

Moliva's Store

Ntonjelana River

LESOTHO

Ntonjelan' Eshonalanga

North Peak

Police Post

Saddle

Isandhlwana Stream

South Peak

Ntonjelan Ephumalanga

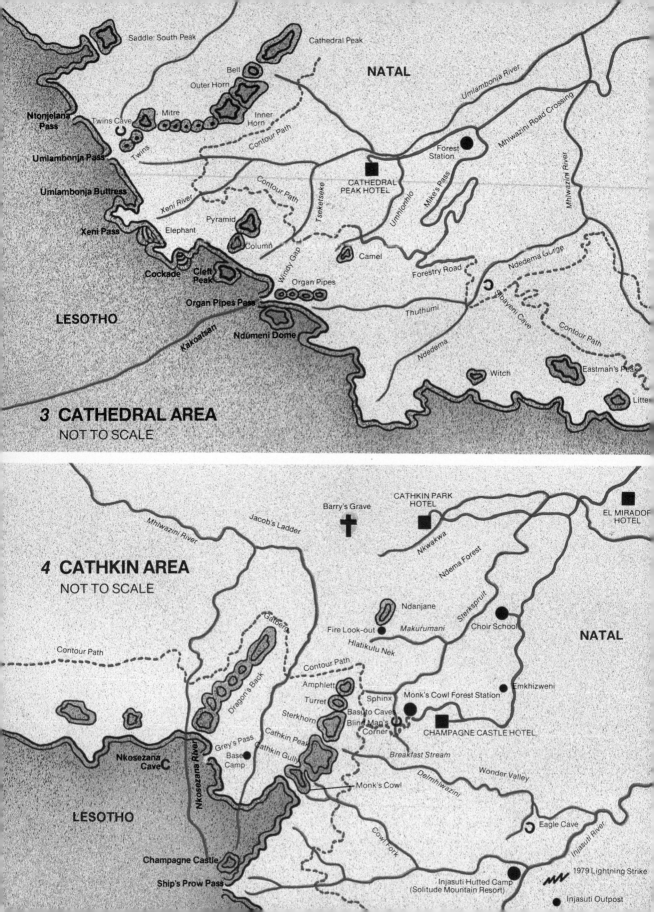

3 CATHEDRAL AREA
NOT TO SCALE

Saddle: South Peak
Cathedral Peak
NATAL
Bell
Outer Horn
Mitre
Inner Horn
Ntonjelana Pass
Twins Cave
Umlambonja River
Mhlwazini Road Crossing
Contour Path
Forest Station
Umlambonja Pass
Twins
Mike's Pass
Umlambonja Buttress
Xeni River
Contour Path
CATHEDRAL PEAK HOTEL
Umhlonhlo
Mhlwazini River
Pyramid
Xeni Pass
Elephant
Column
Tseketseke
Camel
Cockade
Cleft Peak
Windy Gap
Organ Pipes
Forestry Road
Ndedema Gorge
LESOTHO
Organ Pipes Pass
Ndumeni Dome
Kakoatsan
Thuthumi
Sbayeni Cave
Contour Path
Ndedema
Ndedema
Witch
Eastman's Peak
Litter

4 CATHKIN AREA
NOT TO SCALE

Mhlwazini River
Jacob's Ladder
Barry's Grave
CATHKIN PARK HOTEL
EL MIRADOR HOTEL
Nkwakwa
Ndema Forest
Contour Path
Galbero
Ndanjane
Sterkspruit
Choir School
NATAL
Fire Look-out
Makurumani
Hlatikulu Nek
Contour Path
Dragon's Back
Contour Path
Amphlett
Emkhizweni
Turret
Sphinx
Monk's Cowl Forest Station
Sterkhorn
Basuto Caves
Nkosezana Cave
Grey's Pass
Cathkin Peak
Blind Man's Corner
Nkosezana River
Base Camp
Cathkin Gully
CHAMPAGNE CASTLE HOTEL
Breakfast Stream
Wonder Valley
Monk's Cowl
Delmhlwazini
LESOTHO
Cowl Fork
Eagle Cave
Champagne Castle
Injasuti River
Ship's Prow Pass
Injasuti Hutted Camp (Solitude Mountain Resort)
1979 Lightning Strike
Injasuti Outpost

1 Brigadier N. M. McLeod

"Ye'll have to hammer a good deal louder than that, mister, if it's the Old 'Un ye're wantin'," said the woman next door. "It is the Old 'Un yer wantin', is it?"

"Why, yes – Brigadier McLeod."

"That's 'im. Give the door a good hard whack. 'E's deaf as a dumb-nut."

The man at the door knocked more loudly, while his wife gazed around the neat garden, the lawns, and the roses.

"Best go inside, mister," said the woman from next door. "'E won't mind. Never 'ears a thing."

The old man was sitting quietly in a chair by the open window, in the sunlight, reading; a lock of white hair hung over his left eyebrow, and his eyes were bright and clear as wet stones.

"Good morning, sir. Brigadier McLeod?"

"Why, yes, and you're . . . ?"

"Symons, sir, Godfrey Symons★, and this is my wife Norah."

"Ah, yes! Yes, yes, of course. Mr Pearse told me you were coming – all the way from South Africa to bonny Scotland."

"Yes, sir, we're on a trip to England and the Continent, but we wanted to come up and have a chat with you about your famous climb, way back in 1910 – 65 years ago, isn't it? You were the first to climb Sentinel Peak, I believe."

"Oh, that! Yes, I was lucky. Climbed it with a fellow by the name of Wybergh."

"That's right. Would you care to tell us a little bit about it?"

The old man settled himself back comfortably in his chair. "Well," he began, "way back in 1908 I was sent out to Harrismith as a young subaltern in the 59th Battery, R.F.A. I was 25 at the time, and had just completed my training at Woolwich. I hadn't done much in the way of mountain climbing, but it wasn't

Lieut McLeod in regimental dress. The photograph was taken in 1913, three years after his famous climb.

★ Godfrey Symons is a well-known Natal Midlands farmer, noted ornithologist, wildlife photographer and mountaineer. He was a member of the four-man team that first photographed the Lammergeier in 1961.

long before some of us young chaps in the Battery became interested in the Drakensberg, especially in one of the highest points, the peak we called the Buttress. You call it the Sentinel today. [See map no. 1.]

"We used to ride out from Harrismith and stay at a little place called Rydal Mount, near Witsieshoek, run by a chap called Tom Casement. He had a brother, Roger – came to a sticky end a few years later, when he was hanged by the British as a traitor. One day in 1909 I got the idea of climbing the Buttress. Early in October of that year I went out with a Lieutenant Field, and we explored the top and reconnoitred the peak, but we weren't able to climb it. Next year I had my chance, and on 27 September I rode out to Rydal Mount, intending to climb the peak the next day, but Casement persuaded me to team up with a chap called W. J. Wybergh. He had reconnoitred the peak the previous year, like me, but he also had been unable to climb it as he lacked a companion. He happened to be staying at Rydal Mount when I arrived, so we agreed to team up together.

"I understand you fellows today go by car to just below the base of the final cliffs and only commence your climb at about 9 000 feet. In those days it was a much tougher proposition. We used to make our way up the valley of the Eland River, some miles to the west of the peak, at about the 5 500 feet level, and start our climb from there. We would sleep the night in Suai's Cave, and next day climb to the top. But look, why not take this letter. It will tell the story very much better than anything I could do at my age, after 65 years."

And out came a yellowed, faded letter.

My dear Father,

Very many thanks for your letter. I have just come back from the Mount of Sources where I have been climbing with a Mr Wybergh from the Rand. He is very deaf but has an accousticon with which he hears quite well even when riding in a gale of wind. He is a great politician and was a Member of Parliament and with his machine has found no difficulty in carrying on. I think he is deafer than you.

I have been on short leave and travelling about all the time. I went down to Durban and Port Shepstone. I left Port Shepstone on Monday morning 26 September, and arrived at Harrismith on Tuesday at midday and rode out to Witzieshoek that afternoon.

Wybergh was ready for an expedition to tackle the Buttress so we rode out to the Bushman's cave on Wednesday, 28 September. Slept the night in the cave and set off on foot on Thursday morning, 29 September,* at 8.

---

* The date has always been given in South African climbing circles as 5 October 1910. This is incorrect. It was 29 September 1910. Subsequent to the climb Wybergh had sent an account of it to the *Rand Daily Mail*. In it he said the climb had occurred "a fortnight ago". The account appeared in the *Rand Daily Mail* on 19 October, and it has always been assumed that Wybergh meant a fortnight before publication, i.e. 5 October. What Wybergh meant, however, was a fortnight before he wrote the account, i.e. 29 September.

Climbed a long steep ridge for about 3 000 feet, skirted round the base of the Buttress and found a place to commence our climb*.

With a few difficult places we found it much easier than we expected. It was thick mist all day so it did not give us the best of chances. With careful choosing of the way and Wybergh's great mountaineering experience we found quite an easy way up. We could not tell we were on top until we had walked all over it to find out if there was any more to climb, as the mist was so thick. We built our beacon right on the summit and where the cliff falls away sheer to the Tugela Gorge below.

The Buttress is the most imposing and formidable-looking peak of the whole Drakensberg and has been tried by many people I have met. They have all failed at the last krantz at the top, but we avoided that on our first ascent.

I went up a second time to try the krantz which several people told me was impossible. I had a very strenuous climb of about 60 feet up a smooth chimney** with no footholds and reached the top. This cleft will in future

---

* It was to the left of the "Notch", between Sentinel and Beacon Buttress as one faces the peak from the present chain ladder. They had elected to climb the south-west face of the peak.

** A chimney, in mountaineering terms, is not like a fireside chimney, entirely enclosed. It is a narrow crack, running down the rock face, wide enough for a human body to be inserted into it. It often provides the only way up a sheer rock face.

be known as "McLeod's Chimney". I will send you a cutting which will be in tomorrow's *Rand Daily Mail*.[1]

Mrs Wybergh wired the news off at once. It is really the first successful climb of any importance that has been done. There are lots of mountains that have been tried, but all have been unsuccessful. The height of the Buttress is about 11 000 feet.[2] I wish we had an aneroid as the heights of these places are very vague at present.

We descended to the cave again to sleep, and Friday morning (30 September) we rode up to the Goodoo Pass[3] It was very difficult going but the scenery is grander of the Tugela Gorge and the East Bastion of the Mount of Sources. We got back to Casement's about 7.30 after a strenuous day. Yesterday (1 October) as my leave was up I returned and feel I have made the most of my three weeks leave. At any rate it has not been expensive. It will now be awfully dull until we depart for India.[4]

"By the way," said the old man, "in my letter I forgot to tell my father that it was really a baboon that finally led us to the top. We had reached the final crux pitch, which had beaten so many previous climbers, and were faced with a sheer wall of cliff which it seemed impossible to climb. But I suddenly noticed a baboon clambering round a corner of the cliff. We followed it, and we suddenly found ourselves out on the western face of the peak, and on a steeply sloping ledge, which finally brought us out on top.

"Yes, it was a good climb," said the old man, reaching for his pipe, "but I climbed it twice again, you know, three times altogether. A couple of weeks after our first climb, just before we left for India, I was back again with Field and Lieut. J. L. Park (he was a descendant of Mungo Park, the explorer) and we climbed the peak together. Poor fellows, seven years later they were both dead, killed in Flanders. And then in 1912 I took my wife up, on our honeymoon. Yes, I got married in Durban, on 20 April 1912, and the day before the wedding we met Tom Casement in the street. He invited us up to Rydal Mount for the honeymoon, so, as we hadn't made any final plans, we accepted. We had a great time, revisiting my old haunts (immediately after my first climb I'd had two years in India with my regiment) and I took Irma up the Buttress, which in the meantime had been renamed Sentinel Peak. We even spent a night in the cave, which I think you call Crow's Nest Cave today. I'll never forget the sunrise on that second morning, one of the most magnificent sights I have ever seen. Far better than anything we ever saw on our great trek into Basutoland."

---

1. It appeared only on 19 October.
2. Actual height 10 385 ft (3 165 m).
3. Over Basuto Gate, site of the present Witsieshoek Mountain Resort.
4. Wybergh's account of the climb may be found in *Barrier of Spears* by R. O. Pearse (Howard Timmins, 1973), pp. 89 and 90, and in *The Natal Drakensberg* by D. P. Liebenberg (T. V. Bulpin, 1972), pp. 49 and 50.

"What was that?" asked Norah.

"Haven't you heard of our great trek?" said the old man. "Unknown country it was in those days. Saw a military map of it soon afterwards, published a few years before we attempted it, and part of the area was just a blank marked 'Very Wild and Little Known Country Infested by Wild Bushmen'. We trekked from Witsieshoek almost to Giant's Castle, and then across to a little place called Estcourt."

"Tell us about it," prompted Godfrey.

"Hold on a moment. I think I've got my diary somewhere. I'll have to refresh my memory a bit. Yes, here it is. Let's see . . . The first entry is dated Friday, 5 November 1909.

"We set off from Harrismith in a cape cart and six mules at two in the

The south-west face of Sentinel.
1. First route to summit
2. Top pitch around corner
3. McLeod's variation later the same day

5

morning. By 'we' I mean myself, a chap called Sankey (H. J., I think his initials were) and Dorni, my black servant. Sankey was a forestry officer, and had taken part in the London-Brighton road race before coming to South Africa.

"Our packs contained provisions for three days – 6 lb of chocolate, ½ lb of Grape Nuts, two small home-made loaves, one small tin of grated biltong and a piece of cheese. We also carried a small emergency supply of food for a possible fourth day. We didn't have sleeping bags in those days, not even blankets. We just slept out, but I did take an extra shirt and pair of pants, a light overcoat and a burberry cape for sleeping in, as we knew the nights would be cold.

"By 9.30 am we had reached Gray's Store at Witsieshoek, and after a cup of tea and some sandwiches, we set off for Suai's Cave, 16 miles away. [See map opposite.] Here we had lunch and a dip in the stream, and then set off for the summit, reaching the top, at 10 000 ft, soon after 7 pm.* It was bitterly cold, but we made some coffee, had supper, and turned in. We slept until midnight, but after that it was too cold to sleep. During the previous 24 hours we had driven 43 miles, walked 20 and climbed 6 000 ft.

"We set off at half-past four the next morning, still bitterly cold, and with all our night clothes still on. I shall never forget the grandeur of the scenery that early morning, with the great wall of the Amphitheatre on our left, and the dawn breaking over Eastern Buttress and Devil's Tooth (as you call them today). At half-past six we called a short halt for breakfast, and then on again, travelling steadily south, with Cathkin Peak, 24 miles off, in the distance.

"At one stage we saw a Basuto kraal up on the hillside. A fine strapping chap came down to meet us, and asked politely who we were and where we were going. He was obviously there to stop and report on any strangers who had ideas about possible prospecting for minerals.** When we explained that we were merely on a holiday walk, he went off to his kraal and brought us a large can of milk which we were delighted to have.

"When we reached the Mnweni area the country really did become wild and lonely. Dorni looked quite frightened. 'What are you going to do now, Basie?' he said. We realised that the country between us and Cathkin, along the escarpment edge, was quite impossible, so we decided to strike inland, along the Mopeli path.

"Here we were able to speed up our pace, and we walked hard until 6.30 pm, with a short halt at midday for lunch and a bathe in a mountain stream. During the afternoon the path had descended something like 2 000 feet, and at dusk we found a pleasant camping spot in a small kloof – a little damp, but at least out of the wind. We reckoned we had done 35 miles that day.

"The next day, our third, was Sunday. We had intended diverging to the right, to take in the Maletsunyane Falls, but we realised now that this was

---

* They went up the Namahadi Pass, the usual route to the summit in those days.
** This would be roughly the area of the present diamond mine, Letseng-la-Terae.

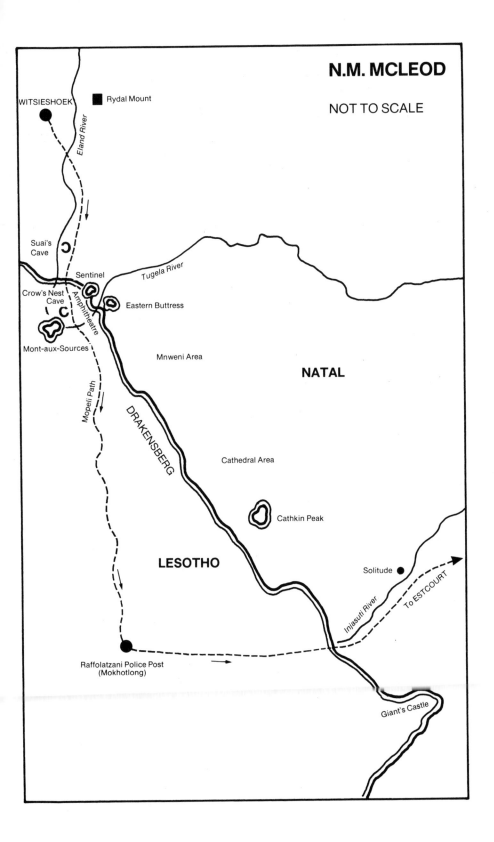

WITSIESHOEK

Rydal Mount

N.M. MCLEOD

NOT TO SCALE

Eland River

Suai's Cave

Sentinel

Tugela River

Crow's Nest Cave

Amphitheatre

Eastern Buttress

Mont-aux-Sources

Mopeli Path

DRAKENSBERG

Mnweni Area

NATAL

Cathedral Area

Cathkin Peak

LESOTHO

Solitude

Injasuti River

To ESTCOURT

Raffolatzani Police Post
(Mokhotlong)

Giant's Castle

7

impossible. We decided to head straight for the Raffolatzani Police Post.*

"Again we were off by 4.30 am, stepping it out at a good pace. We covered seven miles, in a narrow valley, before stopping for breakfast.

"During the morning we met several Basutos who were rather surprised to see us on foot, and were very amused at our packs. They told us we could not reach Raffolatzani Police Post that night, but might do so next morning if we travelled fast.

"The day was hot, and I remember it was at this point that we began to suffer from our feet. We pushed on hard, however, and finally called a halt at 7 pm after covering 33 miles. We found a small kraal on top of a hill, where an old man gave us some hot milk for a handful of tobacco. We slept well in the shelter of some giant rocks.

"Next morning (it was the King's birthday) we were off at dawn, reaching Raffolatzani Police Post at 6.45 am. Here we found two members of the Basuto Police, Aston and Marsh,** still in bed, but we routed them out and scrounged a fine breakfast of ham and bread from them. Here we were able to arrange for two policemen to accompany us as guides to the Cathkin Peak area.

"We set off at 9 am, climbing steadily up a long valley in the direction of the Drakensberg. Lunch was late that day, but we managed to fit in the usual bathe. At dusk, in a rocky pass, we halted, with 31 miles to our credit. Our supper that night was half a loaf of bread, a small spoonful of Grape Nuts and some chocolate.

"We were now approaching the Drakensberg, and the scenery became steadily grander and more spectacular. This was now our fifth day. We rose before it was light, and were on our way by 4 am, still climbing steadily. A short halt at 7 for breakfast, and then we pushed on over rough and stony ground swarming with rats. By 11 am we had reached the edge of the escarpment.

"Here, of course, the scenery was magnificent beyond telling – tremendous precipices, gorges, minarets, and far below, thousands of feet, the clouds floating in the clear mountain air. For an hour we walked along the edge until we came to the pass we were going to descend."

"Have you any idea where you were?" asked Godfrey.

"No, I'm afraid I don't. I do know, though, that after we had descended the pass we found ourselves in the valley of the Little Tugela, or Injasuti River."

"Probably Corner Pass," said Godfrey, "just south of the Injasuti Triplets."

"You could well be right," said the old man. "Before we descended the pass we had lunch – a crust of bread, chocolate and cheese – and at 1 pm we started down. I found this the toughest part of our trip. The pass had been blown up with dynamite to prevent cattle being driven up from Natal with tick fever, and

---

* The old name for the present Mokhotlong.
** Eighteen months earlier Sub-Inspector Marsh had taken part in the epic Natal/Basutoland Police Patrol from Giant's Castle to Mont-aux-Sources. See pp. 50 and 51 of *Barrier of Spears* by R. O. Pearse.

the descent, for something like 6 000 feet, was rough and dangerous.

"I remember I had one very narrow shave. Half a ton of loose rock came tumbling down on me, and I only just managed to save myself by leaping aside. The two Basutos brought their ponies down after us. How they did it, I just wouldn't know. At one point they hauled them down a sheer wall, 12 feet high. Then came a long, steep grassy descent, until at last we stood in the rocky bed of the Little Tugela River.

"By this time it was 3.30 pm. We were tired, our feet sore and swollen. We called a brief halt and finished the last of our supplies – some chocolate, a small hunk of cheese and some water. Then on again, scrambling and battling for miles down the rocky bed of the stream, with magnificent cliffs and forest-clad slopes on either side. At 6.15 pm we reached the small hut of a white man."

"'Solitude' or 'Compensation' almost certainly," said Godfrey.[1]

"The chap was nowhere to be seen, and the only thing we could find in the hut was an empty Quaker Oats packet. We decided to go on and try to make Conche's Store at the foot of Tabamhlope.[2] Fortunately our two Basuto guides had now caught up with us, and they lent us their ponies, on which we rode through rain and thick mist until 9.30 pm. We got completely lost in the dark. Even the Basuto guides had disappeared (we never saw them again), and eventually, tired out and hungry, we simply lay down in the wet grass and slept until dawn.

"Next morning, our sixth day, we woke cold and hungry, with the mist heavy around us. Dorni wasn't so bad. During the night he had killed and eaten a rock-rabbit, but we had had nothing. About 7 o'clock we found a kraal and were told that the store was miles behind us: we had bypassed it in the dark.[3] The nearest white man was a German missionary. He could speak no English, and we could speak no German, but he fed us royally on bread and butter and tea.

"He was a tiny little chap, with a waistcoat and tie, and very long hair, curled up at the back, and you could not see his face for beard. He did nothing but smoke foul-smelling cigars one after another. Everything in the way of furniture was covered with German texts. We heard afterwards that the old chap had five outstations, all within 10 miles of his own station, but in the five years he had been there he had not visited any of them.

"We stayed an hour, eating solidly the whole time, and then pushed on, for our time was running out. Six miles on we came to a small country hotel, just in time for lunch. Here we drank vast quantities of lime juice and shandy-gaff. We were very nearly at the end of our tether, and our feet were dreadful. Sankey's were in a particularly bad way, and Dorni said he was dead, so we gave him a large tot of gin.

---

1. The area of the present Injasuti Hutted Camp.
2. White Mountain Inn.
3. They had veered too far to the north.

The Injasuti valley, at the foot of the main Drakensberg, down which McLeod and Sankey hiked after descending the escarpment.

"After a magnificent lunch we tried to get a conveyance to take us to Estcourt, as we had to catch a train there at four o'clock next morning, but we had no luck. Mr Horner's ponies were all lame. We just had to walk.

"We started off at three o'clock, reached a store* on a branch line at four o'clock, had some tea and pushed on again. By that time we were nearly finished, and it took us five hours to do the last 10 miles to Estcourt. We got to an hotel, and promptly started on another magnificent feed. We had done 36 miles that day.

"At 3.30 am we heard a train and just managed to catch it. Breakfast at Ladysmith station at 7 am, another breakfast on the train at Van Reenen at 10 am, and at midday we were on parade at the Barracks in Harrismith, shaved, washed and in uniform!"**

---

* Possibly Moorleigh.

** A few days after the climb with Wybergh, Brigadier McLeod's regiment was ordered to India where he spent two years. On his way back, in April 1912, he married Irma in Durban. He served throughout World War I in Flanders and on the Western Front, ending up as Brigade Major in the 25th Division of the R.F.A. In 1918 he was gazetted Brevet Lieut. Colonel. In 1920 he was back in India, as Staff Officer, Southern Command. In 1934 he was appointed Officer Commanding British troops in Aden. He retired in 1939, but during World War II was Brigadier, commanding the Home Guard Defences in the North and East London areas. At the time of going to press Brigadier McLeod is still alive and living in a nursing home in Edinburgh.

2 The Stocker Brothers

On a pouring wet day, early in December 1887, a young English clergyman alighted from the train at Estcourt railway station (the line had only recently reached the town). He was the Rev. A. H. Stocker, and he had come to South Africa to visit his brother, F. R. Stocker, who was waiting for him at the station.

The first names of the brothers have been lost in time, but for the sake of easy reading of this story we propose to refer to the Rev. A. H. Stocker as Arthur and his brother as Frank.

Frank, then, had come out to Natal some years previously, and was managing the farm Wellington at Draycott, 20 km from Estcourt. After a brisk two-hour drive the brothers were home and the young minister was settling into his new home. He was to spend the next eight or nine months with his brother.

Forty-five kilometres away – a blue line on the horizon – were the beckoning Drakensberg mountains. Arthur had been a keen alpinist for several years, and Frank had already pitted himself against those immutable mountains. Two years previously, early in 1886, he had had a crack at the North Peak of Sterkhorn and had failed. It was not long before the brothers decided on a joint venture into what was then almost unknown territory.

But it was a wet season. After several abortive attempts, bogged down for weeks at a time in mountain caves, they decided to wait until the weather cleared. By early April the clouds had gone, the sky turned an enticing blue, and early on the morning of Tuesday, 24 April, with the dawn cool and blue, they set off. By the evening of 25 April they were camped, snug and warm in their little tent, within sound of the rippling waters of the Mhlwazini River (probably near the point where the present contour path crosses the river, below Hlatikulu Nek). They had decided to make Champagne Castle their first peak.

Champagne Castle, at 3 377 m (11 079 ft), is a rounded dome on the summit of the escarpment, behind Cathkin Peak and Monk's Cowl (see map no. 4). Although one of the highest mountains in the Drakensberg, it is not a particularly difficult climb if one uses the Grey's Pass route.

Jutting out at right angles from Champagne Castle is the minor Cathkin

11

Range. This consists of Monk's Cowl, Cathkin Peak, Sterkhorn, the Turret and Amphlett.

Next morning they were up early, and by 6.30 were on their way up the Mhlwazini River. Soon they had reached what we call today Base Camp, where the Keith Bush Mountain Hut used to stand. They were now directly beneath the final precipices of the escarpment.

From here the usual route today leads up and away to the right (west), ascending Grey's Pass (a narrow, rocky gully) to the summit. This route actually carries one away from the final summit of Champagne, to the right (north), but it is a comparatively easy climb. The Stockers obviously did not know of the Grey's Pass gully, for they decided to head straight for the peak, to the south, and scale the cliffs immediately facing Monk's Cowl. This is a very difficult climb, known today as the High Route, and seldom used. They certainly encountered some very stiff climbing, with several almost impossible gullies, sheer rock faces and ice-glazed rocks, but by two o'clock they were on the escarpment. They still, of course, had the rounded dome of Champagne Castle to reach (which they called "extremely dull and uninteresting") but by 2.30 pm they were at the top with a keen wind blowing. Their climb was over. Their aneroid barometer gave the height as 11 135 ft. The actual height is 3 377 m (11 079 ft).

They did not stay long on the summit, only ten minutes, for they still had to get back to their tent, hundreds of metres below. They set fire to the grass to announce their success to watchers down in the valley below, noted the view, which Arthur described as "the grandest I know anywhere – a lovely valley with four magnificent peaks at the upper end, two square blocks and two aiguilles lying to the north of Champagne Castle" (Dragon's Back), and by 2.40 pm were on their way again.

They decided to descend via Ship's Prow Pass, which they called Champagne Castle Pass and which they described as "the stoniest and most abominable gully we ever were in". Ship's Prow Pass is a deeply incised gully immediately to the south of Champagne Castle. The V is divided into two gullies by a narrow flange, like the prow of a ship: hence the name. These two gullies meet a few hundred metres below the summit to form the main gully.

The Stockers obviously had gone down the first of the two gullies which comprise the pass. If only they had gone a few metres further on they would have reached the second gully, much easier and more pleasant.

But it was now past three o'clock. Wearily they stumbled down the pass, and then headed north along the lower flank of Cathkin, heading for their tiny tent in the Mhlwazini valley. It grew darker, but soon the moon arose and shone frostily on the naked peaks. With blistered feet and aching muscles they kept on . . . and on . . . hour after hour, through a land of silvered shadows, until at last, at 10.20 pm, they came to the white gleam of their tent in the pale moonlight. Their long trek was over. They had been on their feet for 15 hours 50 minutes and climbed 1 525 m (5 000 ft).

Next month they were back in the mountains, with Sterkhorn as their goal this time.

Sterkhorn is part of the Cathkin chain, already mentioned, and is the triangular-shaped mountain to the right (east) of Cathkin, the flat-topped peak as one looks at the range from any of the present-day Berg hotels in the area. Actually Sterkhorn has three peaks or summits – the South Peak to the left, the highest point and a difficult climb; the North Peak to the right, a comparatively easy climb; and the Middle Peak, the lowest of the three and of average difficulty. The triangular-shaped face of the peak (as seen from the Berg hotels) and the three summits form the east face. Behind it, unseen from the hotels and seldom climbed, is the west face. It is the east face which is usually climbed today. The Stocker brothers elected to climb the more difficult west face.

By the evening of 21 May they were comfortably settled in their mountain cave, halfway up the Little Berg, which they called Gray's Cave, but which we today call the Basuto Caves, just beyond the Sphinx. Sitting beside the warm glow of their camp fire that night, with the great shadowed valley of the Sterkspruit far below them, they discussed their plans for the morrow. But they soon turned in for they wanted to make an early start.

During the night the wind arose, and next day it was howling and shrieking across the valley, with great tufts of grass, leaves and broken branches hurled high into the air. It was impossible to move, and all day the brothers lay in their blankets (there were no sleeping bags in those days) and slept and read. But next day it dawned bright and clear, with a strange silence after the wild clamour of the previous day, and a rose-pink dawn – a perfect autumn morning. It was Wednesday, 23 May 1888.

They got off to an early start, with a pack pony carrying their little tent and their few provisions, and soon reached the summit of the Little Berg at about

1. Ship's Prow Pass showing left-hand and right-hand forks.
2. Champagne Castle
3. Monk's Cowl
4. South Gully
5. Cathkin Peak

13

1 830 m (6 500 ft). From there, at a steady pace, they proceeded for about three-quarters of an hour along the crest of the Little Berg, approaching the main Berg, and then the real climbing began. Their pack pony managed to carry them a further 396 m (1 300 ft) to a height of 2 379 m (7 800 ft), and then the African

The west face of Sterkhorn.
1. Sterkhorn North
2. Sterkhorn South

porters carried their gear another 116 m (380 ft) to a height of 2 495 m (8 180 ft). Here they found a splendid little nook, sheltered by rocks and a tree, where they pitched their tent and spent three very pleasant nights.

Next morning, Thursday, 24 May, they set off on their first attempt on Sterkhorn South. They were a little late in starting (8.30 am) but it was a beautiful autumn morning and their hearts were light, the air clear and crisp, the mountains a splendour of bright light against a diamond-sharp sky. Patches of snow lay on the higher reaches.

Frank and Arthur made their way up the stream that runs down from the nek between Cathkin and Sterkhorn, and by 10 o'clock they had reached the summit of the nek, their aneroid barometer reading 9 460 ft (2 833 m). From there they descended a few metres down the far, western side in order to climb the western face, out of sight of the watchers down in the valley.

This western face is a grim and forbidding crag, but it is crossed horizontally by three grass ledges, the first fairly large, and the two upper ones less prominent. Their first task was to reach the lower grass ledge. This they did by means of some hair-raising climbing up a narrow fissure.

Then they ran into trouble. There seemed to be no way up the sheer rock face that confronted them, up to the second grass ledge. They traversed left (in a northerly direction) along the grass ledge until they reached the nek between the South and the Middle Peak, but although they made several attempts, they could find no way from the lower to the central grass ledge, which, they were sure, would have led to the third grass ledge, and so by an easy route to the summit. They decided to give up Sterkhorn South for the day.

It was 45 years before this west face was finally conquered by Mark Frank, Brian Godbold and F. E. Ellis in 1933.

But they did climb Sterkhorn North, which, it will be remembered, Frank had tried unsuccessfully to climb, alone, two years previously. Passing through the nek between Sterkhorn South and the Middle Peak, they soon found themselves on the east face of the mountain, from which a short thrilling climb brought them to the top at about 1.30 pm. Their aneroid barometer gave the height as 10 093 ft (3 076 m). The actual height is about 2 960 m (9 705 ft).

They spent half an hour at the top, admiring the view (it is one of the finest I know in the Drakensberg); then an exhilarating race down the slopes of the eastern face, and by 3.15 pm they were back in their little tent halfway down the mountainside. That night they slept the sleep of tired young men, muscles agreeably slack and a great contentment in their hearts.

Next day they had another go at Sterkhorn South. They again went up the gully to the nek between Cathkin and Sterkhorn, but before reaching the top of the nek they contoured round on to the east face instead of the west. They first tried a promising-looking chimney, but this proved impossible. Then the wind came up, howling eerily around the battlemented spires and roaring down the valleys, making climbing impossible. They had to abandon the attempt.

The Stocker brothers were a tough breed of men. Sterkhorn had beaten them twice and they weren't going to stand for that! Three months later they were back in what they called Gray's Cave.

But the omens were not good. For three days they were confined to their cave by the weather. We arc not told what the trouble was. With typical British understatement they merely called them "three doubtful-looking days" which prevented any serious work; but the fourth day, 19 August, dawned bright and clear, and they were off. This time they decided to concentrate on the east face, seen so clearly from the present Berg hotels. By 10.56 am they were immediately below the final rock precipices.

They first tried a difficult-looking chimney, and failed. A huge chock-stone blocked their way. The only alternative was the eastern buttress to the right, but this proved even more difficult. Progress was exasperatingly slow, and soon they were almost in despair, but fortunately Frank found a route still further to the right and this proved to be the key to the climb. There still followed two hours of nightmare climbing, which taxed the two men to the utmost, but at 1.45 pm they made the final heave, and were at the top. The peak was theirs.

They spent half an hour of "blissful" rest at the top; the bliss, however, somewhat spoilt by their anticipatory fear of the descent, for both men dreaded going back the way they had come up. They decided to descend the west face instead – the face that had beaten them three months previously – and to rope down. This they did, not abseiling down as would be done today, but hand over hand down the rope.

As dusk fell, they reached their little cave, and as the night closed in they sat with their pipes around the dancing flames of their camp fire, savouring in retrospect the deep joys of the finest day's climbing either of them had ever had.

This was the last of their exciting days in the Drakensberg, but in between the May and the August trips to Sterkhorn the brothers had made two other major climbs. In June they had visited the Mnweni area and early in August they had made a gallant attempt on Cathkin Peak.

The Mnweni area (see map no. 2), 32 km to the north-west along the line of the Berg, lies between the Cathedral area and the present Royal Natal National Park at Mont-aux-Sources. Even today it is one of the remotest and most inaccessible portions of the Drakensberg, little known and seldom visited, with no hotel or caravan sites, *terra incognita* to the ordinary tourist. To enter it a hundred years ago must have been a truly daunting proposition, even to the most venturesome.

They set off on 12 June 1888. How they crossed the wild country between Draycott and the Mnweni we are not told, but it would appear that they used pack-horses and African drivers. It took them six days altogether, but they had been delayed by bad weather. They reached the Mnweni area on 18 June and were immediately overwhelmed by the beauty and the majesty of all they saw. From the account they subsequently sent to the *Alpine Journal* it is a little difficult to work out exactly what they did, but it would appear that they

The Mnweni area. The two pyramid-shaped peaks towards the left are the two Mnweni Needles. The highest point on the horizon is Mponjwane. To the right, almost level with it, is the Saddle.

attempted to climb North Saddle (they called the Saddle "Segwana Cirque"), and then climbed Rockeries Pass and gazed spellbound at Mponjwane, or Rockeries Tower as it is sometimes called. Three days later they were back home.

Cathkin Peak (see map no. 4) is a stupendous, flat-topped block of a mountain, 3 149 m (10 330 ft) high, and one of the most prominent features in the whole of the Drakensberg. It is ringed on all sides by tremendous precipices, but the south face is gashed by a deeply incised cleft, almost vertical, called the South Gully. It affords the only practicable route to the summit. Early in August the Stocker brothers decided to have a crack at it. As far as we know, it was the first of many subsequent attempts.

They approached their objective, this time, not up the Sterkspruit valley, as they had done before, but up what we call today Wonder Valley. High up in a lateral stream, on the (true) right bank of the river, they discovered a new cave, which they called Eagle Cave, and they made this their base camp. From here they pushed on up one of the spurs of the Little Berg which runs down from Cathkin, turned left and descended into the stream which rises just below Monk's Cowl, and which we today call Cowl Fork. Here they pitched their tents, at a height of 2 070 m (6 790 ft). It was Saturday, 11 August.

Next day they began their climb. It must have been an awesome experience. It was winter, and the sun never once touched those black and sullen rocks. The chasm was narrow and completely iced up. They had to use their ice-axes to cut steps in the ice. Inch by inch, the cold striking down into their very bones, they battled their way up the ice-encrusted rocks and sunless cracks and chimneys in the freezing cold. But time was against them. To spend the night in this

A lone climber is dwarfed by soaring peaks.

1. Champagne
   Castle
2. Monk's Cowl
3. South Gully
4. Cathkin Peak

ice-chest would have meant only one thing – death. They reached 3 085 m (10 120 ft), with only 64 m (210 ft) still to go, but it was now 12.30 pm and the hardest part was still to come. They knew they could not do it. With one last lingering look at the beckoning summit, they turned their backs and commenced the descent. That beckoning summit was not to be reached until 24 years later, and a further nine years elapsed before it was conquered a second time.*

These climbs of the Stocker brothers in 1888 are the first officially recorded climbs in South Africa. They were published in the *Alpine Journal* of 1889.

---

* The long and dramatic story of the many attempts to climb Cathkin Peak may be read in Doyle Liebenberg's *The Drakensberg of Natal* (T. V. Bulpin, 1972), and R. O. Pearse's *Barrier of Spears* (Howard Timmins, 1973).

3 A Drakensberg First

The date: Friday, 17 July 1936. The time: 5 pm. The sun had just set over as wild and lonely an expanse of mountains as you could well wish to see. The place: the summit of Cleft Peak (see map no. 3), 3 281 m (10 765 ft) high, towering over a wilderness of lesser peaks far below. In front of a small two-man tent sit four young people, the light from their tiny twig fire casting flickering shadows on their faces and on the tent. Would they survive the night?

It was a Drakensberg first, but measured by modern standards one of the least noteworthy, one of the strangest firsts ever to be recorded: the first time climbers had slept out in the open on the summit of the Drakensberg in mid-winter. Up to 17 July 1936, this had been considered impossible.

To understand the situation we must remember that in those days the Drakensberg was still little understood. Large areas remained unvisited, untested and unexplored by mountaineers. Even to get there was difficult, necessitating a train journey to Bergville and then, in the early days, a journey by oxwagon (later by motor-lorry) to Mont-aux-Sources. If you wanted to get to the Cathkin area it meant, early on, a train journey to Loskop, and then again a journey by an appalling road into the mountains. The only real opportunity of exploring the mountains was the annual July Mountain Club Camp. The time factor made today's casual weekend trips quite impossible.

We must also remember that the men who pioneered those early days, men like Bassett-Smith, Bill Marriott, Dr Park-Ross, Doc Ripley, Brian Godbold and Maurice Sweeney, were very different from today's young tigers, eager to take hair-raising risks. These were men who, in many cases, were approaching middle age; men in their thirties and early forties. They did a magnificent job, but were naturally, and commendably, more cautious. Accidents at the early Natal camps were almost unknown. The taking of unjustifiable risks was frowned upon. It just wasn't done. Without exception these early climbers were convinced that man could not survive a night on the summit in the middle of winter. The extreme cold would almost certainly prove fatal. D. Gordon-Mills, an experienced climber, said in 1930 that it was quite out of the question to sleep out on the summit at any altitude over 2 135 m (7 000 ft). Remember, too, that in those far-off times today's modern mountaineering equipment was not yet on the market. Our soft down sleeping bags, our windproof anoraks, our light, pre-cooked foods were unknown, and even a two-man tent could weigh 10 kg.

But what a world of magnificence and grandeur could be opened up if man could survive a night on the summit! As things were, it took four to six hours to reach the summit, and you could remain there only an hour or so before it was time to head for your camp down in the valley. If you could spend a night there and have days on end to explore that fantastic region at all hours of the day and night . . . !

One man believed it could be done. He was Brian Godbold, with nine first ascents already to his credit. If polar explorers could survive sub-zero temperatures, then surely Natal mountaineers could survive a night on the summit of the Drakensberg.

He had one other burning desire: he and Mark Frank, a Durban climber, had long desired to watch a sunrise from the top of the Drakensberg! During the 1936 Natal Mountain Club July Camp the two men decided to make the attempt.

They persuaded two Cape climbers, Naomi Bokenham and H. C. ("Hooter") Hoets to join them. Brian, gaunt, lean and long-legged, veteran of the First World War, was 37 at the time, paymaster on the staff of Reynolds' Bros Sugar Estate. His first visit to the Drakensberg had been in 1924, when, at the age of 25, he had visited the Giant's Castle Game Reserve. From 1931 he started attending the Natal Mountain Club July Camps, and soon he was recognised as one of Natal's foremost climbers.

Naomi Bokenham, then in her early twenties, was a lecturer in zoology at Cape Town University, cheerful and good-natured. In addition to being a fine climber, she had the reputation of being able to run faster down a mountain than any man! She subsequently married Arthur Millard, a Cape Town climber, and she and her husband accompanied Brian Godbold on his epic frontal assault on Cleft Peak in 1946 (see *Barrier of Spears*, p. 125).

"Hooter" Hoets was a quiet young Cape Town engineer and a first-class climber. As far as we are aware this was his first and only visit to the Drakensberg.

Mark Frank is described by Brian Godbold as "a modern Sir Galahad". He was the type of man whom the gods loved, lean and athletic in build, spartan in his living, chivalrous, loyal. Twenty-seven years old at the time of their climb, he had a maturity of thought and outlook far beyond his years. When war broke out he joined the NMR, and was tragically killed by a booby mine at Alamein.

And so the plot was hatched. They had with them a small two-man tent, food for three days and plenty of warm clothing, including balaclavas.

But the rest of the camp was uneasy. Maurice Sweeney, president of the Natal Mountain Club at the time, who was in camp, expressed his grave

disapproval, saying that it was an unjustifiable risk, and that as camp was breaking up within two days, no search party would be available if they failed to return. Unperturbed, the four young people carried on with their preparations.

They set out after breakfast on the morning of Friday, 17 July 1936. The weather was fine – a clear, sparkling morning as only the Drakensberg knows. A pleasant stop for lunch on the way up, and by 3 pm they were through Organ Pipes Pass and on the summit.

But it was not here they had planned to camp out. Not for them these heights when there were greater heights above. They had selected as their camping spot the summit of what was then thought to be the highest peak in the whole Drakensberg, the wildest and loneliest spot they could find, Cleft Peak.

This peak, 3 281 m (10 765 ft), towers 325 m (1 065 ft) above the summit of Organ Pipes Pass. It is in an area that had not been visited before by the Mountain Club. It had been climbed for the first time only three days previously, by Doyle Liebenberg and Doc Ripley. And it was a formidable climb, especially for climbers with heavy packs, beginning to feel the altitude at 3 048 m (10 000 ft). After a short rest at the summit of Organ Pipes Pass, a few minutes after 3 pm, they set their faces to the climb.

Several days previously there had been a heavy fall of snow. The whole of the summit was covered, but in the low-lying area between the summit of the pass and the lower slopes of Cleft Peak the snow was especially deep, and here they found themselves battling through waist-deep drifts. The going was hard and it was some time before they gained the lower slopes of the peak, where the snow

21

was not so deep and things were easier. Even so, the sun had already set by the time they reached the top. Thankfully they swung their heavy packs down.

The view from the summit of Cleft Peak looking north must surely be one of the fairest in all Africa. Almost immediately below, gaunt and menacing, towered the twin peaks of Column and Pyramid, the Column considered at that time quite unclimbable. Then, plane upon plane, Cockade, Elephant, and the gigantic Umlambonja Buttress, followed by the blue spires of the Cathedral Range. Fainter still, a world of jagged peaks, the far Mnweni: deep haze-hung valleys and the gleam of distant rivers; on and on to the beckoning plains of the Orange Free State, almost lost in the goose-grey distance. This has stirred the heart of many a tired climber.

Brian Godbold, Naomi Bokenham and "Hooter" Hoets had seen it all two days previously when they made the second ascent after Liebenberg's and Ripley's first. But now the peaks were shrouded in the battleship grey of approaching night, the valleys drowned in darkness and the rivers gone. The temperature suddenly dropped alarmingly.

The summit of Cleft Peak is not much more than 12 square metres in area. They found a level patch of frozen gravel and there they pitched their little two-man tent. Dry clothes were the first necessity. They were soaked with sweat and wet snow after their exertions struggling up those steep rock-strewn slopes with heavy packs.

Mark Frank stripped to the skin except for his shorts. "But look," he said, "it's not really cold." He lit a match and held it out, saying "There's the explanation." The match burned in the still air without a flicker. It was dead still. Hypothermia can be a killer, but it is not the temperature alone that kills. It is sub-zero temperature *plus wind*. Worse still is cold *plus wind and wetness*. They were fortunate. There was not a breath of wind, and they were soon out of their wet clothes.

Then they prepared for the night. With an ice-axe they hacked out a large chunk of frozen snow to be melted down for their water supply. They collected a big pile of dry heather twigs (*Helichrysum trilineatum*, a small shrub with a high oil and resin content which makes excellent, if limited, fuel), and soon they had a tiny fire going in front of their tent. Round this they sat and heated up a tin of tomato soup. (There were no packet soups in those days.)

We asked Brian Godbold, now a spritely veteran who celebrated his 86th birthday on 28 May 1985, what he remembered of that momentous night.

"Well," he said, "that night was an experience I shall never forget. First of all we ate our supper huddled together in the tent entrance, looking down on many snowy peaks below us. The atmosphere was crystal clear, the stars were more dazzlingly brilliant than we had ever known them to be, and the sky remained a deep violet [a phenomenon recorded by mountaineers elsewhere at high altitudes after heavy snowfalls].

"The whole top of the Berg as far as the eye could see was shining silvery-

white in the bright starlight. Not a breath of air stirred, there was not a sound of any sort, and we felt that we had been immensely privileged to have such an uplifting spiritual experience. We felt exalted far above our mundane earthly existence."

The view from the summit of Cleft Peak, looking north.

Drowsy at last they doused the fire, crept inside, and wriggled into their sleeping bags, looking like spacemen, thick with all the warm clothing they had piled on. By now the temperature had dropped to well below zero, but they slept the sleep of tired climbers, well content.

At dawn they were roused by the ominous sound of wind sweeping across the frozen wastes of Lesotho and tearing at the guy-ropes of their tent. Their boots were frozen solid, and so too were eggs and oranges. The mercury in the thermometer was down in the bulb and no longer registering.

As the eastern horizon slowly turned a deep blood red they made their shivering way to the edge of the escarpment, a sheer 610 m (2 000 ft) drop, and sat down to await the longed-for sunrise, each one secretly hoping that it wouldn't take too long! Slowly the red deepened, and suddenly, like the tip of a

23

Mark Frank

red-hot poker, came the disc of the sun. They did not wait. As one man they scuttled back into the tent for shelter against the cruel wind, longing for a hot drink.

But how to make the billy boil! There was no wood: they had used up all their heather twigs the previous night, and in any case nobody was prepared to freeze outside trying to make a fire. They had brought a small pressure stove with them, but with four of them packed into the tent, there was literally not a square centimetre of spare room on which to set it up.

Then Brian Godbold had a brainwave. Taking a deep breath, he made a dash outside, grabbed a flat rock rather like a soup plate, and dashed back inside again.

They made Mark Frank lie on his back, the rock was placed on his stomach and the billy, full of snow, was carefully balanced on the little stove. For the next fifteen minutes all jokes, or anything that might raise a laugh, was strictly forbidden!

"Seldom can coffee have been more eagerly or anxiously awaited!" Brian told us. "Then, warmed inside, we snuggled back into our bags to wait for the sun to warm the air before making breakfast."

They were lucky. The wind dropped, the day warmed up, and with perfect weather and visibility they enjoyed the unique experience of having a full half-day in which to wander through the snow along the edge of the escarpment, admiring the magnificent panorama of Natal in the morning sunlight, from Van Reenen's Pass to Zululand and southwards to Giant's Castle, spread out far below them.

The summit of Cleft Peak. From left: Naomi Bokenham, Brian Godbold (seated), the leader of the expedition, and H. C. "Hooter" Hoets.

They descended the Xeni Pass, between Elephant and Cockade (a first descent), into the Umlambonja, and so home to Base Camp as dusk was closing in, just in time for the evening meal. They had added a new dimension to mountaineering and to mountain summit expeditions.

Since then sub-camping on the summit in the middle of winter has become commonplace. One of the finest nights' sleep I can ever remember was a night on the summit in the middle of July, back in 1951. I was out with my son, Malcolm, still a schoolboy, and two friends of his, Robert and Malcolm Moor (Malcolm Moor went on to become one of Natal's great climbers, with many first ascents and mountain rescues to his credit). We were caught in heavy snow, midway between Langalibalele Pass and the Upper Injasuti Cave, at 3 050 m (10 000 ft), with no shelter and no tent, and darkness coming on fast. We first marked off a small rectangle 3 m by 3 m, cleared all the snow off the ground (it was thigh deep), and used the cleared snow to build a snow-wall round the rectangle, about a metre high. The wind was blowing straight off the great snowfields of Lesotho, and we knew that wind was more our enemy than the sub-zero temperatures that were certain to descend on us. On the floor of the rectangle we spread masses of the small heather bushes mentioned above. Experts will tell you that to keep warm at night you need as much below you as above. Then we spread out our sleeping bags, got the gas-cooker going, and soon a spanking hot supper was ready. We turned in early, with a roof of stars above us, and slept the sleep of kings, only to wake as the dawn came creeping up over the grey hills.

Part II

THE DRAGON SHALL NOT HAVE THEM

Why didst thou leave the trodden paths of men
Too soon, and with weak hands though mighty heart
Dare the unpastured dragon in his den?

Percy Bysshe Shelley, *Adonais*

The Drakensberg is a place of matchless beauty and grandeur, where cloud caravans wind in and out of a world of soaring peaks, and ice-clear mountain streams tell of a peace you will find nowhere else. It is the ideal place where your harassed businessman can unwind and discover once again those inward resources and assurances he thought he had lost for ever.

But it is also a place of hidden menace where, for the unwary, disaster can strike in the flash of a second and where death lurks around the least-expected corner. Increasingly of late the rescue squads have had to be called to pull in a stranded climber or to bring in the body of someone who had paid the ultimate penalty.

In the early days rescues were primitive, ad hoc affairs. Stretchers were nothing more than a couple of blankets tied to two poles, and there was no organised rescue system at all. Later new and better equipment came into use, attempts were made to enlist the use of aircraft, and the telephone numbers of individual members of the Natal Mountain Club who were prepared to go out with rope and tackle to bring in an injured climber were listed. Today our modern, highly organised rescue system co-ordinates the potential of the Police, Army, Air Force, Directorate of Forestry, Natal Parks Board, paramedical and specialist medical services, and the highly trained men of the Mountain Club of South Africa in a service able to swing into instant action, almost at the press of a button.

This section of the book examines the rescue techniques of what we might call three periods, the early, the middle and the present.

Yes, year after year the "unpastured dragon in his den" has claimed his victim, but these are the stories of climbers who cheated the dragon of his prey and who lived to tell the tale.

We commence with the stories of two rescues which date from the period of the early thirties.

We then go on to tell the stories of two rescues which took place 23 and 37 years later. By now rescue techniques had improved considerably. Members of the Mountain Club were becoming better trained for the job, and more available. But there was still no accepted rescue organisation, and the use of aircraft was only just beginning. Aircraft were not used at all in the 1953 (Derek Schaeffer) rescue, and in the 1967 (Anthony Keen) rescue the use of a helicopter was obtained, but with great difficulty. The biggest handicap was still the absence of any rapid method of communication between different rescue parties and these parties and their base. This is particularly noticeable in the Derek Schaeffer rescue. Walkie-talkies were not used in Drakensberg rescues until 1959.

4 Doyle Liebenberg

Throughout the early hours of the night the thunder had roared, the lightning had flashed, and the mountains had echoed to the sounds of cascading water. But for the savage lightning flashes the night was inky black and bitterly cold. Suddenly there came a jagged spear of light more terrifying than the others. It momentarily lit up the fearful precipices of Devil's Tooth, the Eastern Buttress, the walls of the Amphitheatre and the dark, narrow depths of the almost vertical Devil's Tooth Gully. Then blackness descended again. But it had also lit up the two tiny figures trapped between the rock walls of this narrow gash in the pouring rain, 3 050 m (10 000 ft) up in the clouds, the one with a shattered leg and the other exhausted, dazed and injured from a recent fall down the gully. From far below came the distant thunder of the Tugela River as it raced through the rock walls of the Gorge in full flood. Would the night ever end? The one figure moved slightly to make his companion more comfortable. The dawn might come, but not, it seemed, the end of the pouring rain and the white water cascading down on the two tiny figures.

It was March 1932. On the afternoon of Thursday, the 25th, four young men had left the Modderfontein dynamite factory intent on an Easter weekend's climbing in the Drakensberg. Their names were Harry Orpen, Sam Leith, Freddie Vogl and Doyle Liebenberg. They had spent the night on the road and had arrived at the (later Royal) Natal National Park the next day. During that afternoon they had carried their packs up to the Gorge, 12 km from the hotel. Here they spent the night (see map no. 1).

Early next morning they commenced their climb. Towering 1 525 m (5 000 ft) above them, to the south-east, was the southern wing of the Amphitheatre, consisting of the Eastern Buttress, Devil's Tooth and Inner Tower. Between Eastern Buttress and Devil's Tooth is a nearly vertical, narrow gash in the mountainside, known as Devil's Tooth Gully. Their objective was to climb Eastern Buttress via this narrow gully, a route pioneered by Father Kelly many years before, in 1914. It had been pointed out to Doyle Liebenberg by Melatu, the Basuto guide who had always accompanied Father Kelly into the mountains.

29

It was an exhilarating climb. Heavy rain had fallen and the rocks were still slippery, but Doyle at least was an experienced mountaineer and they knew how to look after themselves. The air was now sparkling clear.

They made good progress, but near the top of the gully they encountered a series of obstructing waterfalls. To avoid these they left the gully and climbed out onto the right flanking buttress of Inner Tower, using for the first time their ropes.

They were soon back on the gully floor, however, with Devil's Tooth, a thin spire, towering above them. Here Sam and Freddie decided to remain behind, leaving Harry and Doyle to complete the climb alone. At this point the ravine narrows, hemmed in by steep walls of rock, on the right Devil's Tooth and on the left the tremendous precipices of Eastern Buttress dropping vertically from the summit.

Climbing up this narrow gully they encountered a small waterfall, and then a large chock-stone blocking the gully and necessitating some difficult rope work. Then they were on the nek separating Devil's Tooth from Eastern Buttress.

30

Now came a long walking traverse to their left below the Buttress cliffs, round an awkward corner leading into the final gully and summit chimney. Then they were up, by midday.

In high spirits they walked across the flat top to view the escarpment and the distant plains of Natal through rain-washed air. Behind them, on the flat plateau behind the Amphitheatre, billowing white masses of cumulus cloud-statues were gathering. "We needed no champagne to celebrate our ascent," said Doyle afterwards.

But gathering storm clouds when you are perched a thousand metres above the nearest shelter are not conducive to delay, and soon they began their descent. They retraced their steps down the chimney, around the corner, across the traverse, and were back at the nek just before two o'clock. Now, through the gap, they could see to the south the frowning, jet-black base of a mighty storm centre. It was not a pleasant sight. They sped down the gully and over the chock-stone on a fixed rope. And then came the waterfall.

It was here that disaster struck. Doyle was climbing over some boulders piled on the steeply sloping ravine floor. With a sickening crunch the pile moved. Something struck his right calf and he went down on his right knee, stumbling forward. But his left leg held him. Then, as he moved his right leg forward for the next step he noticed that his right boot was turned outwards. He managed to jump forward on his sound leg on to firmer ground and sat down. Here he stayed for the next 20 hours.

Harry, who was below him, immediately climbed up to him over the boulder pile, which moved again, but he managed to reach a secure stance next to Doyle.

The two men then took stock of the situation. Doyle's leg was obviously badly fractured some ten centimetres above the ankle. His knee was slightly bruised. He pushed down his stocking and found that the broken tibia end had ruptured the skin. This skin tear was immediately bandaged with an antiseptic bandage they had with them, an action which probably prevented bone infection, thus ultimately saving his leg.

But it was obvious he could not be moved without splints, and how was this to be done in a narrow rock-bound cleft? All they could do at the moment was to move the right boot, straighten the leg and tie the damaged right leg to the sound left leg. This Harry did by peeling off his khaki shirt, tearing it into strips and bandaging the two legs together.

Harry then left Doyle as comfortable as he could, and, using the rope, climbed down to Sam Leith and Freddie Vogl, who were waiting for them not far below. They decided that Sam Leith should climb back and stay with Doyle while Freddie and Harry went for help.

Using a safety rope they managed to descend the difficult rock pitches on the Inner Tower buttress slopes, and then, back in the gully, the two men made their way down the treacherous slopes as fast as they could. Harry soon outdistanced Freddie and, now in the Gorge, raced at top speed along the bridle path to the hotel – less than four hours altogether, a magnificent feat. But it wasn't until long after dark that Freddie made the hotel.

In the meantime Sam Leith, carrying a rucksack with whatever scraps of food he could find, climbed back to Doyle. It was a gruelling and never-to-be-forgotten climb. He was not as experienced a climber as he would have liked to be, but he conquered, alone, the upper reaches of Devil's Tooth Gully. Twice he fell, once on the waterfall pitch, sustaining a bad injury to a leg, but he kept doggedly on, reaching Doyle about 3.30 pm.

First, the stock-taking. Food supplies gave them no concern. These were more than adequate. But weatherproof clothing was critical, especially at that altitude. Two hats, three shirts, three sweaters and two small waterproof capes were all they had. Their shorts were quite inadequate for the stormy night which lay ahead of them. They drew lots for the shirts and sweaters. Doyle won one shirt and two sweaters. Sam was not so lucky. He had to be satisfied with two shirts and one sweater. They covered Doyle's legs with empty rucksacks.

At dusk the storm burst upon them. The rain came pouring down, turning the mountain streams into raging torrents and the mountainside itself into a series of waterfalls. The gully became a cascade from which there was no escape, the water pouring down upon them from above. The rock side walls were practically within touching distance. Sam gallantly tried to pack a stone wall behind Doyle to divide the deluge swirling around him. At the height of the storm both men were sitting in water, but the capes kept most of the icy rain away from vital organs.

Down at the hotel Otto Zunckel, lessee of the park's hotel and park warden, immediately swung into action. It would be a miracle, he said, if the two men survived that bitter night at an altitude of close on 3 050 m (10 000 ft), but that did not preclude every effort being made to rescue them. Otto's sons, the hotel staff, visitors and the Zulu rangers were quickly mobilised.

The first rescue group consisted of four young men, Gray, Pope and Howard, led by Otto's youngest son, Udo, a genial giant of a man just out of school. They set off at 5.30 pm, just as dusk was falling. By 8 pm they were in the Gorge.

It was a battle such as few men have fought in the Drakensberg. The Gorge itself was choked with the roaring, foaming waters of the Tugela River in full flood. In inky blackness stabbed by the bright flame of jagged lightning, and in pouring rain, the men fought on, hour after hour, with no pause for rest or food. The floodwaters rose higher and higher, and it soon became impossible. Even Udo admitted, just before midnight, that the end had come. They had done all that mortal man could do. They decided that Gray, Pope and Howard should remain at Tunnel Cave for the rest of the night, while Udo made his way back as best he could to the hotel with the news of their defeat. He arrived back at 3 am.

Meanwhile 1 525 m (5 000 ft) above the Gorge, shortly after 8 pm, the two men in their lonely perch were surprised to see torch flashes from down in the Gorge. It seemed incredible that the rescue party could have already reached the Tunnel area. Their spirits were lifted by the assurance that help was on its way, but they realised that no mortal man could negotiate the gully climb in the dark at the height of the savage storm. By nine o'clock the torch flashes, which they had tried to answer with counter flashes, disappeared, the blackness of the night closed in, and they settled down to sit out that grim night.

Towards midnight the storm abated. They started swinging their arms, pummeling and massaging each other's bodies to keep the blood circulation going. Doyle's legs, being immobile, were numb from the cold, but this at least masked the pain from the broken leg. He catnapped now and again, disturbed by dreams of bath and warm bed. So the night passed into a clear, cloudless Easter dawn.

The sun took some little time before it reached them, but when it came it was warm and their clothes started to dry quickly. Sam took a photograph of Doyle with his legs cradled on a rock slab and stockings laid out to dry.

On Udo's return to the hotel at 3 am Otto Zunckel marshalled his forces in earnest. Although a man of 54 and heavily built, he took personal charge of the whole party, which included hotel guests and 16 Zulu guides and rangers.

He first despatched his son Walter, accompanied by three men. They left the hotel before dawn, and, travelling fast and light, they made their way swiftly up to the Gorge in spite of the still raging torrent.

By 8 am they had reached Tunnel Cave. Stopping only to cut two strong poles from the forest for a makeshift stretcher, they collected Gray, Pope and Howard from the cave, and then set off on the long climb up the gully. Of the

Swathed in as much warm clothing as they could find, Doyle Liebenberg lies in the narrow cleft in which he was trapped after breaking his leg, waiting for rescue. Note the wet socks draped over the rocks.

seven men only Walter was an experienced mountaineer. The others were mostly novices.

By mid-morning Sam and Doyle became aware of activity far below them. Then, about 11 o'clock, the head of Walter Zunckel appeared above the rocks, with a solitary exclamation: "Well, Lieb!" The other six were close behind.

They at least expected the two men to be almost unconscious from exposure, but to their amazement were greeted by warm smiles from both men. They were particularly struck by the fortitude of Doyle himself. He was obviously in intense pain, but still bright and cheery.

Then commenced the preparations for the descent. In addition to medical equipment the rescue party had brought an eiderdown. Walter applied half-splints to the broken leg, the two legs were tied together, and the eiderdown wrapped around Doyle's hips and legs. An improvised stretcher was made up out of the two poles (it was heavy but strong), but this could not be used in that narrow, rock-girt gully. It was reserved for easier ground.

They then started the descent. Owing to the confined space and steepness of the gully it was impossible to carry Doyle. Walter held his legs and Doyle, with the help of others, propelled himself down on his bottom, using his arms. At the waterfall section he and Walter were lowered slowly together, Walter keeping Doyle's legs away from the face. Unfortunately the eiderdown soon started to disintegrate, and then the feathers were dispersed up and down the gully like a miniature snowstorm.

Left: Doyle is strapped firmly to the stretcher, and two ropes, held by another group of men (out of sight), prevent the stretcher from cartwheeling down the mountainside.
***Right:** Doyle being carried in the stretcher.*

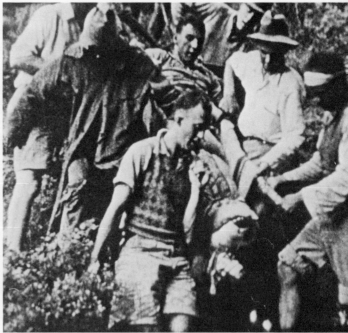

In this way they reached the "root" of the Devil's Tooth (where the left and right-hand ravines on each side of the Tooth meet). At this point they were met by Otto Zunckel and his party of African guides and hotel residents.

Otto, grand old man of the mountains, took full command. He was the first man on ahead, directing operations and pioneering the route. Walter assumed the role of recorder with his cine camera. The film is still shown at the hotel.

Now the improvised stretcher could be used. Doyle was strapped securely into it, and, with three bearers on each side, he was lowered by means of ropes over the buttress section.

Then came the middle and lower sections of the gully, the bearers stumbling over the boulders as best they could, Doyle now in agony with the constant movement. Six men carried the stretcher, and six others, dug in like a tug-of-war team, strained on a tight rope at the back of the stretcher to prevent it running out of control. Progress was appallingly slow.

Finally the sun set and they called it a day. They had still not reached the cave and they slept out under the open skies on a near-level spot in the bed of a stream. A fire was made, supper handed round, and Doyle was injected with a pain-killer. A few rescuers remained with him, the rest hiked on to Tunnel Cave where, by all accounts, an uproarious party was held.

Next day before recommencing their journey Otto made an improved stretcher. Sections of tree branches were secured across the two long poles, and, although heavier than the old one, it provided a firmer base to which Doyle could be strapped.

The route continued down the final sections of the Devil's Tooth Gully, through the main Tugela Gorge, and so on to the path through the forests. Once clear of this Otto decided to leave the path and return to the bed of the Tugela River, where there was an old African sledge-track. Here a sledge with oxen was waiting for them.

But by now darkness was almost upon them again, and the hotel was still six kilometres away. Doyle pleaded with Otto not to try the sledge: he was sure the extra bouncing would wreck any chances of saving the leg. But the stretcher-bearers were exhausted, and nothing would make them move. They tried the sledge, but soon even Otto agreed that it would not work. He offered double rations of brandy to the bearers, but even this would not move them. The impasse appeared insoluble, but suddenly Kleinbooi came to the rescue. He was the only Basuto guide among the Zulu bearers. He jumped on a log and delivered an impassioned harangue in Zulu. What he said will never be known, for no-one but the Zulus could understand him, but it certainly stung them into action. Kleinbooi bent down and lifted his end of the stretcher, and the others followed suit. They reached the hotel at 8 pm.

Here Doyle was met by his sister, Dr A. D. Innes, her husband and Dr Pinniger from Ladysmith. His leg was dressed, he was given an injection, and he spent a comfortable night in one of the hotel's rondavels.

Next morning he was strapped to a mattress, placed in the hotel's old six-cylinder open Buick, and taken to Ladysmith Hospital. Here X-ray plates showed a double break of the tibia and an oblique fracture of the fibula. It was now thought better to transfer him to Johannesburg for specialist treatment, as a plating operation for the battered tibia was thought advisable.

After months of painful treatment the leg was saved, and Doyle made a complete recovery. By the end of the year he was climbing again. Three years later, during the Easter weekend of 1935, he led the first successful ascent of the mighty Amphitheatre wall. Today he is the doyen of the Drakensberg mountains, author of that fine book *The Drakensberg of Natal*. He served as president of the Mountain Club of South Africa for 1978 and 1979.

A word should be said here about Sam Leith, the man who had endured that terrible night of 27 March with Doyle. It will be remembered that in climbing back to Doyle he had damaged his leg. In all the trauma and excitement of getting Doyle down the mountain, he was completely forgotten, and was left to fend for himself as best he could. On the last stretch through the forest his torch failed when the cap end dropped off. He managed to improvise an electrical connection with the metal tip of his shoelace, and battled on alone. After his return to Modderfontein he was confined to bed for a week by the factory doctor. He subsequently became a life-long business colleague of Doyle's, but he never climbed another mountain in his life.

Freddie Vogl, with the prospects of a brilliant career ahead of him, was tragically killed in an accident five years later. Harry Orpen, like Doyle, is now retired from AECI. Both men still go mountain walking whenever the opportunity arises.

One final comment must be made. The story of this epic mountain rescue illustrates vividly the difference between rescues in the thirties and mountain rescues today. In 1932 it took 54 hours before the victim could be taken to medical help, and three whole days before he could receive specialist attention at a hospital. Today a doctor could have been with him within 18 hours (six hours if the accident had occurred in the morning), and two hours after that he could be in the Intensive Care Unit at Addington Hospital, Durban, with the best medical attention in the world.

5 Sally Walker

In the previous chapter we have seen something of the difficulties confronting rescue teams in those early days. One of the biggest problems was the simple matter of communication. There was no way (except by African runners) whereby rescue teams could keep in touch with their base, or with each other. Where it was a matter of search, over a wide area, this made things particularly difficult. In mountain accidents speed in getting medical care to the victim is often the decisive point in whether the victim lives or dies. In the case of Doyle Liebenberg it took two and a half days to get him down to medical care.

Two years previously another accident, in the same area, almost exactly the same in character as Liebenberg's, occurred. The victim this time was a woman.

In 1919 the Natal Mountain Club started the tradition of holding a two-week camp during the month of July. The first camp was held in the Kranskop area, but thereafter all camps were held in the Drakensberg, with the exception of one camp, in 1926, which was held in the Malutis.

In 1930 the choice was the Singati Valley (see map no. 1).

We have already outlined in the last chapter the topography of the area, how the Eastern Buttress Range juts out at right angles from the main escarpment. Where this range joins the escarpment two angles are formed, a north-western, facing the Tugela River, and a south-eastern, known as the Singati Valley, in which the Singati River rises. This river flows through a broad, open valley and joins the Tugela River a short distance below the hotel. It was in this valley that the 1930 July camp was held. As the campers tramped up the valley after leaving the lorry on the main road (in the grounds of a small wayside store) they had Eastern Buttress, Devil's Tooth and Inner Tower on their right. In front was the steep gully, or ravine, known as the Singati Gully, and at its head, and slightly to the left, was Mount Amery.

Mount Amery had been named after Col. L. C. Amery, *The Times* war correspondent. It was almost certainly down Singati Gully that Col. Amery had descended from the summit in 1900. The first ascent of the gully was made in 1920 by D. W. Bassett-Smith and R. G. Kingdon.

Sally Walker

On Thursday, 10 July 1930, a party from the camp set out to climb this gully. Among them was Alice Walker, known affectionately as Sally. Sally came from Highflats where her father Harry, a previous Member of the old Natal Parliament, was farming. She had joined the Mountain Club in 1924 and was an experienced mountaineer.

The weather was perfect, and with gay chatter and banter the party was soon toiling up the steep slopes of the ravine. Above them loomed Mount Amery, and away behind were the giddy precipices of Devil's Tooth and the Eastern Buttress.

Suddenly came the accident. About 250 m (820 ft) from the summit and the end of the climb, Sally put out her hand to steady herself, and in doing so dislodged a rock. It fell on her leg, fracturing the bone badly. A contemporary newspaper account said the rock continued its downward flight, narrowly missing two other climbers before finally crashing hundreds of metres below into the valley. Actually it did not move far, only half a metre or so, but it weighed a full 90 kg, and Sally was in bad trouble.

It was now midday. Sally found she could not place even the slightest weight on the injured limb. It was impossible to carry her. The precipitous nature of the rocks in the gully made anything of this nature quite out of the question. For five and a half hours the injured girl crawled down the jagged rocks and along narrow ledges, knowing that the least slip would mean instant death. Every movement was agony. Whenever possible she was assisted by the men in the party, but they were in such a confined space that there was little they could do. Night fell long before they were out of the gully.

Preparations were immediately made for what lay ahead. Sally was made as comfortable as possible. To ease the pain and to enable her to get at least a little rest, ice was packed around the limb, and two of the party lay on each side of her to keep her body warmth in. She got no sleep at all during the long night, but in spite of that, and her pain, the only words that passed her lips were not of complaint, but of thanks and cheerful encouragement to her rescuers.

Of course as soon as the accident happened word had been sent down to the main camp 16 km down in the valley and help was quickly organised. Long after dark, somewhere around midnight, the relief party arrived with blankets, food, the necessary first aid kit and an improvised stretcher. The hours of the night ticked steadily on.

Next morning an attempt was made to reach the main camp, but progress was agonisingly slow. There were waterfalls to be descended, narrow rock ledges to be negotiated and loose boulders to be watched throughout the descent. The men in the party took it in turns to carry the stretcher. To add to the many difficulties, the lower reaches of the ravine were covered with loose stones. In an attempt to make the way easier for the bearers, other members of the party went on in front, clearing a pathway through the rubble.

Again night fell. The main camp was still many kilometres away, and they

1. Mount Amery
2. Singati Gully
3. Sentinel
4. Devil's Tooth
5. Eastern Buttress

were forced to spend another anxious night out in the open. Again Sally was made comfortable and tended throughout the night. Next day saw the journey resumed, the going getting easier and easier as the valley floor began to level out. When they reached base camp they were weary but triumphant – and Sally was still smiling! It had taken nearly three days to get her down.

She was immediately placed in a car and driven swiftly to the sanatorium in Pietermaritzburg, where doctors were waiting for her. Here she made a rapid and satisfactory recovery and it was not long before she was on the mountain slopes once again.

Sally continued her membership of the Natal Mountain Club and became a much-loved character, a popularity eventually recognised by her election to a vice-presidentship. After her father's death she devoted herself to the running of the family farm and business at Highflats, and her climbing days were largely over. Although a most attractive person, she never married. At one time there had been a rumour that she had been engaged to a young man, but he had been killed in the First World War. She died in March 1965.

6 Derek Schaeffer

"A young mountain climber from Durban is lying seriously ill and delirious with suspected pneumonia 10 000 ft up in the Drakensberg. By his side throughout the biting cold of last night was a young woman companion, who with another man had set off on Friday to climb the Rockeries in the Cathedral Peak district."

So read the *Natal Mercury* report of Tuesday, 7 April 1953. It was the first news to reach the outside world of the grim drama that had been unfolding during the previous three days in one of the wildest regions of the Drakensberg.

The report was wrong in one respect. The tragedy that was soon to fill the newspaper's front page took place not in the Cathedral area, but in the Mnweni (see map no. 2).

The Mnweni River is one of the largest in the Drakensberg. It rises at a point roughly midway between Cathedral Peak and Mont-aux-Sources. It is joined by the two Ntonjelana Rivers, and then flows through a valley, broad and beautiful, to its meeting with the Tugela River 20 km away. At its head is some of the most magnificent scenery in the whole of the Drakensberg, the most prominent peaks being Mponjwane (or Rockeries Tower), the two Mnweni Needles, the Mnweni Pinnacles, and the Saddle, with two flanking peaks, North Saddle and South Saddle. Two mountain passes lead up to this delectable region, the Mnweni Pass, facing north, and the Rockeries Pass, facing south.

On Friday, 3 April 1953, three young people, Martin Winter, Derek Schaeffer and Gillian Bettle, set out to climb Mponjwane, one of the major climbs in the Drakensberg.

Martin himself is one of the most remarkable and perhaps the best loved climber Natal has ever known. As a young man he showed an alarming tendency towards dangerous living, losing his canoe and all his clothes in a test of endurance against the flooded Tugela River. Then in 1947 he took up mountain climbing, and during the next 25 years built up a reputation as one of Natal's foremost climbers. Before long he was credited with fifteen first ascents. He has climbed every major peak in the Drakensberg at least once, often solo

Mponjwane, the peak Martin Winter, Derek Schaeffer and Gillian Bettle had planned to climb.

41

(we know of no other Drakensberg climber with a similar record), while his energy was phenomenal. In July 1954 he climbed the Fourth Cigar (Dragon's Back) on one day; the next day he climbed Sterkhorn North and South; the following day, in heavy snow, he climbed, in one day, both Cathkin and Monk's Cowl, and was still climbing on the fourth day! In addition to all this he has led innumerable rescue parties into the Drakensberg.

Martin, who now farms at Frere, just outside Estcourt, is the grandson of the Hon. H. D. Winter, Minister of Agriculture and later of Native Affairs in the old Natal Parliament. Winterton is named after him.

Derek Schaeffer, 22 years old, was a well-known young Durban musician. The celebrated pianist, Arthur Rubenstein, had predicted a brilliant future for him.

The "woman companion" was bright-eyed Gillian Bettle, 24 years old, auburn-haired and fresh-coloured, a Durban schoolteacher. Her calm courage and fortitude in the drama which was to unfold during the next few days was to draw the warmth and admiration of all who knew her.

All three were experienced climbers and had climbed together for some years, making a fine team. Each seemed able to anticipate the moves of the others, and they climbed with a rhythm and harmony that augured well for the future.

Derek Schaeffer had had influenza. His father tried to persuade him against making the trip, but Derek wouldn't pull out. At that time the Mountain Club had a rule forbidding parties of fewer than three, and if he had pulled out his two companions would have had to forego the trip. He did not want to let them down.

Mponjwane Cave (in the bottom right corner)

Mponjwane, the peak they wished to climb, is in one of the most inaccessible regions in the whole Drakensberg. In those days the most feasible way of reaching the peak was to kick off at Cathedral Peak Hotel (see map no. 3), climb the Umlambonja Pass to the summit of the escarpment, and then trek along the summit in a roughly northerly direction for about 15 km. This would bring one directly to the peak, and to a fine cave, Mponjwane Cave. This summit trek, of course, was over difficult, broken country and would take about a day. The three climbers decided to spend the first night at the head of the Umlambonja Pass, in another cave, Twins Cave.

Derek Schaeffer

They set off soon after midday from the hotel on Friday, 3 April 1953. But the weather was against them. A wet, drizzly mist came down, their packs were heavy, and soon they were wet through. Umlambonja Pass is not the easiest of Drakensberg passes. It is very steep, full of rubble and broken rocks, and towers 1 525 m (5 000 ft) above the hotel. Derek, especially, found the going tough, and it was well after dark before they reached their cave.

They slept well that night, however, and were up early to face the summit trek. But again the mist and the drizzle closed in, and it was bitterly cold. They reached Mponjwane Cave just as dusk was setting in.

Next day, Sunday, the 5th, dawned clear, but soon the mist came down again and a bitter northerly gale blew up. Derek said he felt wretched, and decided to sleep it off while the other two reconnoitred the peak.

Mponjwane is one of the mightiest peaks in the Drakensberg. It is a free-standing peak (that is, standing alone and not part of the escarpment), a great solid block separated from the main escarpment by a tremendous chasm, less than 75 m (250 ft) across and 450 m (1 480 ft) deep. To reach the peak they would have to descend, and cross, this chasm.

Martin and Gillian spent the morning on the edge of the escarpment working out possible routes, and returned to the cave about 1 pm. Derek was asleep, but at suppertime he seemed to revive a bit, and was bright and cheerful. That night, with all the pools and streams frozen over, it was colder still, but Monday morning dawned bright and clear.

Then, suddenly, the alarm sounded. As they were watching the sunrise the other two noticed that Derek was acting strangely. He started rambling in his talk, seemed confused, and to have lost his memory. They examined him carefully, and were shocked at the rapid deterioration in his condition. He was weak and completely helpless.

Urgent action was essential. They had to move, and quickly. They decided that Martin should go for help, along the route they had used on their way up, while Gillian remained behind to care for the sick man.

All along the escarpment edge Martin raced, as he had never raced before. It had taken them a day and a half to cover the route on the way up. Normally it would have been a full day's march on the way down. Martin covered the distance in three hours 45 minutes, an incredible time.

Gillian Bettle (now Mrs Earl) who remained behind in Mponjwane Cave to nurse the sick Derek Schaeffer.

At the hotel it was Albert van der Riet, the hotel's genial owner, who immediately took command. Derek's parents were informed. Fred Zunckel, a pilot of Drakensberg Air Services, was summoned from Ladysmith, the best medical advice obtained telephonically, and supplies of penicillin obtained. At 3 pm Albert drove Martin down to the airstrip, and then they were airborne in an attempt to land the plane and get Derek off to hospital.

But it was impossible. The area immediately above the cave was fairly level, but it was a wild jumble of rock and stone, and to attempt to land a plane would have been suicidal. One hope remained – Mokhotlong. This was a tiny mountain village in the heart of Lesotho, 55 km down the Orange River. There would be a Resident Medical Officer there. They might just pull it off. They turned the nose of the plane south-west.

And what of Gillian? Throughout the long day she nursed the sick man. Fortunately the weather cleared and the sun came out. But it was still bitterly cold. Derek was brought out into the sun, wrapped in blankets and two sleeping bags to keep him warm. By now he was completely delirious, and only seemed to know his name. He refused all food, and even tea, although Gillian managed to get him to drink a little water. And so the long hours dragged on, Gillian, alone with a helpless man, wondering all the time what was happening in the outside world, but unable to know. At 3.30 pm came the roar of a plane, and Gillian at least knew that Martin had got through. But what were the rescue plans? Gillian could not know. All she knew was that another lonely night lay before her, in the silence of the ice-clad peaks. The plane dropped a packet of penicillin, which Gillian failed to retrieve, and then flew on.

Meanwhile things were moving, rapidly. Martin Winter and Fred Zunckel decided that a two-pronged attempt should be made to rescue Derek, one from Mokhotlong and one from Cathedral Peak. If the one failed, the other one might succeed. Fred Zunckel dropped Martin on the Mokhotlong airstrip, and immediately flew on to Cathedral Peak. He arrived there just on dusk.

At Mokhotlong Martin contacted the District Commissioner, and a rescue party, consisting of the Resident Medical Officer, the Agricultural Officer, two police troopers and Martin, was hurriedly organised. They set off at 8 pm, riding all through the night up the Orange River. It was a never-to-be-forgotten nightmare journey, the night pitch black, and progress was painfully slow. The horses slithered and slipped on the mud-plastered slopes. In places it was so bad that the men were forced to dismount and lead their horses. Several times they had to cross the flooded Orange River, the water coming up to their girths. Dawn broke, and there was no sign yet of the escarpment. They rode on.

Back at the hotel Albert van der Riet organised the second rescue party, equipped with a wicker stretcher and with supplies of penicillin. It consisted of eight men led by John (Matateni Xosa), the famous yodelling guide. But they were faced with a three-hour climb up the notoriously steep and difficult Umlambonja Pass, in pitch darkness, in addition to the trek along the escarpment to Mponjwane Cave. They decided to wait until the moon rose, and finally set out at 3.30 am.

Meanwhile other plans were afoot. Back in Durban that night Derek's father was searching for a helicopter to take his son off the mountain. The Army had no helicopters in those days, but it was known that some were available at Mtubatuba, where they were used for crop-dusting and nagana spraying. But the only pilot was Mr P. Moolman, and he was away for the Easter holidays and could not be located. Telephone calls to the Transvaal and Free State were equally unavailing. No pilot was available. (In any event it is doubtful that a helicopter could have reached those heights – 3 050 m or 10 000 ft – in those days.)

Mr Schaeffer then began offering astronomical sums to any pilot who succeeded in landing his plane and taking his son off. Early the following morning Fred Zunckel had another look at the area, and pronounced it impossible. Another Ladysmith pilot, Peter Strong, said he thought he could do it, and was prepared to make the attempt provided he was given a guarantee of £1 500 in case his aircraft was wrecked. Mr Schaeffer gave the guarantee, but before Mr Strong could be informed Derek and his rescuers had already left the area.

Back now to Martin and the Mokhotlong rescue party, who were steadily making their way towards the escarpment edge. At last, at 10 am, after 14 hours in the saddle, they reached it, but 10 km south of where they should have been, at the Ntonjelana Pass instead of Mponjwane. However, away to their right they could see the Cathedral rescue party coming up over the Twins. By this time the horses were exhausted, so, abandoning his mount, Martin made for the stretcher party on foot, and together they raced on to the cave.

Back in the foothills the authorities had not been idle. Fred Zunckel reported the arrival of the two rescue parties at noon, and it was thought that they might travel through the night and reach the Mnweni River within 12 hours. An ambulance was summoned from Ladysmith. It reached the rendezvous point at the Mnweni late on Tuesday afternoon, but it could not cross the river. It remained there well on into the night, but there was no sign of the rescue party, and in the small hours of the morning it had to return to Ladysmith. But one vehicle, that afternoon, did manage to get through the Mnweni and proceed a short way up the valley in an attempt to meet the rescue team. Len Carr, veteran caterer to the Mountain Club July camps, fitted his truck with mattresses, managed to cross the river, and by nightfall was well up the valley. All night he waited in his truck, but at dawn, with no news or sight of the rescue party, he made his way back to Bergville.

We must note here again the tremendous handicap of the lack of radio communication between the various rescue teams and between these teams and the authorities. There was only one way whereby news of the complex rescue operations that were taking place in the Drakensberg could be conveyed to the outside world, and that was by Fred Zunckel reporting to Ladysmith what he saw from the air. Ladysmith could only report to Pietermaritzburg and Durban. There was no way whereby the watchers at the rendezvous point on the banks of the Mnweni could either communicate rapidly with the outside world or be informed of what was happening elsewhere. And, of course, the rescue party itself was completely blanked out.

Meanwhile, back at the cave, it was a scene of bustling activity. It was Tuesday, 7 April, and well after midday, and the two rescue parties, as we have seen, had met in full strength. The Mokhotlong doctor examined Derek and pronounced him fit to be moved, though in a grave condition. Derek was strapped to the stretcher, warmly wrapped in blankets and sleeping bags, and at 3 pm they were off, the Mokhotlong men to return to Mokhotlong and the Cathedral team, with Martin now in command, to face the wicked Rockeries Pass down to the foothills. They had decided it would be quicker to get Derek down into the lower Mnweni area than to use the long route they had already used, along the escarpment edge and down the Umlambonja into the Cathedral area. At 5 pm Fred Zunckel made his last flight of the day over the scene, and announced on his return that the camp had broken up and that the place was deserted.

Taking it in turns, the bearers carried the stretcher slowly down the upper reaches of the pass. Choked with broken rocks and boulders it was a fearful ordeal. By nightfall, exhausted, they were only halfway down the pass, and here they decided to camp for the night.

Fortunately the weather had cleared: it was a bright, starlit night, but freezingly cold. They made Derek as comfortable as possible, but none of them got any sleep that night. Owing to the steep slope the men had to sit, propped up by boulders, throughout the night. They had no sleeping gear and only the thinnest of clothes. Some were in shirt sleeves, as they had set out not expecting to have to sleep out. They had hardly any food, and although they managed to light a fire, it did not last long.

Next morning, at first light, they were off again, battling their way over some of the most difficult country in the whole of the Drakensberg. Three hours after their start they called a halt for their last meal – tea and a few husks of bread. Their food was now finished.

Derek was unconscious as hour after hour the men who carried him squelched doggedly on through swollen streams and slid down precipitous slopes, their strength slowly beginning to fail. It was a race against time.

And all through the long hours Fred Zunckel's plane circled slowly in the sky overhead, unable to help but keeping ceaseless watch. Periodically they signalled to it, a white flag to signify life. Somewhere in their packs was a black flag, to signify death.

Meanwhile, from early afternoon, the watchers on the high point above the Mnweni River were straining their eyes to get the first glimpse of the rescue

party. Reporters and photographers from the city dailies began to arrive. The ambulance returned from Ladysmith and took up position. Derek's parents arrived during the morning, and kept watch all day. A sled, drawn by oxen, was sent off up the valley to relieve the exhausted bearers over the last stages of the journey. In the late afternoon Albert van der Riet rode over on horseback from Bergville, together with two doctors and additional medical supplies. They crossed the Mnweni River and headed up the valley. The two parties met at nightfall, a kilometre beyond the river. Derek was examined by the two doctors. All they could do was to urge the utmost speed. Time was running out. The rescuers pushed on.

Then came the crossing of the Mnweni. The recent rains had brought the river down in full spate. Mustering all their manpower, they carried Derek at shoulder-height. The bearers had been given the order to loosen their holds if they stumbled or fell.

And now the slow uphill climb to the rendezvous point. It was nearly over.

Those waiting at this point first saw the beams of torches as the rescue party wound its way slowly upwards from the river. Powerful headlights of waiting cars were switched on, and there came the answering flashes from the torches below. Then the silence of the evening was broken by the loud wail of the amulance's siren as it sounded its greeting to the weary men below.

The Mnweni area. It was through this maze of valleys that the sick Derek Schaeffer was carried on a mountain stretcher.

47

Martin Winter, veteran Drakensberg climber and leader of many mountain rescues.

First up was Dr van Heerden, followed by Gillian Bettle on a Basuto pony. Immediately after came the stretcher party, with the unconscious Derek swathed in blankets, his face covered with a handkerchief, put there sometime during the trek to protect him from the sun. A short halt for further treatment, and then the ambulance set out in convoy with two other vehicles, Mr and Mrs Schaeffer going on ahead in their car.

Thunder clouds were closing in as the convoy moved off. Within minutes of its departure the storm broke, drenching the countryside in fresh rain. If it had broken ten minutes earlier, those treacherous mountain roads would have become impassable, and it might have been hours before the convoy could have got through.

Two hours later Derek Schaeffer died as he was being placed in a bed at the Ladysmith Provincial Hospital. The time was 10.15 pm.

Three months later Martin was back at Mponjwane Cave for the scattering of Derek's ashes. He was accompanied by five of Derek's climbing friends. The ceremony was very brief and very simple. The six young men gathered at a point on the escarpment edge, opposite Mponjwane, looking straight down into the mighty chasm that separates the peak from the escarpment. The sun was setting as they laid the casket on a nearby rock. On it was a sprig of Berg heather and a few yellow daisies. Nearby was an ice-axe, erect and stark against the western sky. While they prayed Martin scattered the ashes over the edge of the escarpment, and then buried the casket on the lonely hilltop.

Autumn in the valley of the Injasuti.

7 Anthony Keen

Tuesday,* 25 July 1967, was black, wet, and dripping. The dawn was still two hours away. Heavy mist blanketed the mountains and the valleys of the Little Berg. The night pressed heavy on the land. Over the deep snow-drifts which choked the ravines of Cathkin Peak (see map no. 4), dark shadows lay. In the bedroom at the Monk's Cowl Forest Station Steve Rossouw, the foreman-in-charge, was awake. His wife, Joyce, was still asleep. Steve always woke early these days. It was a good time to plan the work of the day. If only the mist would lift he could burn that fire-break down from Ndanjane past the forests of the Upper Makurumani. It was 4.30 am and too early to make coffee. He drew the blankets up close around him, for it was cold. From outside came the only sound, the steady drip–drip–drip of the dank mist from the liquidambar trees.

The freshness of dawn comes to the great Tugela valley.

Suddenly the silence of the night was shattered by a frantic hammering at the back door. It woke Joyce, but Steve was first at the door. On the steps outside was a young man, haggard, exhausted, on the point of collapse. Quickly he told his story. He was Peter Keen. He and his brother, Dr Anthony Keen, had set out along the contour path four days ago on a traverse from Cathedral Peak to Champagne Castle. The previous afternoon, in the Mhlwazini valley, Dr Anthony Keen had suffered a heart attack. The two men had attempted to descend the mountains to Champagne Castle Hotel, but Anthony had collapsed for the second time. His brother had placed him in two sleeping bags, and laid him on a stretched-out tent alongside the path, and had gone for help after Anthony had written down his diagnosis on a slip of paper. Peter had arrived at the hotel about 9 pm, and with an African boy and an Indian waiter had returned up the Little Berg to where he had left his brother in the Mhlwazini valley. Together they had tried to carry the stricken man down, using the sleeping bags as a makeshift stretcher, but had found it impossible. Through the

The Cathedral Range is bathed in early morning sunlight.

---

* Pages 49 to 52 are taken from *Barrier of Spears* by R. O. Pearse (Timmins, 1973), by kind permission of the publishers.

night, in the bitter winter weather, Peter had again descended the Little Berg, and this time had pitched up at the Monk's Cowl Forest Station.

Steve and Joyce (a trained nurse) immediately started the wheels turning: a cup of steaming tea and food for the exhausted man, while Steve phoned the hotel three kilometres away, alerting them to the emergency, and asking for a stretcher and a rescue party to be assembled immediately. Then another call to the Estcourt telephone exchange, with an urgent request that they attempt to locate a helicopter. The reply fifteen minutes later: two local helicopters were unavailable, so a third call to an Estcourt doctor, to whom Peter had read his brother's diagnosis. The doctor promised to alert the Defence Department, with a request to them for a helicopter from either Bloemfontein or Durban, and he also promised to send an ambulance out. Yet another call to Durban, to the parents of the two men. In between the calls Steve despatched an advance party of African forest guards up the mountain, with food and blankets. Then Steve and his wife drove Peter Keen over to the hotel. Here he was immediately put to bed, and was asleep within five minutes. Steve collected the stretcher and then returned to the Forest Station where Joyce swiftly packed a rucksack with hot tea and sandwiches. Then, with Peter's last words ringing in their ears: "Hurry, for God's sake: he may not last long," they sped off, taking a short-cut up the mountainside, while the stretcher party took the longer route up the bridle path. It was 6.45 am, and the day was just breaking. Behind they left their daughter, Caroline, a child of 12, in charge of the Station, to look after their four younger children and to man the telephone for any incoming calls.

Through the heavy mist they climbed up, and reached the summit of the Little Berg at Breakfast Stream in 25 minutes, the usual time for the climb being an hour. Then swiftly along the summit plateau and on to Hlatikulu Nek. An icy wind began to blow off the snow, and the mist was still heavy, but at Hlatikulu Nek it grew lighter, and when at 8.55 am they reached the stricken man, the sun was just beginning to break through.

They found Dr Anthony Keen beside the path, halfway down the Mhlwazini valley. He was conscious, his pulse was strong and steady, and he said he felt better. Soon after that the stretcher party arrived and arrangements were made for the return trip.

In the meantime little Caroline, down at the Forest Station, had been kept busy. Competently she handled the incoming telephone calls – from the parents of the two men, from eager newspaper reporters, from the Estcourt doctor, and from Defence Headquarters. About 7.30 am came a call with the news that an Air Force helicopter was on its way from Bloemfontein. Caroline's younger brother, Stephen, a lad of 10, immediately offered to climb up the mountains with the news. Alone, barefoot, with only a single thin pullover, the boy made the journey of more than 12 kilometres in less than two hours, along treacherous footpaths shrouded in mist and covered in places with snow and ice. He arrived just as the stretcher party was about to set off.

*Steve Rossouw,
Forestry officer at the
Monk's Cowl Forest
Station, who
organised and carried
out the rescue of Dr
Anthony Keen.*

The Sphinx, a well-
known landmark
above the Monk's
Cowl Forest Station,
where the helicopter
picked up Dr Keen.

Down below the mist became thicker, and Caroline took another telephone call to the effect that the helicopter could not get through because of the mist. She realised that the rescue party might be waiting in vain for the machine, and she decided she must go herself to warn them that they would have to depend on themselves to get the sick man down. She did not hesitate a moment. Leaving the three younger children in the charge of an African servant, she set off immediately, taking with her only her father's three dogs, Mutt, Luxy and Toasty, for protection. Up through the mountains, she, too, climbed, delivered her message, together with one from the Estcourt doctor urging them to press on, and immediately returned to her post at the Station to prepare food and hot drinks for the return of the rescue party.

All this time the stretcher party was toiling on, manoeuvring the stretcher over mountain streams and along steep kranses and narrow footpaths. As they climbed up out of the Mhlwazini valley the mist came down again, heavier than ever, thick, black, wet and dripping. It turned bitterly cold, the wind gusting down from the snowfields in icy blasts. Little Stephen, still barefoot, was visibly frozen, even though Caroline had given him her own pullover before she had left for home. The little fellow was almost in tears. By the time they reached Blind Man's Corner they were all wet through. They battled on.

At last, when they reached the Sphinx, the huge sandstone rock just below the summit of the Little Berg, the mist began to lift. Down below the Alouette helicopter had by now arrived at the Forest Station, together with the ambulance and oxygen. As soon as the pilot saw the rescue party at the Sphinx, far above him, he took off, and landed just below the rock, picked up Dr Keen and flew him down to the Forest Station. There his father was waiting for him. A brief halt while the patient's condition was checked, and then the whirling blades began to turn again as the machine took off for Grey's Hospital in Pietermaritzburg. Steve and his wife watched the plane grow smaller and smaller until it was a speck against the drifting clouds. Then they turned to their work. There was dinner to prepare for five hungry children, and it was still early enough to start that fire-break down from Ndanjane. Steve called to his labourers.

Two questions remain. In writing the account in *Barrier of Spears* I was concerned only in using the story of the rescue to illustrate the sort of problems with which Government foresters and their families were expected to cope. I was not concerned with the events which had led up to the emergency. To round off the story, this must now be told.

Secondly (and this is a vital matter), the nature of Dr Keen's symptoms, their diagnosis, and their implications for future climbers must be dealt with. Dr Keen was a medical man, and he was quite sure, at the time, that he was suffering from heart failure. But on arrival at Grey's Hospital, he was found to be comfortable and in no distress. ECG and other tests showed no heart

abnormalities, and there was no previous history of heart trouble. There were no after-effects, and altitude sickness was diagnosed.

But there are grave difficulties in accepting altitude sickness as the correct diagnosis. Part of the object of this book is to identify the various dangers facing mountaineers in the Drakensberg, and to discuss possible preventive measures. The whole of Part IV and Part VI of the book is devoted to this. If a climber can be struck down, as Dr Keen was, for no apparent cause, then, if only for the safety of other mountaineers, the matter must be investigated and the causative factors discovered. This we shall attempt to do.

Dr Anthony Keen, 29 years old, was a qualified doctor, studying pathology in Cape Town. Peter, 31 years old, had come out from Sweden for a few weeks with his family. Both men were experienced mountaineers, and they decided on a quick holiday excursion into the Drakensberg – from the Cathedral Peak area via the contour path to the Mhlwazini River in the Cathkin area, up Grey's Pass to the summit, and along the summit back to Cathedral Peak.

The contour path runs along the summit of the Little Berg, from the south of Cathkin Peak to Cathedral Peak, at an average altitude of about 2 135 m (7 000 ft). It is the only practicable means of travelling from Cathedral Peak to the Cathkin area at this lower altitude. The summit route, of course, is much higher, the average altitude being about 3 050 m (10 000 ft). In view of what happened it is important to remember these altitudes. There are no paths on the summit. Paths are not necessary. All one has to do is to follow the escarpment edge, where the mighty wall of the Drakensberg drops sheer down into the foothills of the Little Berg and the plains of Natal.

They arranged for a lift up Mike's Pass (see map no. 3) to the summit of the Little Berg, and then set off at about 5.30 pm along the contour path, in the dark. Their packs were heavy, for they had planned for a seven, possibly eight-day, trip, but in the starlit night the going was good, and they camped comfortably that night in the Ndedema valley, in the well-known Sibayeni Cave.

Next day they were off at 8 am, climbing for two hours up the long slopes leading to Eastman's Peak. They lunched at the crossing of the Nkosezana River, and by four o'clock were having tea where the contour path crosses the Mhlwazini River, below Gatberg. They had gone well, especially Anthony, who had taken over a few kilos from Peter's pack to even things up a bit.

According to their original plan they would have camped there for their second night, but after a cup of tea and a rest they still felt fine, and decided to push on to the Keith Bush Hut at Base Camp, a mountain hut erected in 1955 (but since demolished) in memory of the young climber, Keith Bush, who had fallen to his death on Cathkin Peak. To do this meant leaving the contour path, altitude 1 906 m (6 250 ft), turning right (west) and following the river up the valley to the hut, altitude 2 333 m (7 650 ft). These figures are interesting, and necessary for an understanding of what happened.

They arrived at the hut just as darkness fell, pleasantly tired after a long hard day with heavy packs. They slept well.

When they awoke next morning, however, Peter had a headache and felt nauseous. They cooked breakfast, but Peter refused his portion for fear of vomiting. Their scheduled plan for the day would have meant a climb of 717 m (2 350 ft) up the face of the escarpment, into Grey's Pass (a narrow, rock-strewn gully), and so up to the summit, where they would sleep the night in a cave known as the Nkosezana Cave. But they just did not feel up to it. Anthony thought he recognised the symptoms of altitude sickness, though he was a little puzzled that it had hit Peter at so low an altitude, 2 333 m. They had a day or two in hand, so they decided to take the day off and spend it in camp, acclimatising.

Altitude sickness – or mountain sickness, as it is sometimes called – occurs at high altitudes, where the air becomes thinner, with a consequent lowering of the concentration of oxygen. The symptoms include difficulty in breathing, nausea, fatigue and a feeling of anxiety. It is rare, however, for this condition to appear at an altitude of anything below roughly 3 000 m (10 000 ft). Above 4 575 m (15 000 ft) most mountaineers have to adjust themselves to it. This is done by gaining height slowly, with frequent rest days. In this way the body adjusts itself to the rarified air, and heights of even 8 845 m (29 000 ft, the height of Mt Everest) have been attained without oxygen. The process is known as acclimatisation.

They lazed and dozed the day away, but by mid-afternoon they felt no better. Anthony had also begun to feel nauseous. They decided to sleep at a lower altitude, so, taking with them nothing but their sleeping bags and a little food, they went down the valley to their afternoon tea spot of the previous day, the contour path crossing the Mhlwazini. Amazingly, they had hardly arrived when their nausea left them, their appetites returned, and they felt full of energy.

Next day they returned to the Keith Bush Hut and then, after a short rest, commenced the long ascent of the escarpment. They took it slowly – they had learnt their lesson from the previous day – but they felt fit and eager for the climb.

But gradually they found themselves going slower and slower. Normally this is a climb of about three hours, but after two and a half hours they were only about a third of the way up. Suddenly Anthony experienced a curious fluttering feeling in his chest, and he felt strangely weak. His pulse seemed to be all right, and he continued the climb, but very slowly. Then came a strange inexplicable feeling of anxiety, and he knew he would not make it. He sat down and said: "Peter, I can't go on. I'm feeling funny, weak. We must go back."

Without another word they turned and started the descent. In half an hour they were back at the hut, where Peter made a brew of tea. Anthony's symptoms continued.

It was obvious now that a change of plan was necessary. Any summit trek at

3 000 m was quite out of the question. They decided to go down to Champagne Castle Hotel, put up there for a few days, and do a series of easy day trips into the mountains.

They packed up all their gear. By now it was dark, and torches were necessary. They managed to find the path which leads up out of the valley to join the contour path on its climb to Hlatikulu Nek, but Anthony was obviously getting weaker and weaker. Strangely enough, there was no shortness of breath, no discomfort and no pain. But his pulse was hardly perceptible, and he was so weak he couldn't even walk downhill. He would never make the hotel.

Peter made him as comfortable as he could, and then, at 6.30 pm, set off alone as fast as he could for help.

During the night Anthony experienced all the symptoms of heart failure. He was weak, had hardly any pulse, experienced acute anxiety and was confused in his thinking. He diagnosed hypotension,* but couldn't make out what was causing it. A horrible sinking sensation came over him, especially in the pit of his stomach. He thought he was dying. He has no clear recollections of the rest of the night. He remembers feeling desperately cold, shivering, his pulse picking up and fading almost to nothing. All the symptoms of heart failure, but why the complete lack of respiratory symptoms?

Then, at last, as we have seen, came the rescuers.

The final medical diagnosis at Grey's Hospital was: "Fairly fit, but not acclimatised to height, mild mountain sickness, and then collapse with only moderate exertion: collapse appearing to be on a hypotensive basis, seemingly cardiac in origin, spontaneously resolving on rest and/or descent from the mountain, with no demonstrable sequelae.**"

All this is very interesting from a mountaineer's point of view. They had both taken the same food and drink, so hypoglycaemia (drop in blood-sugar level) or any kind of poisoning seemed ruled out. At no time did Anthony have any trouble with his respiration. He had never had heart trouble before, and there were no signs of heart trouble in his present condition. A circulatory failure would explain the symptoms, but there was no sign of this. Personally we find it hard to believe that mountain sickness had much to do with it, though it is significant that Anthony's condition improved as he lost altitude. They were mostly at the 2 135 m (7 000 ft) level, and we doubt whether they had gone above 2 440 m (8 000 ft). Mountain sickness at these levels is extremely rare, and remember that Anthony was an experienced mountaineer (he had climbed on Mt Kenya) and had often stayed for days at a time at the 3 050 m (10 000 ft) level, with no ill effects.

---

* Hypotension means abnormally low blood pressure.
** Sequelae means any abnormal condition or disease related to or arising from a pre-existing disease.

So what happened to Dr Anthony Keen? We simply do not know. I believe we are in the presence of something new to medical science. May I give a brief account of something that happened to me years ago.

In December 1970 I set out to climb Hlatimba Pass (just south of Giant's Castle) together with two friends, Lawrence Ralfe and Bill Barnes, of Giant's Castle. The first day we proceeded up the valley of the Hlatimba River, and camped in the valley for the night. I climbed well, with no undue fatigue. Next day I woke, fresh and eager for the day's work. As on the previous day, I experienced no difficulty at all. Suddenly at about the 2 135 m (7 000 ft) level a strange feeling of utter exhaustion came over me. Even on a level contour I had to stop every 100 metres or so for a rest. We arrived at the foot of the pass, where we had planned to camp, at midday, and I was completely exhausted. That afternoon the other two climbed the pass. No power on earth would have got me up even the first twenty metres. I lazed about in camp throughout the afternoon. I tried to collect some firewood for our campfire that night, but had to stop and rest every few metres. There were no other symptoms – no nausea, no feeling of anxiety, no headache – simply a complete lack of energy. I did not think to check my pulse. I thought with dread, however, of the next day's eight-hour march to our cars. How would I ever make it? I was 70 years of age at the time. To me the explanation was simple. "Your climbing days are over, old chap," I said to myself ruefully.

I slept well, woke next morning, and as I was brewing the early morning cup of coffee, I suddenly thought, "I can do it!" It was five o'clock. We had planned to set off for home at 9 am. I told Lawrence and Bill, who were still in their sleeping bags, that I was going to climb the pass and would be back by nine.

It was one of the most exhilarating climbs I have ever made. I fairly raced up that pass, enjoying every minute of it. On top I headed north, along the escarpment edge. The air was gloriously fresh and keen. I went down another pass, and was back at camp by 9 am, as promised. A quick breakfast, and I then marched for eight hours, with a heavy pack, and reached the car at 5.30 pm, only reasonably tired.

How can one account for this? My collapse on the previous day was not due to heart trouble. A medical check-up the next week, and the doctor told me "You have the heart and lungs of a man of 30." It wasn't altitude sickness, I'm sure of that. I have never suffered in any way from altitude sickness, and have often been at 3 355 m (11 000 ft) with no distress whatever. What, then, was it? I just don't know, but I believe medical science has still a lot to learn about the body and its reaction to physical stress.

To return to our original story. In closing we add a brief postscript. Two months later the *Daily News* appeared with the following brief story:

A 10-year-old Natal boy, who braved 14 miles of mist, ice and snow, running barefoot and alone to arrange a helicopter landing spot after a climber had a heart attack, will receive a citation for bravery from the principal of his school.

He is Stephen Rossouw, son of Mr Steve Rossouw, forestry officer at Monk's Cowl in the Drakensberg Mountains.

Stephen's 12-year-old sister Caroline, who followed him an hour later with another urgent message, will also be honoured. She, too, went alone into the mist-covered mountains.

The citation for bravery, courage and initiative will be handed to the two children by the Principal of the Winterton Government School, Mr J. I. de Wet, this week in the presence of all their school fellows.

"We are very proud of them," said Mr de Wet.

Stark silhouette against feathery clouds.

8 Modern Rescues

Previous chapters have told in some detail the stories of mountain rescues carried out by what is regarded today as somewhat outdated methods, on foot or horseback.

What is almost certainly the first climbing accident in the Drakensberg took place as far back as 1897. On one of the short holidays of that year George Coventry, farming at Acton Homes, took his family by oxwagon to Gudu, the site of the present Royal Natal National Park. While climbing one day a rock became dislodged and fell on the foot of Archie, one of his sons, damaging it severely. His brothers carried him back to camp and then Walter, his elder brother, set off for the Upper Tugela hamlet (later renamed Bergville) for a doctor. Roads in those days were only two faint wagon-tracks, and Walter rode all through the night, over impossible tracks and bridgeless streams, to bring back next day the legendary Dr Jones, the first district surgeon to be appointed in the area. The doctor set the bones and managed to save the leg, but the big toe had to be amputated. Many years later Walter Coventry was to purchase Gudu and become the first lessee of the present Royal Natal National Park.

Dr Jones was quite a character. His Zulu name was M'delanguba, meaning that he was the one who did not hesitate to throw his blankets off immediately there came a call for his services. He usually travelled on horseback, but sometimes, when a road was available, used a small gig. He had a whole collection of dogs and never travelled without them, the dogs prancing away on both sides and in front of the gig, monopolising the whole road.

The first occasion when a helicopter was used for mountain rescue work in the Natal Drakensberg was in 1959 when a helicopter was commissioned to transport the rescue teams to the summit during the search for Keith Erasmus and Peter Christensen (see p. 92). This was a private aircraft. Hitherto helicopters could not reach the ceiling of the Drakensberg summit owing to the rarified air. But the development of the super-charged engine changed all this, and from then helicopters have been frequently used to pluck stranded climbers off impossible mountain ledges, to bring swift medical aid to men injured in rock falls, or to bring down the bodies of climbers who had fallen to their deaths in the mountains. In this chapter we have selected five typical rescues during the 20 years between 1963 and 1983 where men and women have owed their lives to the skilled and daring work of the helicopter pilots of the South African Air Force.

It was in 1963 that the SAAF were asked for the first time to assist in a mountain rescue. On Friday, 4 January of that year a small Alouette helicopter, piloted by Major R. V. Lamb, was flown down from Pretoria to Drakensberg Gardens.

On the previous Wednesday Kenneth Saffer, a 19-year-old Witwatersrand University student, studying for his B. Com. degree, had arrived at Drakensberg Gardens for a short holiday. The following morning he set off with a party of five other people to climb the 3 051 m (10 011 ft) Rhino Peak. On the way up Kenneth took a different route to the others, but they did all meet at the top. Again, on the descent, Kenneth took a different route. The rest of the party arrived back at the hotel late that evening, only to find that Kenneth had not arrived. The alarm was immediately raised and the Search and Rescue team of the Natal Section of the Mountain Club alerted. It was a rainy, misty evening.

Most of the men residents of the Drakensberg Gardens Hotel turned out that night and took part in the search under the leadership of a local farmer, Barry Tod. In the early hours of the morning the search and rescue team arrived, under Dr Sherman Ripley. It consisted of Dr Ripley, Malcolm Moor, Brian Hutchinson, Warwick Keating and Jim Thompson. They were equipped with

Malcolm Moor, veteran Natal climber and for many years a key member of the Mountain Club's Search and Rescue team.

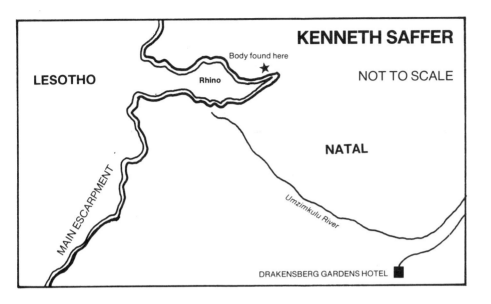

Body found here

Rhino

LESOTHO

NATAL

MAIN ESCARPMENT

Umzimkulu River

DRAKENSBERG GARDENS HOTEL

torches, flares, a Neil Robertson stretcher, resuscitation apparatus and medical supplies. All five members were expert mountaineers who knew the area well.

Throughout that Thursday night and all day Friday the search went on, hampered by mist and rain. At one time it was thought that Kenneth might have wandered off on to the Lesotho side of the mountain, where the nearest village is about 30 km away. The Lesotho police were informed and they carried out their own search on their side of the mountain.

Early Friday morning a SAAF helicopter from Pretoria arrived, but the heavy mist and cloud made flying impossible, and the pilot, Major Lamb, and his flight engineer had to stand helplessly by.

Saturday again dawned with the rain pouring down, and heavy mist still blanketed the Berg. At 10 am, however, the summit of the Rhino suddenly appeared through the swirling mists. It was time for action. The rescue equipment of the Mountain Club's team had already been stowed in the helicopter, and it only took a few moments to assemble four of the team, and they were off.

Ten minutes later Major Lamb set them down on the summit of the Rhino, and then, with the mists beginning to close in again, he was off. They arranged to signal to him with a Very flare when they found the missing climber, so that the helicopter could return for them. As it turned out, this proved impossible. The mist closed in again, rolling across the Lesotho border, making any further flying that day impossible.

The search for Kenneth Saffer then began, hampered by the clinging mist and the steady rain. The men slithered on the wet rocks and abseiled down difficult and dangerous pitches in the eerie stillness. It was Malcolm Moor who actually found the body. Kenneth had fallen down the north slope of the main ridge running down from the Rhino. He had obviously fallen twice (the first fall

61

a minor one), for his right leg was injured and he had wrapped his rugby jersey around it and tied it tightly. The second was a major fall – 150 m (500 ft) – and death must have been instantaneous. He was dressed in rugger shorts and a shirt, and was wearing sandshoes.

The body was strapped to a mountain stretcher, carried to the south side of the ridge, and from there lowered by rope to easier slopes. Here they were met by search parties from the hotel with a wheeled stretcher. At 3 pm they arrived back at the hotel.*

The second helicopter rescue is interesting, not only because it is still ranked as one of the most hazardous, but also because of a strange coincidence: the events leading up to the rescue were almost identical to those of the Derek Schaeffer tragedy fifteen years before (see p. 41). In both cases the time was the Easter weekend. The locality was the same, and the emergency took the same form – a climber went down with pneumonia in Mponjwane Cave. But there the similarity ends. The 1953 victim died because in those days helicopters could not reach 3 000 m (10 000 ft). The 1968 victim lived because of modern technology.

Easter of 1968 seemed to be all set for good weather in the Drakensberg, and on 7 April a large party of students from Pretoria University arrived in the Mnweni area (see map no. 2). There were about 60 young people altogether in the party, and all were members of the University's Exploration Society. They left their cars at the Police Post in the Lower Mnweni and from there trekked to the summit, basing themselves in Mponjwane Cave.

They then divided themselves into three groups of about 20 students each, and commenced exploring one of the most awe-inspiring, but least known, portions of the Drakensberg.

One of the groups was led by Malan van Rensburg, a fifth-year medical student and chairman of the Exploration Society. In his group was a young student, Cornelius Eckhardt, 23 years old and a keen mountaineer. On Good Friday, 12 April, he developed pneumonia.

At first the rest of the party were not unduly alarmed, but to be on the safe side Van Rensburg and another student, J. Geldenhuys, volunteered to go to Cathedral Peak Hotel for a stretcher. They left at three o'clock that afternoon, taking exactly the same route Martin Winter had taken fifteen years previously, along the top of the escarpment at 3 000 m (10 000 ft) altitude, past the Saddle, down the Umlambonja Pass and so to Cathedral Peak Hotel. Travelling partly through the night and camping down for a few hours, probably in the

---

* Of the rescue team, Dr Sherman Ripley has been convenor of the team for many years. He is on the staff of the Medical Faculty of the University of Natal in Durban. Malcolm Moor, with many first ascents to his credit, farms just outside Estcourt, while Brian Hutchinson is a Durban businessman.

Umlambonja Pass, they reached the hotel early on the Saturday morning and were back in Mponjwane Cave by 3 pm with the stretcher.

But that night Eckhardt's condition suddenly worsened, and it was decided to send three men to Bergville to obtain the services of a helicopter. Van Rensburg and Geldenhuys were exhausted after their long dash to Cathedral Peak and back, but there were plenty of others willing to go. Three volunteers left the cave at 10 o'clock that Saturday night, making their way down the treacherous and difficult Rockeries Pass in the darkness. At the bottom they proceeded rapidly down the Ntonjelana River, reaching the Police Post at 2 am. There they collected one of their vehicles and headed as fast as they could for Bergville.

At Bergville arrangements were made to alert the Natal Section rescue team and to despatch a SAAF helicopter to the scene.

The helicopter left Pretoria at six o'clock that Sunday morning, but struck bad weather on the way down and had to turn back. Pretoria immediately arranged for another machine to be sent from Bloemfontein. This aircraft, piloted by Lieut Bartman, picked up the three men at Bergville at ten o'clock that morning, and headed straight for the mountains. Half an hour later they touched down at Mponjwane Cave.

In the meantime, at eight o'clock that morning, it had been decided by the others, on the advice of the rescue team who had arrived during the night, to begin the descent of the pass on foot. They could not be certain that a helicopter would be available, and they also thought it wise to get the patient down to a lower altitude to ease his breathing.

A SAAF rescue helicopter in the Cathedral area flying towards Mont-aux-Sources. Pyramid and Column to the right.

Sunrise over the Cathedral Range.

The helicopter crew were told that the party had left two hours previously.

The problem now was to pluck the patient out of that steep, narrow, rock-strewn gash in the mountainside. The helicopter pilot decided to go below cloud cover and to fly up the gully so as to locate the stretcher party and the patient.

Of course there was no level area whatever for landing. As the helicopter flew up the pass the black walls closed in around it, and faces grew grim. With infinite skill and patience Lieut Bartman slowly manoeuvred the aircraft into a position where the one landing wheel was just touching the steep slope and the other hovered in the air. There was barely room for the huge aircraft with its whirling blades to fit into the narrow space. Bartman kept the craft as steady as he could while the men on the ground lifted Eckhardt carefully into the machine. Then came the tricky backing out, but suddenly they were free and away, soaring up and out into the clear mountain air. "It was a superb feat of airmanship," said one of the rescue party later, "and a dramatic climax to an undertaking which all of us feel owed its success to the splendid co-operation and organisational efficiency of the South African Air Force."

Eckhardt was flown to the Ladysmith Provincial Hospital and later back to Johannesburg, where he made a complete recovery from his mountain ordeal.

Later Eckhardt also paid tribute to three women in the party who had given him first aid for two days and nights to keep him alive. They were Marie Ribbens, Petru Scholtz and Ami Bester, two of whom were physiotherapists. He said he had felt fit at the start of the journey, but on the climb the wind "seemed to be going right through me". He had an uncanny feeling of desolation, and barely made it to the cave.

"My willpower got me there because I had no physical reserves left, and I kept falling down. A tent was pitched for me in the cave."

It will be many years before Klaus Schobinger forgets the tragic events of the night of 24 October 1975. He spent it alone in a small cave in the Drakensberg, barely surviving in sub-zero temperatures, not knowing that his brother-in-law lay dead in the open, only a few metres away.

The two men, Klaus Schobinger and Otto Werder, had climbed together for many years. They had recently ascended Mt Kilimanjaro, and they knew the Drakensberg well. They were both experienced mountaineers. They had planned to spend the weekend of 24 to 26 October climbing in the Cathedral area (see map no. 3).

They arrived at the Forestry gate about midday on the Friday. Then, shouldering their packs, they set off for Organ Pipes Pass.

This is an easy climb, entailing a pleasant walk up the Umhlonhlo valley, a bit of a zigzag to the summit of the Little Berg, up past the Camel, through Windy Gap and so to the pass proper. Here the going gets a little steeper, but there are no real difficulties and it is not long before you are out on the summit plateau.

Light floods into the valleys of the Mnweni area.

All went well until the two men reached the pass proper, with the Organ Pipes, long basaltic spires stabbing the blue of the sky, on their left. Here Otto Werder ran into trouble. He developed stomach pains and leg cramps. He struggled on for a short while, but soon it was obvious that he needed a rest. But time was getting on. The grey hush of twilight was beginning to spread across the waiting peaks. It was decided that Schobinger should go on ahead and prepare their cave for the night while Werder followed on more slowly behind. It is one of the cardinal rules of mountaineering: never, under any circumstances, split your party if you can possibly help it. They did split. They should have known better.

It had been their plan to spend the night in Ndumeni Cave. When you reach the head of Organ Pipes Pass you have the vast Lesotho plateau sloping gently down before you, but on your left rises the huge dome of Ndumeni Peak. In the rock faces of the dome are several small caves and one large one, known as Ndumeni Cave. The only trouble is, it is a "dry" cave. There is no water nearby. But at the base of the dome, running down into Lesotho, is a small stream, the Kakoatsan. You have to fill your water-carrying utensils at the stream before climbing up to the cave.

As Schobinger approached the stream he noticed a few ominous black clouds swirling around the peaks to the north. He started to fill his utensils, and then . . . it hit him, a blizzard of unprecedented fury and intensity. There had been no warning. Suddenly there was the terrifying scream of tortured wind, the roar of falling hail, the steel-like hiss of rain against rocks and blinding sheets of snow swirling across the plain. Experienced mountaineer that he was, Schobinger knew what this meant. He grabbed his sleeping bag, abandoned his rucksack and the rest of his gear, which he knew would slow him down, and fled, terrified, up the rocky slopes for the shelter of the nearest cave as fast as he could.

For the next six hours he was pinned down there, in sub-zero temperatures, with no food or water. He could not move. Survival out in that wild storm was an utter impossibility. He did not worry unduly about his companion. There was plenty of shelter on the lower slopes of the mountain, and Werder had all his kit and food with him. At midnight there came a lull in the storm and Schobinger was able to venture out. He searched around for his friend for a short while, failed to find him, and then returned to his cave for a few hours of troubled sleep.

Next morning, as soon as it was light, he set out, exhausted, cold and hungry, to find his friend. He first climbed up to the main Ndumeni Cave where they had originally intended spending the night. There was no sign of Werder. He then went down to the stream to retrieve his rucksack, and there he found Otto Werder. He was dead. He had obviously fallen 20 m (65 ft) down a sharp incline and broken his neck.

Horrified, Schobinger set off as fast as he could for help, 14 km down the

Windy Gap and Organ Pipes Pass. The scale is apparent from the two figures in the Pass.

65

rugged Organ Pipes Pass for the Forest Station 1 800 m (5 900 ft) below him. He arrived at 3.30 pm. "The man was completely exhausted when he got there," said Ken Carter, the chief Forestry officer. "It must have been terrible for him to have almost died of exposure himself only to find that his brother-in-law was already dead."

The Natal Section Search and Rescue team brought down the body.

There are two things we can learn from this tragic episode. Both men were mature, experienced mountaineers. They had done this particular climb at least a dozen times before. They knew the area well. And yet they came to grief and one man died.

One thing to remember is the terrifying suddenness with which Drakensberg blizzards strike. This one (the worst he had ever known, said Mr Carter) struck without warning. Without shelter no one could have survived a night out in it.

The other is a point we have already made, but must repeat: never, if you can possibly help it, split a party.

Accidents in the Drakensberg, of course, do not always fall to the lot of the inexperienced. As we have just seen, even experienced and well-tried men can fall victim. Another case is that of Bernard Shuttleworth, in November 1975.

Bernard Shuttleworth is a lecturer in economics at Natal University. Few men know the Drakensberg better. He is an experienced mountaineer, and at the time of his accident was a committee member of the Natal Section of the Mountain Club of South Africa.

Bernard was in a climbing party with three friends that Sunday morning, 9 November 1975. They hiked up from the Tugela Gorge below the Amphitheatre (see map no. 1), heading for Inner Tower Gully, with the idea of climbing Inner Tower. This is the well-known peak that abuts on the main escarpment at the southern end of the Amphitheatre, between Devil's Tooth and the actual escarpment edge.

Having arrived at the nek between Inner Tower and the escarpment, they traversed out onto the southern face of the peak, and just before midday began ascending a narrow chimney. We shall let Bernard himself tell the story of what happened.

"I was 15 minutes from the top when I saw a huge boulder, about a metre high, rolling down the gully towards me.* I instinctively covered my head with my arms and tried to move aside, but I knew it would hit me. I rolled down the gully with the boulder for nearly 10 metres, the rock broke, and the smaller pieces hit me in the back.

"I just remember scrambling frantically to get out of its path and thinking

---

* One of the party climbing above him had dislodged the rock.

'This is it!' Had the boulder hit me on the head or chest, it would almost certainly have been the end."

Fortunately, among the party was Dr J. W. ("Jaap") Earle, a neurosurgeon and ten years later president of the Natal Section of the Mountain Club of South Africa. Dr Earle immediately examined him and made him as comfortable as possible, and then arrangements were made to send for help. The accident happened on an MCSA meet. The remaining members of the party were still at Tunnel Cave when one of the climbing party raised the alarm. Two other members then ran down to the hotel. The men got the message through to the hotel within four hours, half the time taken to hike the route.

The Mountain Club's rescue team was immediately notified and the SAAF contacted. At 4.30 pm that afternoon a SAAF helicopter took off from Louis Botha Airport, Durban, with one mountaineer. In the fading light of their arrival the pilot found it impossible to pluck the victim out of his narrow chimney, but he was able to lift several members of the climbing party who were also members of the search and rescue team to the top in two flights before night finally fell.

Using torches, the team battled for five hours to haul Shuttleworth up to the summit. Throughout the ordeal Dr Earle was in attendance upon him. They all spent the rest of the night on the flat summit of the peak, with the unbelievable panoply of the stars above and the rustle of the night wind in the short tufted grass around them. The helicopter spent the night at the hotel at Royal Natal National Park.

1. *Escarpment*
2. *Inner Tower*
3. *Devil's Tooth*
4. *Eastern Buttress*
5. *Accident happened here*

67

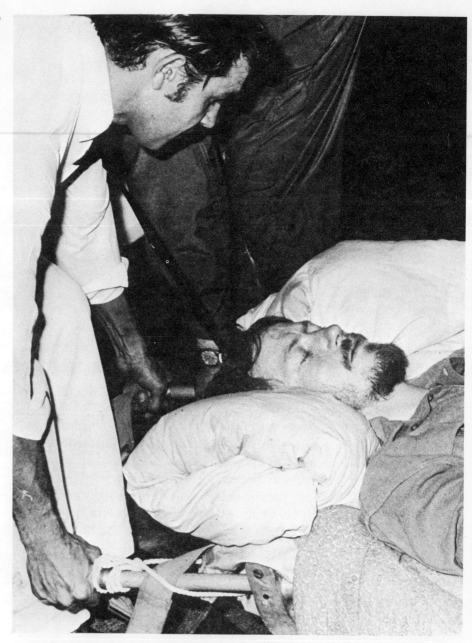

At first light the helicopter appeared, accompanied by the Chief Medical Officer from Natal Command. He was very pleased with the action Dr Earle had taken at the scene of the accident. "My task," he said, "was made much easier because the doctor had already stabilised Mr Shuttleworth for the flight." As in the case of shark-bite victims, victims of mountain accidents should never be moved until they have been first properly stabilised.

Bernard and the rest of the team were transported to the hotel. A short pause for rest and refreshment, and then they were off again, for Addington Hospital in Durban. There it was found that Bernard was suffering from two crushed vertebrae, a cracked pelvis and numerous severe grazes, cuts and bruises. He eventually recovered completely from his injuries.

Worth noting here is the speed and efficiency of the rescue teams and of the SAAF. Within six hours of an accident at the summit of a 3 000 m (10 000 ft) remote and practically inaccessible Drakensberg peak, trained and skilled rescuers had reached the victim, and the ease and swiftness with which he was taken to hospital undoubtedly was a major contribution to his ultimate complete recovery.

July 1983 saw what many knowledgeable Drakensberg climbers had long feared. "26 LOST ON ICY BERG PEAKS" were the newspaper banner headlines on Tuesday, 26 July 1983.

Prior to 1967 the matchless summit of the Amphitheatre could only be reached by men and women who were fit (see map no. 1). It meant a long, hard, eight-hour slog, climbing all the way, up the valley of the Mahai, through Basuto Gate, the exhausting climb up the Zigzag, past Sentinel Peak and then up the chain ladder. But in 1967 the Orange Free State Provincial Administration built a modern road from Witsieshoek up the mountainside to within two hours of the top. It was possible now for your ordinary tourist to park his car at the end of the road, climb to the top, spend six hours there and get back before nightfall. The result has been that on occasions, especially on holiday weekends, literally hundreds of people visit this summit plateau in a day. What would happen, many of us wondered, if a sudden blizzard were to strike and catch large numbers of people on the top? There are virtually only two ways down from that icy plateau, the chain ladder and the Gully. In a bad blizzard the Gully becomes choked with snow and ice, and the chain ladder ices up. Both are impassable. And your ordinary tourist, up for only one day, is scantily clad, with no experience of how to cope with snow and ice, possibly only a few sandwiches in his pocket, and there is no shelter on the summit apart from Crow's Nest Cave, small and wet. What would happen? We knew in 1983.

Early that morning Beryl Reid, manager of the Witsieshoek Mountain Resort, was woken by a telephone call from Johannesburg. It was a relative of a party of climbers who had gone up to the summit the previous Saturday. The caller's family had not returned from their mountaineering trip and she was worried.

It was a cold, wet, misty morning. It had snowed heavily the previous night and it looked like more snow. Mrs Reid immediately got out her car and drove the eight kilometres to the end of the mountain road below the Sentinel. There she found four cars, all with Johannesburg registration plates. She sped back to the Mountain Resort and telephoned the Witsieshoek Police. The police, in their turn, telephoned the SAAF in Durban and the Mountain Club Search and

Rescue team. Parks Board officials down at the Royal Natal National Park were also put on standby.

It was soon recognised that this could be an emergency of major proportions. Four cars probably meant up to 20 people, including children, stranded on the summit in deep snow and unable to descend. It was bitterly cold, with dense mist. Heavy snow blanketed the area. The police visited the car park, noted the registration numbers of the cars, and from these traced the various families concerned. All were from Johannesburg.

Heavy snow fell again that night, but next day, Tuesday 26 July, the cloud cover lifted sufficiently to allow two Alouette helicopters to take off from Durban. In addition to the rescue team, six teams were put on standby, as well as a Super Frelon helicopter. The helicopters took off at 6.40 am and, after a fuel stop, arrived at Royal Natal National Park at 8.30 am.

The shuttle service started immediately, up and down, up and down, ferrying starved and frost-bitten people down from those frozen heights. The rescued stared down in disbelief from the helicopters at the mountain paths they had used on their way up, completely obliterated and covered by the heavy snow drifts. The helicopter crews took the rescued, whose ages ranged from 6 to 63, to the Witsieshoek Mountain Resort.

At 10 am another light fall of snow occurred and the pilots had to call off their search for a couple of hours, leaving behind, however, two of the mountain rescue team to care for those trapped people on the summit whom they had not yet been able to lift off.

Just after noon the airlift of the stranded was over, and at 5 pm the tired pilots made a last reconnaissance of those howling wastes. They were empty. Everyone was off the mountain.

Down at the Mountain Resort 22 weary but happy people (the tally was 22, not 26 as the newspapers had at first said) gathered around a roaring fire to thaw out and relax in the lounge, together with the pilots, the flight engineers and the mountain rescue team, and the tales began. The swift response of the SAAF and the superb efficiency of their men and machines had resulted in 100 per cent success: there was not a single casualty.

Long into the night the tales went on. It had started to snow at 6 pm on the Saturday night. It snowed off and on throughout Sunday, but on Sunday night a blizzard had struck. Most of Monday it snowed and visibility was down to a few metres. Shivering with cold, everyone still remained cheerful and hopeful, though around the fire they all agreed it was doubtful whether any of them would have survived another night.

"It was very cold, and I have learned a lot," said Dr Jack Hickel of Alaska, an experienced climber. "In Alaska we get the low temperatures, but the snow is dry. It was wet up there, and that makes it uncomfortably cold."

Particular anxiety had been felt for a party of five, consisting of a father and his four children, aged from 6 to 12. They were among the first to be rescued –

Dave Jackson and his four children, Michael, Ingrid, Paul and Helen. Fortunately Mr Jackson was an experienced climber, and he knew how to survive. But all five of them had slept throughout Monday night under a collapsed tent, "praying," Mr Jackson said, "for the blizzard to die down".

Sheldon Yetts, an American visitor, and 14 other trippers spent Monday walking around in circles in the blizzard.

"The mist was low," said Mr Yetts, "and the driven snow blanketed everything, even the horizon. We eventually worked out that we must have been walking in a gigantic circle before giving up and pitching our tents." It was at this camp site that all 15 were found by the helicopters on the Tuesday. Mr Yetts had been particularly concerned about the safety of the younger members of his party. "I made them stay in their sleeping bags all day," he said, "and so avoid going out into the wind. Hypothermia can be a killer."

Captain Mike Lombard, one of the pilots, admitted that the rescue had been "a little bit tricky". Loose powdered snow, he said, and high winds had made manoeuvring very difficult, the deep, loose snow swirling around the two helicopters in dense clouds and cutting visibility. Landing and taking off were particularly difficult for this reason.

There is no doubt that had it not been for the superb skill and the cool efficiency of the SAAF, the events of 24 to 26 July would have gone down in South African history as a major disaster.

9 Rescue Organisation Today

The then president of the Mountain Club of South Africa, Colin Inglis, opening a symposium on mountain rescue at Hilton College in September 1983, said: "From the very earliest days of mountaineering there has existed the tradition among mountaineers of rescuing those injured in the mountains, or of recovering the bodies of those who have been killed."

He also quoted D. Gordon-Mills, who, in 1937, had written: "There is a self-imposed and sacred obligation resting on mountaineers the world over. In the case of fatality, if the relatives want the body, it must be delivered if humanly possible. This has been among the traditions of first importance for many generations. And of still greater importance is the obligation to bring down the injured climber."

And so it is that the Natal Section of the Mountain Club of South Africa has assumed the mantle of responsibility for rescues throughout Natal. It is a task that is taken seriously, a task that requires considerable organisation, dedication and sacrifice in terms of personal risk and cost in time and money.

Since those early days when mountain rescuers took days to bring the victim to safety, a thoroughly efficient and rapid rescue organisation has evolved. Better roads, radios, air support from the South African Air Force, modern equipment and advanced medical treatment procedures have all contributed to the better survival rate of accident victims.

Although the Natal Section's rescue service covers the whole of Natal, and elsewhere if required, most rescue operations take place in the Natal Drakensberg.

Each year a rescue convenor is elected, and it is his responsibility to appoint an *ad hoc* committee to assist him with mountain rescue administration. This subcommittee is responsible for general rescue administration and policy, financing, equipment procurement and maintenance, appointment of rescue organisers and rescue team members, training of the rescue team and of general club members and non-members such as Natal Parks Board and Department of Forestry staff. The subcommittee reports to the sectional committee.

The subcommittee appoints rescue organisers – the number and their locality can vary depending on their availability. Usually most are stationed in Durban and Pietermaritzburg, with occasionally some organisers living in the Berg area. They are men with authority, a sound knowledge of the Drakensberg, mountaineering ability and special rescue training.

From club member ranks the rescue organisers have access to a rescue team of 12 to 15 men, including doctors. These are all competent climbers who have had specialist training and are capable of impeccable rope work. The rescue team also has on call the back-up services of as many as 40 club members of varying ability. Outside the club the organisers can obtain assistance from a number of individuals and organisations. Natal Parks Board and Forestry Department staff stationed in the Drakensberg, a number of whom are likely to have had some training by the Mountain Club, are available, as are any parties of climbers in the Berg at the time. The South African Police can provide transport, fuel, and radios, and the Provincial Ambulance Services can be called upon for ambulances, radio assistance and other transport. Further medical back-up comes from about 15 anaesthetists, none of whom are mountaineers, but who are prepared to accompany the rescue teams if needed. The SAAF helicopter squadrons in Pretoria and Durban have provided invaluable assistance to the rescue teams. The part played by these helicopters has dramatically altered survival chances of accident victims, and we shall return to them later in this chapter.

A helicopter in the Drakensberg lowering a rescue stretcher.

Available to the rescue organiser is a fairly extensive range of equipment. This includes a number of stretchers of various types at strategic places in Durban, Pietermaritzburg and in the Berg. A number of Natal Parks Board and Forestry Department stations are also equipped with stretchers. With some of the stretcher kits are wheels, helmets, inflatable splints, roof-racks and hoisting bridles. Four comprehensive medical kits, designed to be robust, lightweight and compact for easy transportation to the scene of an accident are owned by the club. The kits are comprehensive enough to deal with the type of injuries or problems likely to be encountered in the mountains. The Natal Provincial Administration has equipped most Berg resorts and Forest Stations with similar kits.

The club has hundreds of metres of 9 mm and 11 mm kernmantel ropes. It also has three portable transceivers which allow communication from one to another, as well as communication with SAAF helicopters. Available to rescue organisers is the use of Parks Board, Forestry Department and farmers' association radio communication systems, and SAP and SADF portable radios. The difficulties of early rescue teams caused by lack of communication between different teams and the various teams and their base are vividly illustrated in the recovery of Ross Osborn's body in 1953, where Peter Pope-Ellis's team went many fruitless kilometres out of their way and lost valuable hours, simply through lack of a radio (see p. 187).

Nearly all Drakensberg holiday resorts maintain large stables of horses, as do some Parks Board and Forest Stations, which can be used if required by the rescue organiser.

The names and telephone numbers of the rescue organisers are distributed to all Drakensberg hotels, foresters, Natal Parks Board officials, the South African Police in Berg areas, South African Air Force, the Durban-based South African Defence Force medical personnel, and all Natal Section members.

When a runner arrives with the news of a tragedy in the mountains, or when a person or party has not kept a rendezvous at a scheduled time and is posted missing, the news reaches the Mountain Club from various sources – hotels and holiday resorts, Parks Board or Forest Stations, the police, or even the helicopter squadron based at Louis Botha Airport in Durban. The call can go to any one of the rescue organisers on the list. There is no roster of call-outs – and the organiser who gets the call accepts responsibility for it. He must decide on all the details of how the operation will be undertaken.

"All too often," says Roy Gooden, "the information about a casualty is scant and decisionmaking can be difficult. It is important that prime consideration is given to the patient, and the means to reach the patient and transport him off the mountain must be in the best interests of the patient. We emphasise the necessity for speed in the initial phase of getting medical help to the injured person, but not of necessity in getting him off the mountain. We would treat an accident victim *in situ* until he is in a fit state to be transported.

"Because of the nature of the Drakensberg and the distance from Durban, the fastest method for both search and rescue is by helicopter and, weather permitting, this would be our first choice. In adverse weather, car and then foot parties would have to be used. This is undoubtedly to the detriment of the patient as it is slow (it could possibly take several days to reach a victim and carrying an injured or ill person down the front of the Drakensberg on a stretcher is far from ideal transportation). Not only is the use of a helicopter advantageous to the patient but also to the rescue organisation. It generally means that far fewer people are required for considerably less time. When one considers that all rescue personnel are volunteers and most have to leave their jobs when called out, the advantage of using a helicopter becomes readily apparent. This could become an important factor if the number of call-outs continues to increase as it has done in Natal over the past few years. There is a danger that the limited resources of the club could become strained."

Earlier chapters have described some of the hardships endured by rescue teams in those years before South African Air Force helicopters became available. There is no doubt the availability of these machines has given many victims of accident and illness in the mountains a chance of life. There have been many examples of this, but the most dramatic illustration is to compare the

Major Peter Wilkins inches his helicopter between the Mnweni Pinnacles of the Drakensberg. Sudden updraughts and gusting winds make this sort of operational flying extremely dangerous.

Dr Sherman Ripley, convenor of the Search and Rescue team of the Mountain Club of South Africa, Natal Section.

cases of Derek Schaeffer, who died of pneumonia after a harrowing ordeal in which he was carried out of the mountains, and Cornelius Eckhardt, who went down with pneumonia in the same remote Mponjwane area 15 years later. Cornelius was lifted out by helicopter – and survived to climb another day.

But it was not always like this. Remember the heartbreak suffered by Derek Schaeffer's parents as they tried to find a helicopter to rescue their son? In 1959, a small private helicopter was used to ferry men and equipment to the top of the Amphitheatre for the search for Christensen and Erasmus. But this was all on an *ad hoc* basis.

Then, in 1973, Dr Sherman Ripley of the Natal Mountain Club made direct contact with the men of the helicopter squadron in Durban. They agreed to help.

"For a long time we simply liaised on an off-hand personal basis," he said. "We used to say, 'Look chaps, we need your help. Can you come?' And they would say yes or no."

But there was a problem. What was an emergency flight and what was a mercy flight? Emergency flights were free, and mercy flights were paid for – and there was never an accurate definition to separate the two.

"If a man had a heart attack on top of the Little Berg and somebody wanted a chopper to pull him off, what was that? Was it an emergency flight or a mercy flight? The debate went on for a long time," Dr Ripley told us.

SAAF helicopters were first called out in 1963 when Kenneth Saffer was killed in a fall on the Rhino, but this was still on an *ad hoc* basis. The Mountain Club teams and the helicopter pilots needed to practise together to become really proficient, so Dr Ripley wrote to the head of the Air Force, General Rogers, at the beginning of 1972. He received a reply saying the Air Force was happy with the joint activities of the squadron and the rescue teams, and General Rogers gave formal permission for regular liaison in the Drakensberg and in Durban. He also gave permission for Mountain Club rescue team members to remain in the helicopter throughout an operation. Since 1972 the Natal Section of the Mountain Club and the helicopter squadron in Durban have enjoyed the happiest of relations, and many joint exercises have been held.

After a call has been received by a rescue organiser, a team with equipment and supplies for two days can be at Louis Botha Airport and ready for take-off within an hour. Travel time to the Drakensberg is three hours by car – one hour by helicopter. If it takes three to four hours for a runner to bring the news of an accident, an hour to assemble the rescue team and another hour for the flight, the victim could be receiving medical attention within five hours. In the event of inclement weather it may be possible to fly a helicopter to the Drakensberg from Pretoria – the flying time to the northern section of the range would be the same as from Durban. The delay could stretch into a fatally long time if the team had to drive to the Drakensberg and then climb to the victim.

In the mountains no patient is moved by the rescue team until he or she is medically stabilised. With the medical kits carried by rescue teams and the training they have received, it is believed they can cope with almost any serious illness or trauma for up to 12 hours.

Rescue work by helicopters is, of course, difficult and dangerous, and requires constant practice. Split-second timing is often called for, and precision work of a high calibre in tight situations is necessary. Rescuers working with helicopters are trained to cling to the rocks when they have been dropped on a peak to prevent the down draught from the rotor blades blowing them off. When the helicopter returns to lift them off they must allow the winch cable to touch the ground first before grabbing it. The high static electricity in the turbulent air below the machine can result in a very high charge, and a nasty jolt to the man seizing the cable.

But what is the morality of taking a rescue team into a situation where there is a risk of personal danger?

"My attitude on this is very clear," says Dr Ripley. "I expect my rescue team, if there is any chance that the person is still alive, to go – come hell or high water. If we know the person is dead this is a completely different situation. There is no point in endangering life simply to retrieve a body.

An Alouette helicopter drops two members of a rescue team. One man clings to the rock face to save himself from being swept off the mountain by the wind of the helicopter blades.

"But I would point out that there have been only two or three cases where we have known the person was dead. Even with Al Palmer, who fell on Cathkin, we knew accurately where he fell and we were certain he must be dead. But the youngster who was with him was undecided when we asked 'Are you sure he was dead when you last saw him?' Under those circumstances we had to go and do something about it. Although we felt pretty sure about it, there was still a chance that he had survived the fall.

"When we know the victim is dead it is the responsibility of the police, not ours. We only go if the police can't do it, or if the Air Force asks us to go because we are more experienced than the police.

"But when the weather is bad there is no point in jeopardising an aircraft and its crew and a lot of rescue team members to go and pull a body off the mountain. I have had two friends killed doing exactly that sort of silly thing," said Dr Ripley. "If the police need help we will go – but we will go when we can do so under reasonably controlled conditions, even if we have to wait for a day or two. If the weather is persistently bad we would probably send a foot party in to see that the body was covered up or put on a stretcher, or moved out of harm's way so that the jackals don't get it."

Another poser in mountain rescue work is whether the Mountain Club should charge for their services (even an amount to cover travel or lost or damaged equipment). The Mountain Club of South Africa has always been adamant on one thing: they do not want to charge for their services. But the cost of equipment and travel is high. Should they be subsidised by either the Government or the provincial authorities?

Speaking at the Mountain Rescue Symposium in September 1983, Roger Barrowclough, chairman of the Otago section of the New Zealand Alpine Club, said his organisation could not afford the costs of using helicopters without government help. He said the club's contribution was in time, labour and skills . . . "and if we costed them it would be formidable".

By the very nature of the work and the environment in which it is carried out, the wear and tear on equipment is high. Add to this the time of rescue team members – particularly the self-employed (no work, no pay!), and the cost of a rescue would be exorbitant. Add to this again the cost of the helicopter (about R1 000 an hour for an Alouette, and twice that for a Puma or Super Frelon), and the rescue fee would be financially crippling for most people. Various suggestions were made at the symposium – from subsidies to a levy of a nominal fee on every person entering mountain regions. Significantly, however, consensus was that no charge should be made or tax levied. Mountaineers did not want to be dictated to by providers of money as to how mountain rescues should be organised and run.

Nobody going into the mountains wants to become ill or have an accident. But these things do happen. The Mountain Club of South Africa and its Search and Rescue teams train and prepare to provide a service to the community who go into the mountains in search of leisure and adventure. They do not want to be paid for this service. But we believe that travel and the cost of equipment should be the responsibility of the Government, and that a subsidy without strings attached should be levied.*

* The organisation of the Mountain Club's rescue teams in Natal was outlined by Dr Sherman Ripley in a talk to the Mountain Club of South Africa; "Mountain Rescue Organisation in South Africa", and again by Roy Gooden at the Mountain Club of South Africa's National Symposium on Mountain Rescue in October 1983. With acknowledgements to Dr Ripley and Mr Gooden and the MCSA; we have used notes on their talks extensively for the contents of this chapter.

Part III

RENDEZVOUS WITH DEATH

I have a rendezvous with Death
At some disputed barricade.

Alan Seeger, killed in action, 1916

We deal in this section with two tragic accidents in the Drakensberg where, in contrast to the majority of cases in Part II, the Dragon seized, and held, his prey. We have no desire to open up old wounds, but we believe there is much to be learnt from these two cases. Above all, they shine out as matchless examples of man's courage, endurance and compassion in the service of his fellows. They should be recorded for all time.

10 Tom Pinkney

Why did Tom Pinkney fall to his death?

Few incidents in the Drakensberg have caught the imagination of the public more than the Pinkney tragedy of 1947. This is largely due to the horrifying and unexplained nature of his death, and to the two epic attempts to recover the body. In 1975 we commenced the long and involved process of unravelling the details of exactly what happened. Our search was made all the more difficult by the fact that the five actors in the second attempt to reach the body had decided against any publicity. Eventually, however, we managed to trace four out of the five main participants in the drama (the fifth had died), and we either interviewed or corresponded with all four. In spite of the fact that after nearly 40 years the memories of some were naturally a little faulty, we believe we now have the full and correct story.

At 2.45 pm on Friday, 3 October 1947, two cars left Johannesburg for the Drakensberg. In the first were two young men and a girl, Dennis Johnston, Bob Hinings and Auriol Smith. In the second were two girls, Valerie Parker, Betty (we do not know her surname) and Mike Kruger. Bob Hinings, Valerie Parker and Mike Kruger were experienced mountaineers. They had planned to join George Thomson in the Cathkin area that weekend, and climb Monk's Cowl, but each had received a wire from George which read "Plans changed. Go straight to National Park". George was one of the most remarkable climbers the Drakensberg has ever seen, and we tell his story on pages 197 to 212.

The six young people spent the night at Central Hotel, Newcastle.* They were off at five o'clock the next morning. The first car proceeded to Cathedral Peak to pick up George. The second car dropped Betty at Winterton, turned round, and also headed for the Royal Natal National Park. By midday the whole party was together at the Park.

---

* By a strange coincidence I spent the same night at Cathedral Peak Hotel with the man they were going to meet, George Thomson. I heard from him his plans for the ensuing two days. See p. 79 of *Barrier of Spears*.

Why had there been this sudden change of plan?

Two weeks earlier, on the morning of Monday, 22 September 1947, a party of four young people had left the hotel in the Royal Natal National Park (see map no. 1) for the summit of the Amphitheatre. The party consisted, first, of two university students. Some time previously they had left on the summit some photosensitive plates as part of a radiation experiment they were conducting. They were going up to collect them. The other two were holidaymakers: Marjorie Franklin, a young girl from Durban, and Tom Pinkney, aged 32, from Johannesburg. There was no romantic link between Marjorie and Pinkney. They had only just met at the hotel.

The group took the well-known path to the summit, cut by Walter Coventry in 1924, through the wooded valleys of Dooley Waters, up Gudu Pass to Basuto Gate, turning left, and climbing all the time to the zigzag beneath Sentinel Peak (this section now turned into a mountain road). At the base of the cliff the path curves round the peak and then skirts two kilometres of tremendous precipices to the chain ladder (erected in 1930) which surmounts these final cliffs. At the top is a huge plateau bounded on the north-east by the mighty wall of the Amphitheatre, dropping 915 m (3 000 ft) into the depths below. They reached the top in the late afternoon and settled in for the night at the Mountain Club Hut (since demolished).

Early next morning Marjorie left the hut where they had slept and went down to the edge of the Amphitheatre Wall near the Tugela Falls. She was joined a little later by Pinkney. The two sat for a short while, admiring the tremendous view spread out before them, and then Marjorie suggested that they should return to the hut as the two university students wanted to get back to the hotel by ten o'clock.

She got up and prepared to leave. Pinkney told her to leave the jerseys and other odds and ends and he would join her with them in a few minutes. She turned to go.

"I had already left the spot," she told the investigating magistrate, Mr R. E. T. Reichardt, at the inquest a few months later, "and could not have gone more than six paces, when I heard Tom calling out 'Oh, my God!' I turned round to see what the matter was and saw Tom standing on the edge with his hands stretched out, like a sleep-walker. Suddenly he pitched forward into space and fell out of sight."

She immediately ran back to tell the others. "At that moment," she said, "I felt I must get away from the place or I would go over the edge myself." She did not return to the spot as she felt unable to go near the edge again.

What, then, had happened to Tom Pinkney? All sorts of stories have been told and theories advanced. The story that Marjorie's scarf had slipped out of her hands, and that in bending forward to retrieve it Tom had overbalanced and fallen, is obviously incorrect. It has been said that Tom was a bit of a show-off, and that at the hotel he would horrify people by dancing along the edge of

84

The rock face down which Tom Pinkney fell. Note the two figures at the top.

85

1. *Point from which*
   Pinkney fell
2. *Tugela Falls*
3. *Tugela River*

waterfalls. This must also be discounted. Marjorie's evidence at the inquest is clear, and is almost identical with what Marjorie's brother, Kenneth Franklin, told us 33 years later. We believe the explanation lies in some further details which Mr Franklin was able to give us.

Mr Franklin told us that his sister was now widowed, and asked us not to interview her or use her married name as she was not well, and that recalling the incident still upset her.

Mr Franklin said that before the party left the hotel the students had made it clear it was not a sightseeing trip. They had work to do, and wanted to get to the top of the escarpment in a hurry, sleep over, complete their work and return as soon as possible. Marjorie wanted to join them, and they agreed to her going with them. Tom also wanted to go, and he was advised of the same conditions – it was going to be a rush trip. After going a fair distance from the hotel Tom discovered he had left his tobacco and medicine (Luminal) at the hotel. He was believed to be a heavy smoker, and appeared to be anxious about leaving his tobacco and medicine behind. He was told he could go back to the hotel, but the two students would not wait for him. He elected to go on with them.

One vital fact is that Pinkney had to take a daily dose of Luminal. Mr Franklin was adamant about the name of the medicine being Luminal. He was questioned closely on this. It was, he said, one of "those funny things which stick in one's memory". He did not know what Luminal was taken for.

Luminal is the trade name of phenobarbital, a barbiturate drug that became available in 1912, and was used in medicine as a sedative, hypnotic and anti-convulsant. Epileptics would need to carry the drug with them constantly. Was Pinkney, then, an epileptic? And did his lack of nicotine make him agitated and tense, and more susceptible to an epileptic seizure? And was his desperate call "Oh, my God" that of a man who felt the onset of an attack? And why did he tell Marjorie to go on, that he would follow shortly? There is even another small link in the evidence. There is an entry in the log book kept in the hut, dated the previous day, to the effect that Tom was not feeling very well. We believe this is significant, and that it could explain why Tom remained behind for a brief moment telling Marjorie to go on, and then "suddenly pitched forward into space". This explanation comes closest to fitting the facts, and we believe it to be the true one.

The problem of the authorities, of course, was how to recover the body. It could be clearly seen from the edge of the escarpment, lying on a narrow ledge about 300 m (1 000 ft) down the sheer, perpendicular cliffs. The authorities enlisted the help of George Thomson.

Thomson had come from New Zealand to South Africa in 1943. He soon established himself as one of the most fearless and expert mountaineers this country has ever known. No better man could be found to do the job.

Thomson teamed up with Peter Pope-Ellis, warden at the time of the Royal Natal National Park, and on Wednesday and Thursday, 24 and 25 September, they made their initial attempts, first to climb up from the bottom, from the Gorge, and then to descend from the top. Both attempts failed. By Thursday night they were back at the hotel for further supplies. At first light on Friday, the 26th,* they were on their way up again. Halfway up they met Peter Henning, a climber on his way back to the hotel, and he joined their party. The three men arrived on the summit of the plateau by 2 pm. They decided to make their descent via Beacon Buttress Gully.** This is a narrow, almost vertical crack at the point where Beacon Buttress, immediately to the south of Sentinel Peak,

---

* On the same day Natal newspapers carried a short report saying that King George VI had graciously consented to the word "Royal" being added to the name of the Natal National Park. Earlier that year the Royal family had spent a holiday in the park during their visit to South Africa.
** Actually there are two Beacon Buttress Gullies, one on the south-eastern side of Beacon Buttress, close to the Tugela Falls, and the other (the old route to the summit plateau) near the chain ladder, and facing north-west (see map no. 1). To avoid confusion throughout this book we are calling the former Beacon Buttress Gully, and the latter simply the Gully.

joins the main escarpment. It is a dangerous, but the only feasible, route from the summit on to the face of the Amphitheatre cliffs. It had been climbed once before, in 1911. Two forest guards let them down to the first ledge on a length of rope and then threw the rope down after them. There was no turning back.

They then commenced their descent to the body. Thomson described the climb later as the worst he had ever made. The wall of the Amphitheatre is sheer rock, 915 m (3 000 ft) of it, down into the Gorge below, interlaced with a series of narrow, broken ledges. They first had to descend a full 152 m (500 ft), and then make their way along these incredibly difficult rock ledges, in the direction of the Eastern Buttress. By nightfall they were down on a narrow ledge, below the body, and 50 m (150 ft) from it. In between was a slippery, sheer rock face. Here they camped for the night.

Twenty-four hours of stark terror lay ahead of them. At 8 pm the weather changed. It started to rain. By midnight a blizzard had blown up, and it was snowing heavily. An icy storm of rain, hail and snow of unprecedented ferocity, blowing up from the Antarctic, had hit the whole of Natal. From Northern Natal and Nongoma came reports of devastating hail, with stones as large as fowls' eggs destroying crops and killing lambs. Driving winds increased the destruction, with telephone lines down, windows broken, and in the mountain regions sub-zero temperatures.

Weary and frozen, with no blankets or sleeping bags, the three men clung, shivering, throughout the night to their narrow ledge on the sheer face of the mountain, taking it in turns to be the middle man. Every now and then the roar of the storm was broken by the louder roar of great boulders, loosened by the rain, as they came tumbling down the mountainside.

Next morning it was still snowing and the mountain was shrouded in mist. It was impossible to reach the body, and the only escape was to continue the descent down the mountainside and into the Gorge at the bottom. There followed twelve hours of nightmare climbing. They were well off the standard route, and were soon completely lost on the mist-shrouded face of the cliffs. There were three waterfalls to be negotiated, and the only way was to abseil down through the icy water. It was freezingly cold and their fingers were so broken and frozen that they had to use their teeth to tie knots in the rope. Peter Pope-Ellis admits that it was only George Thomson's skill, courage and cheerfulness that saved them.

But at last they were down, at 6 pm, on the point of exhaustion, to find two African game rangers, sent up by the hotel, waiting for them with food and a roaring fire.

In the meantime the affair had aroused considerable interest, and the Natal Provincial Administration had to close the whole of the summit area to the public, so as to thwart morbid sensation-seekers who wished to gaze down at the body. They also placed a ban on all further attempts at recovering the body, not wishing to incur any further loss of life.

But bans of that nature did not worry a man of George's determination, and that is why, six days later, two cars left Johannesburg for the Drakensberg with six people aboard, three of them intent on joining up with George Thomson to make a final effort to recover the body.

They all met at the hotel at midday on that Saturday – George Thomson, Valerie Parker, Mike Kruger, Bob Hinings, Dennis Johnston and Auriol Smith – and left for the long haul up Dooley Waters at 2.30 pm. Halfway up they met another party coming down. Among them was Harold Corbett, a young man who had climbed with George before. He asked George if he could join the party, and George gladly agreed. They climbed the chain ladder in the dark, and arrived at the hut at 9 pm.

Next morning George, Valerie, Mike, Bob and Harold all went down to Beacon Buttress Gully. Dennis Johnston and Auriol Smith were not climbers, and they elected to stay at the hut.

The first thing George decided was that one of them should remain on top as a back-up in case of need. It was a wise, and proved to be a fortunate, decision. But who was it to be? Ultimately, to his great disappointment, the lot fell on Mike Kruger.

One of the factors that had contributed to the failure of the first attempt had been their lack of rope. In a climb such as this an abundance of rope is needed, sufficient to be able to leave some of it behind on sheer rock faces, to assist the climbers on their way back. George had seen to this. They had more than 300 m (1 000 ft) with them.

First came the precipitous descent of Beacon Buttress Gully. They abseiled down this, leaving a length of rope behind for the ascent. Then came the long traverse, south, to where the body lay. It was exhausting and dangerous work. The ledge they were on would peter out, and they would have to climb up, or down, to another ledge, which in turn would peter out. And all the time the exposure was extreme.* Above them towered 300 m (1 000 ft) of basalt, while below was the appalling 600 m (2 000 ft) sheer drop into the Gorge and the blue depths.

The traverse lasted for nearly a kilometre, and there were the three waterfalls to negotiate, one of them the Tugela Falls. By midday they were below the body, but within sight of it. Here they called a halt.

George insisted that Valerie remain behind. The body had lain out on the exposed ledge for nearly two weeks, in the hot sun by day and the freezing cold and snow at night. The sight of it would have been anything but pleasant. By this time Bob was terribly tired, and he elected to remain behind with Valerie. Harold and George were the fittest. Valerie, a trained nurse, made masks for them, and they began the climb up to the body.

---

* "Exposure" is a term used by mountaineers to describe the feeling of empty space around them.

They reached the body at 1.20 pm. It was lying on a ledge about half a metre wide. There was a large hole in the head, but otherwise it was untouched.

Retrieval of the body was impossible. There was no chance whatever of bringing it either up or down. Nor was burial possible – the body lay on solid rock. They built a large cairn of stones over it, stood for a moment in silence, and then left. What fairer resting place could a man wish for!

Then came the return trip, weary hour after hour, with death never far away. At one point Harold slipped and fell, but Bob held him, the rope burning his neck. He still bears the scar, faint but noticeable, to this day. At the Tugela Falls they stopped for something to eat. Then on again.

The last pitch, the climb up the Beacon Buttress Gully, was the hardest of all, for they were bone-tired. But Mike Kruger was waiting on top to help. He first sent down a knotted rope after tying himself to the rock face. George came up first, then Val, pale and exhausted. They tried to pull up Bob, but failed, as he was absolutely finished. Instead they brought up Harold, who was in slightly better condition, and then all four hauled on the rope and pulled Bob up, "white as a ghost". It was 6.30 pm: it had taken them nine hours.

That night in the hut Harold led them in a short burial service, "one of the most moving services I have ever known", said Valerie's letter to us 28 years later.

No details of this remarkable climb have ever been published. George wanted to send an account of it to the papers, but the others disagreed. Silence, they thought, was a more fitting memorial to young Pinkney than publicity. But we were able to contact the main actors in the drama, and they have agreed that after the lapse of many years the story should now be told. We spoke to, or had letters from, Marjorie Franklin (through her brother), Harold Corbett, Mike Kruger, Bob Hinings and Valerie Parker (now Mrs Neill). George Thomson had died. All five gave us the story as they remembered it, after a lapse of nearly 40 years. From these accounts we have pieced together what we believe to be the true story. We are grateful to them all.

Today Tom Pinkney still sleeps on in his mountain grave, high above the dreaming valleys 600 metres below. Surely, after death, there is no more idyllic setting in which to await eternity than the timeless tranquillity of these mountain peaks.*

---

* There is a rumour that some time afterwards George went back with two or three African game rangers, at the request of the Pinkney family, and that he brought the body down. We can hardly credit this. George could never have achieved such a feat without the help of a team of trained and experienced mountaineers. Even the best African game guards would have been of little use. In a letter to us just before going to press, Ethel Thomson, George's widow, confirmed that the body was never brought down.

11 Waldemar Peter Christensen

For many years there stood on the lofty summit plateau of the Amphitheatre, in the Royal Natal National Park, a slab of black marble let into a free-standing piece of Drakensberg basalt. The inscription on the slab read:

IN LOVING MEMORY OF
WALDEMAR PETER
CHRISTENSEN
WHO FELL ASLEEP HERE
29th APRIL, 1959
AGED 23 YEARS

Today you will not find this simple memorial. It has been removed, vandalised by the uncaring, and only the black eagle, soaring in the sky above, knows what exactly happened and of the exact spot where Waldemar Peter Christensen gave his life for his friend.

It was Tuesday, 28 April 1959, shortly after the Easter holidays. A light-hearted party of 15 students from the Johannesburg College of Education left Johannesburg for the Drakensberg. They arrived at the Royal Natal National Park, and next morning set out for the summit along the well-known bridle path, up through Dooley Waters and Basuto Gate to the chain ladder (see map no. 1). The warden, Joe Stanton, had warned them not to go. The weather report that morning, he said, had forecast a cold front moving up from the south, and heavy snow could be expected on the Drakensberg that night. But it was a warm, sunny day, not a cloud in the sky. A bit of snow, if it did come, would be an added thrill. They ignored the warning. The students had no warm clothing with them, and sufficient food for only 24 hours. They had planned to spend one night in the Mountain Club Hut, and then to descend the following day.

Noontide came, and a hurried snack-lunch beside a mountain stream. The sun was still shining, and they were still happily climbing. But in the late afternoon, with unbelievable suddenness, the storm struck. First came an uncanny drop in the temperature, and a wind. Soon ink-black clouds were boiling and swirling around the peaks high above them, and there came the growl of distant thunder. It suddenly grew ominously darker, and then, with a roar, the first icy lash of rain, whipping and tearing, was upon them. Soon it was snowing heavily, and visibility was down to a metre or so.

By this time the party was strung out along the path in a long line, from Sentinel Peak to the chain ladder, a distance of about 1,5 km. Those in front made a dash for the chain ladder.

This ladder, built in 1930, and a little over 30 m (100 ft) high, is suspended on the final precipitous cliff face of the escarpment wall. It requires a good head and steady nerves. Even some experienced climbers dislike it, many preferring the good hard rock of the Gully. Most of the party managed to surmount the ladder, and then, in driving snow, made a dash for the mountain hut, about 2,5 km away.

But three girls and a young man, lagging behind at the tail end of the line, had been unable to make the chain ladder. Night had now fallen, and in a howling blizzard they were stranded down below, cut off from the others and from the only building on those lonely heights. In the light clothing they were wearing, and without food, they could never hope to survive the grim night that now lay ahead.

Three of them were saved by a most fortuitous coincidence. Approaching the Amphitheatre from the other direction, across the plains of Lesotho and by a route hardly ever used, was another party. That morning Dick Reed, the Lesotho Government's meteorological officer at Oxbow, together with Arthur Bowland, *Natal Mercury* photographer, Miss Dorothy Rees of Amanzimtoti, and a *Natal Mercury* reporter, Miles Mattson, had set off for Mont-aux-Sources with pack-horses and a good supply of food and blankets, from Oxbow. They arrived at the hut just after the first batch of students.

As soon as Reed heard that a small group had been left behind, below the chain ladder, he immediately took command of the situation. He collected three of the men students, Brian Kerr, Peter Christensen and John Edgerton, and, in thick mist, carrying food and warm clothing, they set off for the chain ladder. Whipped by driving rain and snow, in a freezing gale, they managed to reach the bottom. There they found two of the girls, Cynthia Bennett and Joan Jansen, each aged 19. There was no sign of the third girl, nor of Keith Erasmus.

But the girls were in a state of collapse, almost in a coma. Reed said afterwards that they could not have survived another hour. In the state they were in, it was impossible to get them up the ladder.

Fortunately Reed was a tough mountaineer and he knew the area well. He remembered the cave. This is at the base of the summit cliffs, midway between Sentinel Peak and the chain ladder. In the early days, before the erection of the chain ladder and the Mountain Club Hut, it had been used as the only means of

93

Dick Reed

shelter by all climbing parties visiting the summit. By the 1950s it was rarely used. But Reed knew of it.

The four men managed to get the two girls into the cave, feed them and bed them down, but the situation was desperate, for by now the girls were in a coma, there was no fuel for a fire – and where was the third girl and Keith Erasmus? Reed decided to go back for further help, leaving Kerr, Christensen and Edgerton to care for the girls.

Reed will not easily forget that nightmare climb back to the hut. By now the chain ladder had begun to ice up. Chunks of ice had formed between the steel rungs of the ladder and the precipitous rock face, making it extremely difficult for the toe of the boot to obtain a firm stance on the rung. He fought his way up, inch by inch, in driving snow and wind. Near the top he missed his footing on the slippery ice, and fell. Fortunately, by a sheer miracle, his boot caught in the rung, and for a few moments he hung there, upside down. Then, with a huge effort, he heaved himself up, caught another rung, and pulled himself back on to the ladder again. Arrived at the top, he raced for the hut.

There he quickly organised a second, and stronger, relief party. This consisted of Arthur Bowland, Tom Edgerton, Neville Davis, Mike Brown, George Tempest and Miles Mattson.

They were just about to leave when the third girl staggered into the hut. She told them she had left Keith Erasmus on the path in a serious condition, and had come for help, not knowing of the first relief party, now settled down in the

94

cave not far from where she had left Erasmus near the cave and below the ladder.

But this second relief party never reached the chain ladder. In that howling blizzard and racing mist they completely lost their way. For nearly two hours they staggered helplessly around on the summit plateau, plunging thigh-deep into snow-filled gullies and ice-encrusted clefts, blinded by the lashing rain and snow.

Miles Mattson said later that once they realised they were lost, their main worry was that they would wander towards the edge of the escarpment, and, in the driving mist, plunge to their deaths.

"The whole top of the mountain was running with water which, in places, was turning to ice," he recalled. "All the paths and recognisable landmarks were snowed over. Whether we would ever have found our way back to the hut is a moot point. What saved us was that for a brief moment somebody at the hut opened the door."

The shaft of light flashed into that death-black night, giving the party a homing beacon to make for.

When they arrived back at the hut Dick Reed was determined to go out again in search of Erasmus, and to take more blankets and food to the party down in the cave.

"We tried to persuade Dick that he had done enough. He was in a pretty knocked up shape from his earlier ordeal, but he was determined," said Mattson.

So back into the night went Dick Reed again, leading a party of the more experienced of the students – Jan van der Merwe, George Tempest and John Vorster. They negotiated the now treacherously iced chain ladder and delivered clothing, food and blankets to the cave. Had this attempt failed, there is little doubt that those in the cave would have perished.

Meanwhile, what had happened to Erasmus? He had been almost the last of the long line of climbers on the bridle path. For some time he had been lagging behind. Altitude sickness had begun to hit him. By the time he had reached the base of the Sentinel darkness was on him and the blizzard had struck. He staggered on, growing weaker and weaker, and soon was in a state of complete mental and physical collapse. The third girl remained behind with him until it was obvious that he could go no further, and then, after making him as comfortable as she could, she ran for the chain ladder, climbed it alone, and then raced for the hut for help.

Away up in the cave, 30 metres above the path, things were a little better. They had some food now and they had blankets, but the two girls were still in a coma and the men were worried about Keith Erasmus and the girl, both of whom were missing. Peter Christensen decided to go and look for them.

Back along the path he went, and soon, huddled up against a rock and unconscious, he found Keith. Nearby was his rucksack and ice-axe, all encrusted with ice. Even the very clothing he wore was stiff with ice. Peter immediately took off his own lumber-jacket and covered him as best he could, thus surrendering his one hope of personal survival. He then sped back to the cave.

Here he told the other two that as there was no sign of the second relief party that Reed had gone to get, he would go back himself for help. They accompanied him to the foot of the ladder from where they watched him go up the first few rungs and disappear into the mists above. He was never seen alive again.

But he may have been heard. The second relief party, lost and floundering around in the snow-drifts on that ice-bound plateau, thought at times they could hear faint cries in the mist. They must have come from Peter Christensen.

Meanwhile, conditions in the hut that night were anything but pleasant. As in the cave, there was no fuel for a fire. Had it not been for the food and blankets brought by Dick Reed and his party, they would indeed have been in a desperate condition. Twenty-five people and a dog, Reed's fox terrier Chips, were crammed into the small stone building, and inside it was so cold that wet clothing froze.

Again Miles Mattson recalls: "Dorothy Rees did sterling work massaging blue bodies into pink bodies. She stripped the clothing off the nearly frozen students and rubbed life back into them."

Huddled together, they got what sleep they could, as the long hours ticked slowly by.

Next morning, Thursday, it was blowing big guns. They took stock of their position. Their own party, it seemed, was now intact. They assumed that the two girls and Keith Erasmus, together with Dick Reed's first rescue party (Brian Kerr, Peter Christensen and John Edgerton) and the second group led by Reed, were all safely down in the cave below.

Contact was soon established with the cave, and then it was discovered that Keith Erasmus and Peter Christensen were not there. A runner was sent down to the hotel with an urgent message for the warden, Joe Stanton, telling him of their plight.

Stanton immediately started the wheels of rescue turning. It soon developed into one of the biggest rescue operations the Drakensberg has ever seen. A priority telephone call was put through to Martin Winter at Frere asking him to come up and take charge of the rescue operations. Crack climbers from Durban, Pietermaritzburg and Estcourt began to arrive at the Park. For the first time in Drakensberg climbing history walkie-talkie radios and a helicopter were used. The helicopter was piloted by Captain Scott, and came from its base in Lesotho. The machine was used to ferry men and supplies up from the Park below to the mountain hut, and for searching the summit plateau.

Soon the mountaineers were joined by staff members of the Natal Parks Board, headed by Wardens Joe Stanton and Bill Trauseld, African game rangers,

The first helicopter to be used in the Drakensberg in a mountain rescue/search. It was a private plane from Lesotho, and was used to ferry men and supplies up to the summit.

Forestry officials, local farmers, police from Bergville, Winterton, Estcourt and Ladysmith, and a doctor. Even Basuto chiefs from Lesotho offered help, and sent contingents of their men. By Thursday evening 29 experienced mountaineers had gathered at the hotel or were on their way up. They were equipped with ropes, climbing gear, a stretcher and two-way radios. A complex operation was set up to keep the men supplied with food, fuel and other necessities from the hotel below. That evening conditions in the hut, designed to take a maximum of 12 people, must have been impossible, with victims and rescuers trying to make what little use they could of the available space.

Throughout the Thursday conditions on that lonely plateau grew steadily worse. The Tugela River was frozen over, and heavy mist made search operations almost impossible. Although any hope of the two missing men being found alive was by now almost nil, the rescue teams continued their search throughout the day. There were four possibilities. The men might have died of exposure on that terrible night; they might have fallen or toppled over the edge of the escarpment, as had happened to Tom Pinkney 12 years previously; they might have wandered off into Lesotho and found refuge in some Basuto kraal; or, miraculously, they might have found shelter under some rock overhang and still be alive, though few thought this possible.

Friday dawned bright and clear, and the task of evacuating the students back to their base began in earnest. This was a long and wearisome business, for the snow was in places waist-high, and the chain ladder was not thought to be safe enough, as it was still iced up. This meant using the Gully for the descent of the cliff face, necessitating a long and dangerous descent down the ice-choked gully. Three of the students – Mike Brown, Deon Glover and Will Ellis, chairman of the Students' Representative Council – refused to go down and elected to remain behind with the search party. While there was work to be done, they were not going to abandon the search for their comrades to others.

The sun shone that day on the vast snowfields, and a systematic search of the summit area began, with the helicopter methodically quartering the snowfields and criss-crossing the bewildering maze of jagged spires and ice-filled chasms.

Erasmus's body was found late on Friday afternoon, not far from his frozen rucksack and ice-axe on the path. He had fallen over a 20 metre cliff and been killed instantly. But of Peter Christensen there was no sign. He had simply disappeared into that frozen night.

Saturday also dawned clear, and the search went on, but Sunday experienced another heavy fall of snow, and on Monday it was still snowing hard. All hope of finding Christensen alive had now faded, but still the search continued. On Wednesday eight members of the Natal Mountain Club had to leave the summit and return home. The rest stayed on. Finally, on Sunday, 10 May, the search was officially called off.

But this was not the only attempt to find the body. Nelson Palmer's was one of the most interesting. Nelson Palmer was a Durban clairvoyant, a retired schoolmaster, who claimed to be able to find missing people by picking up thought waves in the same way that a receiver picks up radio waves. He could even, he said, locate bodies, and he had proved this in the Van Buuren murder case a few years previously by telling the police exactly where they could find the body of the murder victim, Myrna Joy Aken, under a bridge on the South Coast road. His help was sought, and he came up to the Park. He went into a trance and said the body had fallen down a steep, narrow ravine, 30 m deep. It was so narrow and difficult, he said, that he doubted whether it would ever be found. Arrangements were made, however, for Bill Trauseld to be lowered down the ravine on a length of rope, on Saturday, 9 May. He found nothing.

Others offered their services. Late on Saturday afternoon, 2 May, a light aircraft set out from Ladysmith with two Ladysmith businessmen on board to join the search. Conditions were so treacherous, however, that the aircraft had to return to Ladysmith.

On Friday, 29 May, nearly three weeks after the search had been officially called off, a Landrover with five men left Johannesburg. The men were members of the Blue Scarf Mountain Rescue Club, a mountain rescue team assembled and trained by an expert Swiss mountaineer, Dr George Ribi. At the time they were believed to be the only organised mountain rescue club in South Africa. They failed to find the body, but they did save the lives of five amateur mountaineers who were also searching for the body. This latter group had set out badly equipped (one man was wearing tennis shoes) and once again the snow had come down. Trapped on the summit, nearly frozen and with their food running out, they were fortunately found by Dr Ribi and his team. Dr Ribi managed to revive them, and then helped them down the mountain.

A searcher finds the rucksack of Keith Erasmus on the path at the spot from which he fell.

When Chief Wessels Mota, Chief of the Batlokoa tribe at Witsieshoek, heard that the Parks Board had officially called off the search on 10 May, he said, "Then it rests with my people to try to find the young man." At 8 am on Saturday, 16 May, the Chief took 100 of his men up to the summit. They, too, failed.

Two months later: *Natal Mercury*, Monday, 6 July 1959.

BODY OF STUDENT FOUND ON BERG

The body of Peter Christensen, 23-year-old student who perished in a blizzard on the top of the Drakensberg range in April, was found late on Saturday afternoon by a party from Witsieshoek.

Mr A. D. Terblanche, Agricultural Supervisor in the Witsieshoek Reserve, found the body in open country about 600 yards from the mountain hut on top of the escarpment where a large party of students was marooned in the first heavy snowstorm of winter.

Mrs A. J. de Villiers, wife of Sgt de Villiers of Witsieshoek Police Station, who led the search party, told me last night that the body had been preserved by the heavy blanket of snow under which it had lain.

The search party, she said, had covered it with a tarpaulin, weighted with rocks, and had erected a cairn to guide the recovery party to the spot.

Several search parties must have passed quite close to the spot where it was found during the last few weeks.

Sgt de Villiers reported that snow was still lying on top of the escarpment, and that it began to snow heavily again yesterday.

Dick Reed received a medal from the Humane Society for his outstanding service to his fellow men during that harrowing night. Ben Venter, chairman of the College's Hiking Club, wrote to Arthur Bowland and Miles Mattson later thanking them for their "unselfish and unrestrained help" in rescuing the students. He stressed particularly the fact that the maintenance of the students' high morale throughout their ordeal was largely due to these two men. "It has often been asked," he said, "what would have happened had Dick Reed and his party not taken the students under their wing? That question I dread to answer."

Part IV

THE BRIGHT FACE OF DANGER

It is the nature of man to journey
where there is hope of great danger.

From an old medieval
Norse MS, "The King's Mirror"

Part IV pinpoints some of the dangers that may be encountered in the Drakensberg. This mountain region is becoming increasingly popular among the general public as a place for recreation, where one can escape, if only for a brief while, from the pressures of life. But it has its dangers, and unfortunately all too often visitors to the area are completely unaware of these dangers. The result is that the accident toll is steadily rising. More and more people are becoming victims to these hazards, and every accident means the calling out of a rescue team, entailing loss of valuable time to the team members, and often endangering life and limb. Accidents should not happen in the Drakensberg. They are almost always the result of carelessness or sheer recklessness. It is hoped that this section will help to create among the public an awareness of the latent dangers and a desire on their part to do all they can to minimise these dangers.

At the same time we remind the reader of what one of us said in the Preface, that the Drakensberg should not be regarded primarily as a potentially dangerous place. Rather it is a gateway to joy and peace, to physical exhilaration and fitness, to relaxation and spiritual renewal. Let us do all we can to keep it so!

12 Blizzards

In the last two chapters we have considered two of the worst blizzards the Drakensberg has ever known. Blizzards have been the cause of a number of tragedies and deaths in the Drakensberg. What can we say about them?

The weather pattern in the Drakensberg is fairly predictable, but it is wise to remember that the unpredictable can happen. A basic knowledge of Drakensberg weather, and of what sudden changes may be expected, is of tremendous value to the mountaineer, for sudden changes can spell disaster. Obviously one must prepare to face, and to cope with, such changes.

Weather patterns are governed by a complex interaction of a number of different factors. It is not our purpose in this book to discuss and examine these factors in detail, but the mountaineer should be familiar with the general pattern.

Broadly speaking, there are four main factors that govern Drakensberg weather.

First is the configuration of the land. The Drakensberg forms the edge of a high, inland plateau which, towards the west, slopes gradually down into Lesotho and on to the west coast, and to the east drops almost sheer from a height of 3 000 m (10 000 ft) down to the plains of Natal, first to the Little Berg, at a height of roughly 2 000 m (6 500 ft), and from there more gradually down to the foothills and the plains of Natal. The sheer drop from 3 000 m to 2 000 m is known as the escarpment. Altitude plays an important part in weather changes.

Secondly we have the high and low atmospheric pressure systems. Generally speaking, in summer high pressure systems form over the south-east Atlantic and the Indian Ocean, while inland, especially over the northern Cape and north-western Free State and Transvaal areas, we find low pressure systems. In winter this is reversed, low pressure systems being found over the southern ocean areas, and high pressure systems occurring inland over the Free State and Transvaal. These high and low pressure systems determine the direction of airflow, winds blowing from high pressure areas to low pressure areas.

Thirdly, we have a regular system of cold, wet air moving up periodically from the Antarctic Polar regions towards South Africa, always in a north-easterly direction and travelling roughly parallel to South Africa's east coast. This movement of cold, wet air is called a cold front.

And finally we have the warm Agulhas Current, flowing in a south-westerly direction along the east coast of South Africa, above which is a layer of warm, moist air.

This may appear to the experts to be an oversimplification, but it is all the mountaineer needs to know if he wishes to understand Drakensberg weather.

Rain occurs in the Drakensberg in two different ways, as a result of the movement of two entirely different systems.

In summer the warm, moist air over the Agulhas Current moves inland, from the high pressure system over the Indian Ocean to the low pressure area of the interior. It strikes the Drakensberg escarpment and is forced upwards, into the cooler air of the heights, where it condenses to form huge masses of cumulo-nimbus cloud, towering high up into the atmosphere. In summer, from midday onwards the whole summit of the escarpment is often covered, day after day, with these heavy cumulus clouds. Soon they break into afternoon storms, with lashing rain and sometimes hail.

The second system is the moving up, from the south, of a cold front, which creeps slowly up from the Cape to Natal, in a north-easterly direction. In winter these cold fronts, laden with moist air, can be particularly severe, for in the higher areas the rain turns to snow and that is how our blizzards occur. Only rarely does this happen in summer, but it can happen, and there is not a single month in the year when snow has not been known to fall at some time or other in the Drakensberg. A few years ago Cathedral Peak Hotel had the thrill of a white Christmas.

These blizzards strike with unbelievable ferocity and speed in the Drakensberg. We have already told the story of the Christensen tragedy. There is a common belief that South Africa is a land of sunshine and of balmy, warm days: blizzards are associated with places like Switzerland and the Himalayas. This is certainly so, but blizzards can occur in the Drakensberg, and they are sometimes as lethal as anything experienced in Europe.

For the ill-equipped mountaineer these blizzards can be terrifying, but there are one or two reassuring facts. Although at the time they strike with lightning speed, they can, in the long term, be foretold, so long as one can interpret the weather signs. For instance, they are often preceded by several days of hot bergwinds. These westerly winds are regular features of late winter and early spring weather in Natal. On the 3 000 m (10 000 ft) summit plateau they blow for days on end with a ferocity that is hard to believe. It is impossible to stand upright against them, and the hiker simply has to call it a day, find some sort of shelter, and sit it out. Then comes a sudden drop in temperature, and the blizzard is upon you. But remember that this cold front usually takes several days to move up from the Cape. Although it adds to the weight of your pack, it

is a wise precaution, especially in winter, to include in your pack a small radio set capable of picking up weather reports. The experienced mountaineer, fortunately, can usually sense beforehand, subconsciously, a change in the weather, and plan ahead accordingly for it.

Against this is the fact that the summit plateau, at 3 000 m (10 000 ft), is bleak, desolate and inhospitable. There is hardly any shelter. In the whole 150 kilometres from Bushman's Nek to Mont-aux-Sources there are only two permanent buildings – the Mountain Lodge in the Sehlabathebe National Park, above Bushman's Nek, and the chalet on the summit of Sani Pass. The Natal Mountain Club's hut at Mont-aux-Sources has long been unusable, vandalised by neighbouring Basutos. The Transvaal Mountain Club once had a hut on the summit of Organ Pipes Pass in the Cathedral area, but this disappeared long ago. At one time the old Basutoland Government tried to establish a police post on the summit at Mont-aux-Sources, but this had to be abandoned as it was found that the area was too bleak, and at too high an altitude, for permanent occupation. There are a few caves on the summit, but even the best of these is open to the weather. I have often found snow and ice packed at the far end of the Upper Injasuti Cave, one of the best of these shelters.

It follows from all this that the mountaineer, on the summit at least, must always be on his guard against a change in the weather. In addition to the signs we have already described, watch the clouds. The sudden appearance of high cirrus clouds in the west is often a sign of approaching snow. An unexpected rise in temperature during very cold conditions can also herald a snowstorm. A build-up of thick, black cumulo-nimbus in winter is a sure sign of thunder conditions and the certainty of a bad blizzard.

The Little Berg, of course, the mecca of your average tourist, is a different matter altogether. Here hotels and permanent dwellings are never far away, there are innumerable caves, and the snow is never very deep, nor does it last long.

What should one do, then, if one is caught on the summit in a blizzard?

First of all, make sure that you are properly equipped. Practically all of the blizzard tragedies have been due to the party being improperly equipped. Always, even in the hottest summer weather, carry plenty of warm, windproof clothing, wear heavy boots, and, if one is up for more than a day, carry at least one sleeping bag, preferably two.

Nowadays it is especially necessary to give a warning against thieves. Many a climber in recent years has had his spare clothing stolen by Basuto thieves. They have even been known to slip their hands under the flaps of your tent while you are asleep, and steal spare items of clothing and equipment. Also, be sure that you have at least two or three days' reserve food, even if it is only an extra packet of oatmeal and a few slabs of chocolate, enough to keep body and soul together in an emergency. A pressure stove is better in the cold than a gas cooker, but if you have the latter carry with you more butane gas cooking cylinders than you

need. Make sure your first-aid kit is adequate, and don't rely on caves for shelter. A light patrol tent is the answer.

Ominous clouds herald a storm.

If you see a blizzard coming on, it is best to get down from the summit in good time if you can. The danger is that the passes leading down from the summit, through the precipitous rock wall, are few and far between, and even the best of these can become so choked with snow and ice as to render them impassable after a blizzard. Remember, too, the extreme danger of breaking or twisting a leg or ankle while walking over snow on the summit. That glistening sheet of snow that so entrances you can cover huge rocks and fissures, into which you can slip or fall with dire results.

If you can't get down, and have no tent, find what shelter you can, a cave or rock overhang. You are more likely to find these on the actual edge of the escarpment than further inland.

If the worst comes to the worst, your food is running out, you are mist-bound

109

and lost, and there is no hope of descending into Natal, head for Lesotho. Here, within a day or so, at lower altitudes, you are sure to find a shepherd's hut, or shelter of some sort. Make sure, though, that you are heading in the right direction. Don't depend on a compass. In this rock-strewn mountain area a compass will often give you a faulty reading. Simply follow a stream. On the summit streams will always flow in one of two directions, either eastwards over the escarpment edge (you'll soon know if, in the mist, you have chosen such a stream!) or westwards to south-westwards into Lesotho. Keep to the stream bed and you can't go wrong, though it may take you a few days to reach help. Today there is a rough mountain road from Butha-Buthe to Mokhotlong, running parallel to the escarpment and from 20 to 50 kilometres inland, along which vehicles periodically pass. You will strike this road eventually.

The biggest thing to guard against in a blizzard is hypothermia. This is a lowering of the temperature of the body's inner core to a point where the vital body functions, such as of the heart and lungs, are impaired, resulting in death. It can, indeed, be a rapid killer.

Cold, alone, rarely causes hypothermia, certainly in the Drakensberg where temperatures rarely go below –15 °C. It is cold plus wind plus wetness that causes the condition. Cold is difficult to avoid, but with due care one should be able to avoid the other two determining factors. So if you have to sleep out in a blizzard, at least try to get out of the wind, and have dry clothing to wear.

The main symptoms of hypothermia are slurred speech, a dreamy, confused state of mind, loss of memory, stumbling and falling, and bouts of shivering and cramp, followed by eventual collapse, loss of consciousness and death.

To treat a victim of hypothermia, there are two essential things you should do. First of all, raise the victim's body temperature – not an easy thing to do if you are out in a blizzard. Warm baths are obviously out of the question! What you can do is to get the victim out of the wind and into dry clothing. Then put him into a sleeping-bag – if possible a warm bag. You can do this by first putting someone else into the bag for a short while, preferably stripped so that his own body heat can be more quickly and easily transferred to the bag. Another way is to put someone else into the bag with the victim. Then give him warm, sweetened fluids to drink, and feed him well with high-energy foods, such as chocolate, dates or glucose tablets. Throughout the treatment the victim should be kept awake. Don't give alcohol.

We give now accounts of two accidents in the Drakensberg caused by blizzards, in the first of which the victims survived, by a very narrow margin, and, in the second, where one man paid the ultimate penalty.

13 Gunter Stein

For sheer naked courage it would be difficult to beat the story of Gunter Stein.

Gunter Stein was a cripple. At the age of nine he had been stricken with one of the most virulent forms of polio, and at the time of his great adventure, in October 1954, at the age of 24, he could only hobble along with the aid of two sticks. His legs were in calliper splints.

Two years previously he had spent a holiday at one of the Drakensberg hotels. Here he met a young honeymoon couple, Ephney and Roger l'Hoest. Gunter was a professional photographer, and Roger, a Belgian, was an experienced climber. Enviously he watched the young couple setting out each morning with their packs on their backs, bound for the high places.

It was during this holiday that Gunter fell in love with the Drakensberg. One day he told Ephney and Roger of his driving ambition: he too would climb a mountain – and not a small one! It would be a big one, a real big one, the biggest he could find.

Would Roger help?

Roger looked at the two sticks that lay beside Gunter's chair, and shook his head. No way, he said, could it be done. But Gunter persisted. There was no opportunity during this visit (rather to Roger's relief!), but Gunter would not give up. Eventually they agreed to meet at some future date, if possible in the Royal Natal National Park.

And so it came about that Monday morning, 3 October 1955, saw three young people, Ephney and Roger l'Hoest and Gunter Stein, setting off from the Royal Natal National Park, heading for the Mahai valley. It was 8 am.

The previous day they had enquired of the chief warden, Peter Pope-Ellis, about climbing to the Mountain Club Hut on the summit of the Amphitheatre (see map no. 1). Yes, he said, no problem. There were three Transvaal men there at the time, but they were due back any day now. Their names were A. W. Jones, a Mr Goldbold and a third man whose name he had forgotten.

But he was a little taken aback when he heard that all three were going up. "Mr Stein," he said, looking at the two sticks and the callipered legs, "are you

Gunter Stein at the time of his great adventure.

111

sure you can manage it? It's fourteen to fifteen miles to the hut, a climb of nearly six thousand feet, and at the end of the climb the chain ladder, more than a hundred feet high. How will you ever manage it?"

"Mr Pope-Ellis," said Gunter quietly, "I'm going to climb that mountain, and I'm sure I can manage it."

"You see," replied Pope-Ellis, "I'm responsible for your safety. I've got to be careful." But after Ephney had told the warden that her husband was an experienced mountaineer, he eventually, somewhat reluctantly, agreed.

They left at 8 am the following morning, making good time in the lower reaches of the valley, Gunter in the middle and Roger and Ephney on either side. Roger carried the main pack with most of their food, spare clothing and sleeping gear. Ephney carried a lighter pack. Gunter, in between, tapped away with his two sticks, carrying only his camera.

It was a beautiful spring morning, with just a hint of mist in the valleys. Above them, diamond-sharp in the clear air, towered the peaks, etched sharp against a turquoise sky.

By midday they had reached Basuto Gate on the Qwa-Qwa border, not quite halfway. By this time Gunter was beginning to tire, and it was time for a stop for lunch. But Roger persuaded them to go on. "Let's try to get at least halfway before we stop," he said. "We've still got a long way to go."

At 12.30 pm he suddenly threw down his pack. "This'll do," he said. "Quite a good spot." With a sigh of relief Ephney discarded her pack and, flopping down, stretched out her arms and legs on the young green grass. Gunter followed suit.

It was indeed a magnificent spot for the break they all needed. Through a gap in the ridge they could see, far below, a sight not seen by most visitors to Royal Natal National Park – the top of the Policeman's Helmet! In front and ahead of them lay the twisting pathway, and towering over all, the majestic precipices of Sentinel Peak. Away to the right, in the misty distances, rose the enigmatic spires of the Maluti Mountains. Clouds were gathering over the higher peaks, like gigantic clumps of cotton wool, white and gleaming, but to Roger they did not seem worth worrying about.

After a short rest Gunter hobbled over to the gap in the ridge with his camera and started taking photographs. "Roger," said Ephney quietly, "do you think he can make it? He doesn't look too good."

After a pause: "Yes, I think there's a chance. He's got all the determination in the world, and that's half the battle. It means a lot to him to get there. There's a chance."

At 1.30 pm they set off again. The path was narrower now, and steeper, with almost a sheer drop on the right. It meant careful going. If one of those sticks should slip . . . !

It was 6 pm before they reached the Three Witches, three small prominences to the left of the path, just below Sentinel; six kilometres still to go to the chain

ladder, and eight to the hut. By now Gunter was obviously reaching his limit, the darkness was closing in rapidly, and the clouds were piling up, black and ominous now around the Sentinel.

Roger was worried. Bad weather was obviously on the way. Should he push on in a determined effort to reach the hut and shelter, or should he opt for the cautious decision, call it a day, and head back for home? It would be downhill all the way. But, surely, it couldn't be snow! This was October, well past the season for blizzards. At worst it could only be a rain storm. He decided to push on.

Darkness fell and they were still some distance from the ladder. Using torches, they groped their way along the path, keeping well to the rock face on their left, away from the almost sheer drop on the right. Gunter slipped once, but managed to keep his balance. Grimly they pressed on.

Suddenly the storm hit them, a swirl of rain, followed by a bitter icy blast that sliced through their thin clothing, and then snow. In a few seconds they were drenched.

By now Gunter was at the end of his tether. Even without the storm he was on the point of collapse. Against the storm he had no defence. But Roger knew the danger. "We must go on or we will die here," he shouted. In a daze the three young people struggled on. There was no shelter at all. Roger took the lead, the other two behind him with their heads down and their eyes glued to the pool of light at their feet from Roger's torch. Mercifully they could not see the drop on their right.

Flesh and blood could take no more. Suddenly Gunter sank to the ground. "I'm sorry," he gasped, "dreadfully sorry, but I can't go on. I'm finished."

"OK," said Roger calmly. "Take a short rest. You'll soon feel better. Not to worry."

They eased him down against the face into a comfortable position and tried to keep him warm. But by now the snow was falling heavily, a blinding white sheet, soaking through their thin clothing and streaking their hair and eyebrows. They had one chance: the three men already up in the hut, five kilometres away.

"Ephney, can I see you a moment." Roger was standing a few metres off, near a large rock. "Look," he said, "I'm worried. Gunter will never make the ladder. It's soon going to be iced up. It'll need two strong men, one behind him and one up in front. You'd never be able to hold him if he slipped. We're in a jam." He gasped as a flurry of ice and snow hit their faces and nearly blew them over the edge.

"You see," he continued, "we can't stay here – it would be the end. I'd go to the hut for help, but I can't leave you alone here with Gunter in this weather. We've had it!"

"Let me go," said Ephney. "I'll leave my pack behind. I'll make it. I'll send the three men back to help. You stay here with Gunter."

"My dear, you'd never make it," Roger said. "You've never even seen the ladder. At the best of times it's grim. In these conditions it will be impossible."

Threatening clouds over the Amphitheatre.

"It's our only chance," she said as she slipped away into the darkness.

"Always grip hard with both hands," he called out after her. "Keep well into the rock face, and don't look down."

As Roger had said, even at the best of times the ladder needs strong hands and stout nerves. It is made of steel chain, pegged and riveted into the sheer, vertical rock face, with rungs, entailing more than 30 m (100 ft) of steady, dizzy climbing. In a blizzard it becomes slippery and eventually ices up, and then even the stoutest-hearted will not attempt it.

Twenty minutes later Ephney reached the ladder. It looked terrifying in the light of her torch, soaring up and away into the blackness. As she put her foot on the first rung the wind rose to a howl of fury and slammed her frail young body against the rock face.

Step by step she slowly made her way up, the snow tearing at her clothes. She began to sob as she desperately fought her way up, rung by icy rung. Eyes shut, she blindly felt for the next rung, hanging in empty space. Once her foot

115

slipped, but one hand held and she regained her footing. She grew steadily weaker and weaker.

Incredibly she actually reached the top. Blinded by driving snow, she flung herself down, exhausted, on the iron ground. She had reached the top, but where was the hut? Two kilometres away, a tiny speck in a wilderness of snow. She screamed and shouted. The only reply was the banshee howling of the wind. Half crazed with fear, she began to descend the ladder.

Meanwhile, down below, Gunter stirred. "I think I can go on now," he said in a husky voice.

"Good man," Roger said. He helped Gunter to his feet, put one arm round his shoulder, and the two men stumbled on towards the foot of the ladder.

And it was here that Roger found Ephney, curled up under a sodden blanket, sobbing her heart out.

Quickly he ripped open his own pack, found a couple of dry blankets and pulled the sodden blanket off Ephney. Then he made them both don all the spare clothing he could find, some of it he himself was wearing. Then, making them lie side by side for extra warmth, he rolled them in dry blankets and, satisfied he had done all he could, he headed straight for the chain ladder.

He reached it. Steadily he climbed higher and higher. How he ever made that nightmare climb he never knew, but he did make it, and reaching the top, he headed straight into the wild storm for the hut.

One of the remarkable things about this epic story is how he ever found the hut. Christensen, it will be remembered, never found it on that tragic night four years later, in 1959. He perished. Twenty years before Roger's nightmare, in July 1939, Brian and Miriam Godbold crawled on all fours through the snow from the top of the ladder, following the faintest track of a skier. They just made it to the hut – but the ice in his boots cost Brian five toenails! When Roger was on the mountain it was one of the worst October blizzards ever known in the Drakensberg. And yet, in the middle of it, and at night, he managed to locate the hut and to alert the three Transvaal men to the developing crisis at the foot of the chain ladder.

Jones and Goldbold set off immediately with Roger for the ladder, leaving Bernie, the third man at the hut, to prepare hot meals and beds for Ephney and Gunter.

An hour after Roger had left Ephney and Gunter at the foot of the ladder, he was back with the two Transvaal men. Gunter was almost in a coma. They managed to revive him. Then came the climb up the ladder. Neville, one of the Transvaal men, went first holding the torch; Gunter came next, followed by Aubrey, the other Transvaal man. Behind them came Roger, carrying both packs on his back, helping his young wife up, rung after rung.

By now the ladder was encrusted with ice, and it was almost impossible to obtain a toehold. It was a climb none of them would ever forget. How Gunter managed it will remain for ever a mystery.

At the top Gunter and Ephney sat in a pool of mud holding on to rocks and staring down into the inky blackness. All they saw were the torchlights far below where the other three men were now bringing up the blankets and the rest of the gear.

Once they were all up the three men began to carry Gunter, but as they neared the hut, to the amazement of them all, he insisted on hobbling the last few metres himself. He had climbed his mountain, and he was damned if he would do anything else but walk the last few metres on whatever legs he had. It was 10 pm.

Next morning it was still snowing. The three Transvaal men decided to return to the hotel far away in the valley below. They promised to inform the warden of the plight of the other three. The warden never received the message.

All that day, Tuesday, 4 October, Gunter, Roger and Ephney remained in the hut, staring out through the two small windows at the world of swirling white outside. It snowed all that day, and was still snowing when they woke up the following day. But by now their food was almost finished, and Roger decided that no matter what the weather, they had to get down and off the mountain.

They packed up – their packs were a little lighter now – and said goodbye to the little stone building that had been their shelter from the storm. They left early, and by 7 am they were back at the chain ladder.

The Mountain Club Hut on the summit of the Amphitheatre.

*Gunter and Ephney
leaving the summit
on their way down to
safety. They are
nearing the top of the
chain ladder.*

The ladder rungs were now even more coated with ice, making the descent extremely dangerous. Ephney went first, trying with her fingers to guide Gunter's feet on the rungs. Once he trod on one of her fingers, crushing it against the rung. Roger came last, carrying both packs and Gunter's two sticks, which he hitched through the straps of his rucksack. Once Gunter slipped, and hung precariously over a drop of 15 m (50 ft) before Ephney's slender hands came to the rescue. But at last they were down.

Then began the long march home. It was, indeed, a terrible journey. The snow in places was waist deep and all the paths were completely obliterated. The only help they had was the occasional faint mark of a footprint left by the three men the previous day. Gunter was nearly finished. He had not yet recovered fully from Monday's ordeal, and was barely able to stand. Every now and then he would say, "Can't we rest for a moment, Roger?" and Roger would reply "No. If you do that you'll freeze to death. Keep going. Follow me."

For five hours they battled through the heavy snow, and by midday had only reached the Three Witches, a distance normally covered in under an hour. The snow still lay thick around them, and at last, with a groan, white-faced, Gunter sank to the ground. "It's no use," he said, "I'm kaput. I can't go on. Don't worry: leave me. You two go on."

Looking at him Roger realised that he was indeed finished. He himself was in little better shape. Wearing only shorts, he was stiff with cold, teeth chattering, beard and hair encrusted with snow and icicles. It had taken them an hour and a half to cover the last couple of hundred metres. "Right," he said. "I'm leaving you two. I'm going for help. Leave all the packs behind, leave the gear. They don't matter. We can collect them later. But keep moving. Don't stop. Don't rest. If you stop, you're dead. Move slowly, but move all the time."

Then off he sped, down the valley. First came the battle through the remaining snow-drifts, but soon he was through and in open country. From then on he raced at top speed, and reached the hotel at 3 pm in a dazed state.

Help was quickly organised. It only took half an hour, and by 3.30 pm Peter Pope-Ellis, the warden, and Bill Barnes, Fisheries officer, together with five police guards, were on horseback, galloping up the valley with blankets, food, brandy and hot drinks.

Up on those lonely wastelands, high above the snow-line, two tiny figures moved pitifully slowly, like ants, across the frozen wastes of snow. There was no hope, but still they kept on. Life still called. By now Gunter was moving automatically – he has no memory of those nightmare hours. Ephney remembers him muttering incessantly to himself: "Keep moving . . . moving . . . moving . . . Mustn't stop . . . Keep moving." Then his voice was silent. But he kept moving.

Suddenly, just before Basuto Gate, Ephney looked up through bleared eyes and saw . . . horsemen, galloping across the plains below them, "like a cowboy picture," she said later.

Pope-Ellis was the first to reach Gunter. Jumping from his horse he ran to support him. "All right, Stein," he said, "you can stop walking now . . ."

"Keep moving . . . must keep moving."

"Come on, lad," the warden said, as he eased him to the ground, "It's over now." And then, with a quick look at Gunter: "Bill, bring the brandy, quick."*

"Right," came the crisp reply.

"Bill," said the warden later, "there's only one thing to do. They're just about all in. We've got to get them to Mahai Cave where they can thaw out. We can get a fire going there. Come on."

Ephney was just able to sit a horse. Gunter was in a state of complete collapse. He has no memory of what happened. He was semi-conscious by then. He was carried to a horse by Bill Barnes, covered with a blanket, and then strapped to the back of an African police guard. Then the whole party moved slowly down the trail to Mahai Cave.

Peter Pope-Ellis said afterwards: "We had to adopt emergency measures to revive them. We built a fire in the Mahai Cave, massaged them to bring back the circulation, shed most of our own warm clothing for them, and rushed a police guard back to the hotel so that a doctor could be on hand when we returned. In the state they were in, they could not possibly have lived through the night had we not found them. We only reached the hotel at 8 pm."

Roger l'Hoest said: "I have had wide knowledge of mountains and snow-falls in Europe, and have been in many snow-storms, but I have never experienced

---

* The incident happened before it was realised that alcohol should not be given in these circumstances.

anything like this. When I set off to seek help, the snow was well above my waist, but once I got through it I ran all the way to the hotel."

Bill Barnes said: "We hammered the horses all the way, and I believe we must have broken all records in getting to them. Just as well we did, because they were really in a bad way. We had to use our torches to find our way through the dark forests."

Ephney said: "We thought we were going to die in the mountains."

But it was Gunter Stein who had the last word: "I climbed my mountain. So can you. There's nothing you can't do if you are determined to do it."*

---

* Today Gunter Stein is a Chartered Accountant in Dusseldorf, West Germany. Shortly after his great adventure he gave up photography and studied for six years at Witwatersrand University. In 1964 he graduated as a Chartered Accountant, and then emigrated to West Germany. In 1967 he returned to South Africa for a short period during which time (1969) he met and married his wife, Jean-Anne. In 1977 he and his wife returned to Dusseldorf where Gunter is still in business.

Ephney went back to the Drakensberg twice after their great adventure – and both holidays hold special memories. Soon after the first holiday Roger was killed in a motor accident in Johannesburg. The second holiday Ephney spent with her son and daughter, just before her son went to do his National Service. He was killed in action. Today Ephney lives in Randburg, Transvaal. Her daughter and family live next door.

14 Martin Marsoner

*Far left: The chain
ladder to the top of
the Amphitheatre.*
Left, from the top:
*Puff-adder; Rinkals;
Berg Adder; A fire
rages on the slopes of
the Little Berg.*

Why did Martin Marsoner die, and why, experienced mountaineer that he was, did he break four of the most fundamental rules of mountaineering? We shall probably never know.

On Saturday morning, 5 July 1975, nine young people set out from the Oxbow Ski Lodge (see map, p. 127) on a light-hearted trip into the mountains. The Oxbow Ski Lodge, in the north-east corner of Lesotho, had only recently been opened. In winter the slopes of the Maluti Mountains offer some good skiing, and the Lodge had been opened to meet a growing need.

Among the group were Martin Marsoner, aged 32, the manager of the Lodge, and John des Ligneris, 27, a Johannesburg machinery salesman. John had planned a skiing trip to Austria for the following year. He was only a beginner, however, and had come to the Lodge to get a little experience in skiing. Both men were superbly fit, though a little tired, as they had spent the previous evening in a somewhat riotous party which lasted until well after midnight. The objective of the outing was to reach the escarpment at Mont-aux-Sources, about 20 km away.

For the first half-hour they went by Landrover along the Letseng-la-Terae road, to the foot of Mahlasela Hill. Here the Landrover was parked, and they carried on on foot. After an hour or so they called a halt. The rest of the group were obviously feeling the effects of the party the previous night, and they decided to return. Martin Marsoner and John des Ligneris carried on, keen to reach the edge of the escarpment.

But time was against them, and they began to jog a little. (At the time there were reports that a spirit of rivalry had developed between the two men, and that they were racing each other, but des Ligneris denies this.) Then Martin's ankle began to hurt; a leg, which he had broken a couple of years earlier, started to cause trouble, and it was obvious that John was the fitter of the two. After nearly five kilometres they decided to separate, John going on to the escarpment alone, and Martin turning back, hoping to catch up with the others. He told des Ligneris that he would wait for him at the spot where the Landrover had been

121

The present Oxbow
Ski Lodge. The
building used by
Marsoner and his
party was burnt down
a few years ago.

parked. The time was now 1.30 pm, and Martin told John des Ligneris that the escarpment was only about an hour's walk away.

It is one of the basic rules of mountaineering that you never split a party unless it is absolutely necessary. Also, that you never go off alone into the mountains. Twice that day Martin, the leader, had allowed the party to split, and now two of them were alone, Martin heading back towards the Landrover and John going all out for the escarpment. It was bitterly cold. The men were wearing only slacks and jerseys, and neither was properly shod. Martin was wearing light-weight shoes that were too small for him. He complained that they were hurting him.

Recalling what had happened, des Ligneris said later:

"When we reached the point where we parted, we discussed the possibility of reaching the escarpment. Martin seemed keen to accompany me, but said he could only do so if we walked. His ankle was giving trouble and he was limping.

"Having got so far that day, I thought 'What the hell? I may just as well continue.' I wanted to achieve something – and the escarpment was it. I decided to jog ahead alone, and Martin agreed. He said he would return to the Landrover where he would wait for me.

"He walked a short distance with me and pointed out the route. We then bade each other farewell and as I began to jog I turned around and saw him walking back slowly in the direction from which he had come."

This was the last time Martin Marsoner was seen alive.

By 3 pm John was beginning to feel tired, and there was no sign of the escarpment. Snow still lay heavy on the ground after the last snowfall, making the going particularly hard. Martin's estimate of the escarpment being only an hour away was obviously wrong. Worse still, ominous black clouds began to gather around the peaks, and there came the distant mutter of thunder. The air was strangely still. John decided to turn back.

He reckons he was three-quarters of the way back to the Landrover when the blizzard struck. It was 4.30 pm. It struck with amazing speed and fury. Within minutes he was engulfed in an icy hell of roaring snow, hail and rain. Visibility was down to less than a metre and soon he was lost, staggering blindly around in a 70-knot gale of lashing fury.

With all sense of direction lost, in the freezing cold, he blundered on, hour after hour, until darkness fell, and he was finished. He had had nothing to eat since breakfast; he had no food with him, and he was thinly clad. But still he kept on in the pitch darkness – a fight for survival. At 2 am, exhausted, he found some sort of shelter under an overhanging rock, so small that his forehead and knees projected out into the icy wind and driving snow. Here he spent the remaining hours of the night.

Next morning – Sunday, 6 July – it was still snowing. He set off again as soon as it was light, 7 am, and battled grimly throughout the day. Soon his right shoe came apart and he had to discard it. He had nothing with which to replace it and had to walk on with a stockinged foot. Before long the stocking was a solid block of ice. By 2 pm he could go no further, but fortunately he found an abandoned shepherd's hut. He managed to creep under some straw on the floor, and here he spent his second night. He tried eating melted snow to stave off his hunger and stay alive.

The lonely wastes of snow over which des Ligneris wandered for three days and nights.

Meanwhile the alarm had gone out. The rest of the party had managed to make it back to the Lodge before the storm broke, but where were Martin and John? The police at Fouriesburg and Witsieshoek and the SAAF were alerted, and soon teams of rescuers began moving into the area.

It was now Monday, 7 July, and a SAAF helicopter took off from Ficksburg, but conditions were impossible – a howling gale gusting up to 70 knots made flying impossible, and the search had to be called off.

John made a late start that morning. It was 9 am before he got going, but he walked all day, and at night found another abandoned hut with some dirty sheepskins on the floor. These gave him a little warmth, and out of one of them he managed to put together a makeshift covering for his right foot. He was still completely lost, with no idea whatever where he was.

During the afternoon, however, the weather cleared a little, and the helicopter was able to take off again. Ironically, in the late afternoon it actually flew right over the hut. Frantically John waved one of the sheepskins in the air to attract the pilot's attention, but it was not to be. It flew on without noticing him.

By Tuesday, 8 July, rescue operations were in full swing. Several more helicopters flew in to help in the search, and a volunteer ground rescue team, consisting of 40 men led by Keith Whitelock of De Beers in Ficksburg, was airlifted to the summit. All day they searched in the blinding snow, for the blizzard had started up again. That night they slept out in the open in deep snow. One of the men who had been dropped on the summit plateau that Tuesday was Bill Hiscutt, a veteran mountaineer with experience of the Swiss Alps. He said later: "That night out was an ordeal. It was very, very cold. And *we* were dressed in mountaineering gear, and had sleeping bags . . ."

Meanwhile, John's long ordeal was nearly over. At 10.30 am on that Tuesday he found himself staggering down a steep slope, and then, suddenly, he saw it – a hut in the vast wilderness of snow, and outside it a figure. It was David Phenya, a Lesotho shepherd, and in his hut were food (mielie pap and tea – but how magnificent!), shelter, and warm blankets. The shepherd immediately routed out his herd-boy and sent him off, hot-foot, to the nearest police post at Witsieshoek, and then turned to care for the exhausted man.

Next day the herd-boy's father arrived on horseback, and he, too, rode on to the police at Witsieshoek. The Witsieshoek police alerted Fouriesburg, and at 2 pm a Super Frelon helicopter, piloted by Captain Willie van Breda (it was his 51st mountain rescue!) took off from Ficksburg.

Waiting for the helicopter at Ficksburg was petite Christa Marsoner, Martin's young wife. News that a survivor had been found and picked up had been radioed ahead, and Christa, breathless, was waiting for the aircraft. When she found that the survivor was not her husband, she collapsed.

From Ficksburg John was flown to the Rand Airport and taken straight to the Rand Clinic. There, to the amazement of the doctors, he was found to be in good shape. The only damage appeared to be a frost-bitten big toe. He had

survived a four-day water-only diet, in freezing snow and ice, and had lived to tell the tale. It was only his superb physical condition that had enabled him to do this.

Meanwhile, all that Wednesday the search for Martin Marsoner went on. During the morning his scarf was found, not far from where the Landrover had been parked, and that helped to concentrate the search. But of Martin himself there was no sign. Hour after hour the whirling helicopters criss-crossed those icy wastes, with no results. "Every inch of ground in the area," said Commandant J. W. Guyt, in command of the air search, "has been meticulously combed, without any success."

By now there was little hope of finding him alive. It was still snowing, and it was decided that the following day, Thursday, would be the last day of the air search. "There could be a new drama tomorrow," said one of the pilots, "when it comes to airlifting some of the search party out of this freezing hell."

But most of the ground search still went on, and at last, at 3.15 pm on the Thursday, Martin's body was found. It was lying on a ledge under a slight overhang, in a sleeping position, half a kilometre from the road to the Letseng-la-Terae mine, near the foot of Mahlasela Hill, and only an hour and a half's walk from the spot where the two men had separated. Owing to the overhang it had been impossible to see the body from the air. The discovery was made by Martin's friend, Warrant Officer Nathaniel Posholi of the Lesotho Mounted Police.

One of the strange things among the many that characterise this tragic affair is that the body was lying on the windward side of the rock, facing east, instead of in the lee of the rock. Simple common sense, apart from the standard practice of mountaineers, would have dictated a resting place away from that howling gale. No satisfactory explanation of this strange anomaly has ever been offered,

Mahlasela Hill
1. Landrover parked here
2. Body found here

except one from John des Ligneris, which we explain later, but which we cannot accept.

There were no signs of injuries on the body. Martin had simply died of exposure. Quite close to his rock shelter were two empty huts. Why had he not used them? He was only five minutes away from the road to Letseng-la-Terae, along which vehicles had been passing during the long search for the two men.

What is particularly puzzling is that after the parting of the two men at 1.30 pm, Martin had had three hours of clear weather before the blizzard struck, to cover only eight kilometres back to the Landrover. Why had he taken so long?

What, then, had happened?

We cannot accept the theory that he had simply walked back towards where the Landrover had been parked, been overtaken by the blizzard, sought shelter, and died that Saturday night. If John des Ligneris could survive four nights out in that icy blizzard, then surely he could have survived one?

We have examined all the evidence carefully, and we believe that what happened was this: After leaving John he hiked back in a leisurely fashion (remember that he was limping) to where the Landrover had been parked. It probably took him two hours – after all there was no need to hurry. Arrived at the foot of Mahlasela Hill, he found that the Landrover had already left. He decided to wait for des Ligneris's return. But at four o'clock he noticed the gathering clouds, and realised that a change of weather was imminent. What was he to do? He was faced with a dilemma. As manager of the Lodge, and leader of the party, he was responsible for the safety of his guests. But seven of his guests were in one direction, to the west, and the other, alone, away off to the east. Where was the greater need? The seven, in the Landrover, were probably safely home by now, or nearly so. At least they were together. But John des

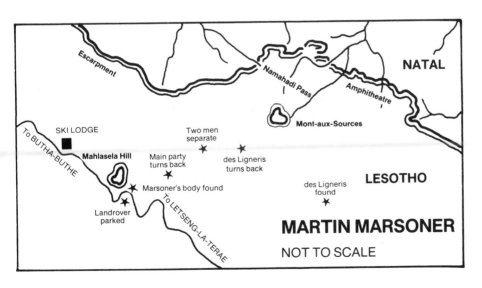

127

Ligneris was alone and inexperienced. Obviously his was the greater need. Martin decided to go back and look for him.

We believe that all through that terrible Saturday night, exhausted as he must have been after the merrymaking of the previous night and his long walk that day, he searched desperately for the lost man. All through Sunday he continued the search, growing weaker and weaker, driven by a fierce sense of duty to his client. By Sunday night he was finished. He lay down under a rock overhang, too tired to even know where he was, too exhausted to realise that he had chosen the windy side of the rock. And there, in the darkness of the night and in that white hell, he died.

There are several factors that support this theory. Experts and mountaineering colleagues who knew Marsoner well say that it would have been completely out of character for him to have gone back to the Lodge and to have left an inexperienced mountaineer to face a blizzard alone. They regarded him as an extremely thorough and responsible man, with a strong sense of duty, and with years of experience in the Austrian Alps.

Marsoner's wristwatch, an automatic, had stopped at 2.35 am on Tuesday. It was taken to a Johannesburg jeweller, and his verdict was that the watch could not have operated for more than 30 hours without body movement. This suggests that Marsoner died sometime on Sunday night or even later. The inquest findings were that Marsoner had been dead at least three days before his body was found on Thursday afternoon.

And there is a further clue. Marsoner's shoes had been borrowed from Martin Watkinson, an outdoor instructor at the Lodge. When Marsoner's body was recovered, Watkinson observed that the shoes were very badly worn, more so than they should have been, suggesting that he had walked a considerable distance before he died.

We believe that Martin Marsoner died in a desperate attempt to save the life of his client.

John des Ligneris does not share this view.

"I believe," he said when interviewed, "that he did not set off at all on the return journey to the Landrover. I think he decided to wait near our parting point for my return,* and it was there, inside a nearby crevice, that he fell asleep, not knowing that a blizzard was imminent.

"I do not believe that he set out in search of me at any stage during the blizzard. In fact, everything points to this possibility: He sought a vantage point. He crawled into the crevice, and fell asleep. And it was there that he died, trapped by the blizzard. He was exhausted when we set out in the morning, and the first-phase hike must have sapped his energy even more. Intending to keep a

---

* Des Ligneris is wrong here. It is quite definite that Marsoner's body was found near where the Landrover had been parked, on the lower slopes of Mahlasela Hill.

watch for me from the crevice, he must have dozed. At that stage there was no sign of a snowstorm building up, and he must have been asleep for several hours before he was covered in snow. And remember, he was lying in a sleeping position.

"Another point is that he had sought shelter on the wrong side of the crevice, the windward side. He would never have done so if he was seeking protection from the blizzard. He chose the side from where he could see me approaching on my return. This was the right side from which to watch for my return."

Always there will be the mystery: How did Martin Marsoner come to die?

This tragic episode is of tremendous interest to all mountaineers who go hiking in the Drakensberg, a warning that all should heed. Experienced mountaineer that Marsoner was, he made four fundamental errors:

1. The party had done no adequate pre-walk planning, nor was Marsoner's leadership adequate.
2. It was July, the middle of winter, with sub-zero temperatures gripping those mountains every day, especially from 3 pm onwards. And yet the walkers set out inadequately clothed, and without emergency rations, first-aid kit, or maps.
3. When the hikers set out on their walk, they were not in peak physical condition. On the night before their walk, and well into the early hours, most of them had taken part in a drinking party at the Ski Lodge.
4. One of the most sacred codes of all mountaineers is "Keep together, whatever happens." Twice on that tragic hike Marsoner broke this rule.

15 The Ship's Prow Pass Disaster

In newspaper parlance, a news story that develops over a period of days or weeks is a "running story". We have investigated one of these running stories as it built up from edition to edition in the daily and weekly newspapers, and in tribute to the reporters who gathered and sifted facts for their readers, we find that there is no new evidence to add, and only very little comment to make, on the stories they wrote during the fateful three days of 10 to 13 January 1981.

We are grateful to the Editors of *The Daily News, Natal Mercury, Sunday Tribune, Sunday Times,* and *Natal Witness* for permission to tell this story again through their news reports. There is some repetition, but it recreates the feeling of living from edition to edition – morning to evening to morning ... that feeling of waiting, hoping, praying.

Daily News, Saturday, 10 January 1981:

HUNT FOR BERG HIKERS HIT BY MIST AND RAIN

Fears for the lives of three mountain hikers missing for 11 days are growing. Rescue attempts have been severely hampered by heavy mist and light rain in the Monk's Cowl area of the Drakensberg [see map no. 4].

Dr Sherman Ripley, leader of the nine-man volunteer Mountain Club team which has been in the area since yesterday morning, said today they were completely bogged down by mist and rain.

Three Air Force helicopters from 15 Squadron based in Durban are standing by with the rescue team waiting for the weather to clear.

"We are getting worried because this weather shows no signs of lifting. They could be anywhere and probably out of food by now unless they ended up in Lesotho – where their chances are still slim," said Dr Ripley.

The hikers – Andries Liebenberg (27) of Welkom, his brother Jan (20) from Steynsrus in the Free State, and Dalthasu Vorster (27) of Pretoria –

left the Monk's Cowl Forest Station at 7 am on 31 December and were due back on 4 January.

Dr Ripley said the hikers could be "almost anywhere" because they had failed to record accurate details of their proposed hike.

"We are really in the dark at the moment. This morning we sent out a three-man party to look in an obvious area, but that's the safest shot-in-the-dark we can take at the moment," said Dr Ripley.

There is a feeling among the rescuers that the hikers may have been struck by lightning during one of the heavy storms in the area or wandered over the border into Lesotho. But Lesotho police claim no knowledge of their whereabouts.

The helicopters, led by Commandant Dudley Foote, flew along the lower slopes of the mountain yesterday but were unable to reach the mist-shrouded mountain tops.

Dr Ripley said it was doubtful the mist would lift today.

The Reverend J. P. G. Liebenberg, a retired church minister living in Steynsrus in the Free State, travelled to the Drakensberg yesterday and is anxiously awaiting news of his sons.

Andries Liebenberg, the eldest, is a teacher in Welkom. His younger brother, Jan, has just finished his army training and intends going to university next year.

Miss Vorster comes from Gatsrand in Pretoria.

Sunday Times, Sunday, 11 January 1981:

DRAMA ON THE BERG: RACE TO FIND HIKERS

Hope is fading fast for three hikers missing in the Drakensberg for six days.

The party were expected home on Tuesday and when they had not returned on Thursday, Miss Vorster's brother Chris phoned the Winterton police and raised the alarm.

They were last seen by two other hikers halfway up Grey's Pass, which leads to the escarpment, several days ago.

Three SAAF helicopters from 15 Squadron in Durban and a nine-member rescue team from the Natal Section of the Mountain Club of SA are helping in the search.

It was thought that the party may have lost its way across the border into Lesotho, but checks with the authorities in that country have drawn a blank.

Several rescue teams yesterday scoured other areas.

A member of one team, Mr Brian Shuttleworth, said that visibility was down to 50 m in places and that it was cold inside the cloud.

Rain on the Drakensberg put a stop to the search yesterday afternoon.

The mountain rescue team, led by Dr Sherman Ripley, is reported to have gone as far up the escarpment as Grey's Pass but had to return to base when the rain set in again.

Dr Ripley described the situation as "pretty desperate".

At Monk's Cowl Forest Station, which has been turned into an emergency operation centre, several family members of the missing hikers are waiting anxiously for news.

Miss Vorster's brother, Chris, said: "I came here because I wanted her to see that someone cares."

The Rev. J. P. G. Liebenberg, father of the men, said: "The rescue people have warned me to expect the worst and I know the chances are not good."

He said Jan had not been keen to go on the hike and "that makes it worse if he is dead. But whatever happens I will accept it as God's will."

Sunday Tribune, 11 January 1981:

BERG SEARCHERS FEAR HIKERS DEAD

Three young hikers missing for a week in the Monk's Cowl area of the Drakensberg are now feared dead, but the search continued at first light today.

Three Air Force helicopters airlifted a Mountain Club rescue team into the upper Berg to comb gorges where it is thought the hikers may have got lost or been injured.

But hopes for the three dwindled yesterday when the helicopters were grounded by mist and darkness after nearly two full days of search, in which they covered an area of 200 square kilometres.

And at the Forest Station at Monk's Cowl, base camp for the rescuers, questions were being asked about why there had been a four-day delay before the search began.

The missing hikers – Miss Dalthasu Vorster of Pretoria, and Mr Andries Liebenberg and his brother, Jan, of Steynsrus – set off towards Cathkin Peak on 31 December, saying they would be back by Sunday, 4 January.

The search did not get under way until Thursday this week.*

---

* Dave Osborne, the Forestry officer at the Monk's Cowl Forest Station, was away on holiday at the time. A rather inexperienced young man had been sent to fill his place, and he admitted that he had failed to check on the Mountain Register on the Monday, as he should have done. The register would have shown clearly that the party was overdue by that Monday, 5 January. The MCSA was only alerted on Thursday evening (8 January).

By this time the hikers' food, light and heating would almost certainly have run out. They are thought to have carried supplies for no more than five days. Their car was left at the forestry station campsite and was found to contain money and clothing.

The three walked up Grey's Pass – one of the few routes through the precipitous cliff face behind Cathkin Peak – and were seen there by another party of hikers on New Year's Day. That was the last time anyone saw them.

Dr Sherman Ripley, leader of the nine-man Mountain Club rescue team, said yesterday there was little hope for the three unless they had left the mountains by another route.

The Rev. J. P. G. Liebenberg, father of the two men, said his sons were resourceful and level-headed, but did not know the Drakensberg. Only Miss Vorster had hiked there before.

Mountaineers said the plateau behind Cathkin Peak was filled with deep valleys where it was easy to get lost, even for someone who knew the Berg.

Dr Sherman Ripley, leader of the Natal Mountain Club's Search and Rescue team, discusses strategy with a group of SAAF pilots.

133

Natal Mercury, Monday, 12 January 1981:

BERG TRIO DEAD
WALL OF WATER SWEPT HIKERS DOWN GULLY

Cathkin Peak. The battered bodies of three hikers were recovered from a gully in the Drakensberg yesterday after an intensive search by helicopters and a mountain rescue team.

The hikers, Andries Liebenberg, his brother Jan, and Miss Dalthasu Vorster, had been swept to their deaths by a wall of water which had roared down a narrow gully ripping through their tent and leaving their torn belongings scattered for more than a kilometre along the mountainside near here.

Rescue workers, who were dropped at the spot by a Puma and two Alouette helicopters from 15 Squadron in Durban, worked for more than three hours to free the bodies from the boulder-strewn bed of the gully.

The force of the water, thought to have been fed by a fierce storm on 2 January, had ripped the clothing from the hikers and battered their bodies beyond recognition.

"The water hit so hard that it picked up a huge boulder and tossed it into the branches of a tree," one of the rescue workers said yesterday.

"They didn't have a chance. It probably happened so fast they never even knew what was happening."

The missing trio were found, three days after the aerial search had begun, when a pilot spotted a haversack lying near a gully in Ship's Prow Pass.

A team of volunteers from the Mountain Club were dropped to scour the area and made the gruesome discovery about 30 minutes later.

The three hikers had left Monk's Cowl area on 31 December with the intention of returning to the Forest Station there on 4 January.

However, the alarm was raised on 7 January when Miss Vorster's brother, Chris, telephoned the police in Pretoria after she failed to return in time to resume her teacher training course.

By that time, rescuers say, all three had probably been dead for five days.

Mist, rain and hail had hampered the Air Force search for hours at a time and helicopters, blinded by mist, actually overflew the scene of the tragedy several times before finding the bodies.

Commanded by Commandant Dudley Foote, the three helicopters scoured a 250 square kilometre area so thoroughly that they stopped to retrieve pieces of refuse and discarded bottles in the hope that the hikers may have scrawled a message for help.

The Liebenberg brothers, Andries, a Welkom music teacher, and Jan,

who recently completed his national service, were on their first visit to the Berg.

"What makes it even more tragic is the fact that Jan did not want to come hiking in the first place," his father Ds J. P. G. Liebenberg said.

"He had said he would have rather spent his holiday in the Heidelberg area, but we persuaded him to go."

The Vorster and Liebenberg families had spent 60 anxious hours at the helipad at Monk's Cowl before a Winterton policeman broke the news of their children's death.

The bodies were flown from the gully to the Winterton Police Station.

A Natal Parks Board spokesman said the accident was the worst of its kind in the Drakensberg.

Unbelievable destruction! The stream below Ship's Prow Pass, where the bodies were found, is a horrifying jungle of rocks, debris and smashed trees. In the white circle is one of the bodies.

135

When the storm hit on 2 January it washed out the road to Solitude resort and nearly swept away a family who were camping out there, he said.

Daily News, Monday, 12 January 1981:

DIARY OF HORROR IN VALLEY OF DEATH

The Ship's Prow Pass is a steep-sided valley running up the side of the Drakensberg between the Solitude rest camp and the Champagne Castle peak above.

During the past 10 days the area has been subjected alternately to fierce storms and thick mist.

Thirteen days ago a party of three hikers arrived in the Cathkin Peak area to spend five days walking in the mountains.

Of the three walkers – the Liebenberg brothers, Andries and Jan, and a friend from Pretoria, Dalthasu Vorster – only Miss Vorster had been in the mountains before.

As a student, having taken time off from teaching to improve her qualifications, Dalthasu was able to squeeze in a few days' holiday.

Andries, eldest son of the Rev. J. P. G. Liebenberg of Steynsrus, had no music classes to give during the school holidays at the Welkom Gymnasium School, and probably notified the Welkom North Dutch Reformed Church that he would be unable to play the organ on Sunday, 4 January.

He did not expect to be back until that evening.

Jan Liebenberg, who had finished his military service at Tempe in Bloemfontein in December, was reluctant to go at first, but was eventually swayed by the enthusiasm of the others.

He was to start studying anthropology at Bloemfontein's university in a month or so.

On Old Year's Day they parked their car at the Monk's Cowl Forest Station, noted their intention to "walk up Cathkin Peak", to return by 4 January, and set off up Grey's Pass into the Drakensberg.

They saw in the New Year in the popular Nkosezana cave on the trail, where they told another hiker they planned to walk along the plateau to Champagne Castle, then down Ship's Prow Pass to the path which led back to their car.

The next day they met another group and told them the same story.

They were never seen alive again.

The alarm was first raised by Dalthasu's brother, Chris Vorster, who realised something was wrong when his sister did not return to Pretoria by Tuesday to resume her classes.

A close-up of Ship's Prow Pass (foreshortened). The "prow" is in the centre of the picture, which was taken shortly after the disaster. The whole pass has been destroyed by a wild avalanche of rocks, stones and debris after the storm.

He told the police. By Thursday a nine-man Mountain Club rescue team had been formed under the leadership of Dr Sherman Ripley.

The Air Force and Mountain Club rescuers gathered on Friday, using the Monk's Cowl Forest Station as their base. By mid-morning they had scoured the lower reaches of the mountains but were forced to call off the search above 3 000 m while dense mist persisted.

On Sunday the cloud lifted, enabling the helicopter pilots to get above the mist to search the mountain plateau, only to report no success to the group of relatives of the missing trio and a growing contingent from the Press.

Yesterday dawned bright and clear. The three helicopters rose with the dawn to check the remaining mountain reaches. They also flew 20 km into neighbouring Lesotho, checked refuse on the mountain trails and interviewed hut dwellers.

They reported nothing but some hail along the edges and an air temperature on the top of five degrees.

At mid-morning the searchers decided to re-examine the hikers' most likely trail before moving the base of the search further south.

In particular the Ship's Prow Pass had been examined only through binoculars as air currents made flying treacherous.

When they managed to enter the valley they were horrified by the devastation they found – "the worst I have ever seen," as more than one seasoned climber described it.

Trees had been torn out and boulders thrown about like marbles.

They also found the first traces of the missing hikers.

It did not take long to discover their bodies. Two were seen almost immediately, and the third, glimpsed from the air, was located by a *Daily News* reporter an hour later.

There seems little chance of being sure of what happened. But the three had obviously been dead for some days and the devastation around them told its own tale.

Many members of the rescue team felt they had been caught in a flash flood while picking their way down the pass in a heavy downpour.

The vast mountain walls would have fed enormous amounts of water into the stream in the space of a few minutes, filling all the pools and gullies to capacity.

Somewhere high on the pass a rock would have slipped, releasing a tiny dam of water into the next pool and knocking out the retaining rock.

In a few seconds a wall of water, tossing boulders ahead of it, tearing out and shredding fully grown trees to matchwood, would have scoured the pass from top to bottom.

The hikers stood no chance. They were found, partly buried under debris, with a distance between them of 150 m, while scraps of their shredded belongings appeared over as much as a kilometre.

BERG TRAGEDY
FLASH FLOOD KILLED THREE HIKERS

Ship's Prow Pass. The party would have descended the left-hand fork.

The bodies of the three hikers missing in the Champagne Castle area of the Drakensberg were discovered yesterday by South African Air Force helicopters and members of the Mountain Club rescue team.

Mr Andries Liebenberg, his brother Jan, and Miss Dalthasu Vorster were apparently on their way down Ship's Prow Pass from the top of the escarpment when they were overpowered by a flash flood and either drowned or battered to death on boulders and scree.

Their bodies were flown from the scene of the tragedy to Winterton late yesterday.

The leader of the rescue team, Dr Sherman Ripley, said the bodies of the hikers were found after one of the helicopters reported sighting debris floating in a stream about a kilometre from a rest camp named Solitude.

Although it is believed that the three were drowned while trying to cross a stream, a member of the rescue team said that he thought the party might have been camping by the stream when the flash flood struck.

"Over an extensive area we found pieces of tent, open sleeping-bags and rucksacks," he said. "In one place I saw a large boulder lodged in the branches of a tree at least a metre from the ground."

Flooding ten days ago in the stream at Solitude – which has its source at the head of Ship's Prow Pass – suggests that the three young people died on Friday, 2 January.

139

Natal Mercury, Tuesday, 13 January 1981:

NEW THEORY ON BERG DEATH HIKE TRIO

Three hikers swept to their death in a Drakensberg gully were probably overcome by a flooded stream as they attempted a crossing.

This was the theory offered yesterday by Dr Sherman Ripley, rescue convenor of the Mountain Club.

It was likely the hikers had no idea that a flooded mountain stream could become a "torrential grinding machine" in which boulders were thrown around, said Dr Ripley.

He said he did not believe that Andries Liebenberg, his brother Jan, and Miss Dalthasu Vorster had been hit by a wall of water fed by high-altitude streams.

"I believe they were trying to cross the already flooded stream on their way back to the forestry camp at Monk's Cowl when they were swept away," he said.

"I think that a lack of knowledge tempted them to cross the stream. They were probably a few hours late and decided to cross before the stream became a heavy flood.

"They probably had no idea that a flooded boulder stream is so dangerous. It is a torrential grinding machine," he said.*

Dr Ripley said that the sketchy plan of the intended hike route supplied by the trio at the forestry camp had also complicated search operations by three Air Force helicopters and a nine-man rescue team.

The meagre outline of their route merely said they intended walking up Cathkin Peak, he said.

"We knew it was wrong as the last 300 m of Cathkin Peak is vertical. But we had no idea where they were."

The eventual possible route of the three was discovered after people who had met them on their ill-fated hike told the Mountain Club of the trio's plans.

"If people go into an environment that can be dangerous they should be sufficiently knowledgeable and give more details of their intentions when they fill in forms," he said.

Dr Ripley said he was against legal obligations being imposed on people who chose to go hiking and climbing in the Berg.

---

* It was later established that the storm which struck the catchment area started around 9 pm, and it would therefore seem unlikely that people would still be hiking down Ship's Prow Pass at this time (or even later) at night.

There is not much to add to this grim story. A few days later we spoke to the District Surgeon who had done the post mortem examinations. He told us they were the most horrifying he had ever done. The two men were quite unidentifiable. Bill Barnes, of the Natal Parks Board, told us that it looked as if the bodies had been through a mincing machine.

How they died we shall never know. Were they still descending the pass when the wall of water and tumbling boulders came roaring down upon them? Were they trying to cross the stream at the contour path? Or had they camped for the night, and in their sleep knew not what had struck them? We do not know.

Never, under any circumstances, make camp beside a Drakensberg mountain stream, no matter how small it is. If you have to cross a flooded stream, use a rope, with two of the party keeping a tight hold on it from the bank. The terrain in the Drakensberg is so steep that a placid stream can become a thundering torrent in a few minutes, and if you miss your footing in it, hope dies.

In 1976 the Sterkspruit broke its banks and came roaring down the quiet valley. A Forestry game guard, Majonini Mpinga, trying to cross just above the Sterkspruit Falls, lost his footing and was swept over the falls to his death. In 1975 Martin de Villiers, a Transvaal schoolboy, tried to cross the flooded Umlambonja River in the Cathedral area. He lost his footing, and he too was drowned in the raging waters.

Among the many joys of the Drakensberg are the mountain streams, chuckling and brawling in the sunlight over the pewter-grey stones, their song a madrigal of quiet contentment and joy. But when a cloudburst strikes like a clenched fist, they become vicious and relentless killers. Watch them.

16 The All-Dreaded Thunder-Stone

Beneath the brooding red precipices of Golden Gate, in the eastern Orange Free State, stand two graves, side by side. The one has the single word WILCOCKS in large capital letters; the other, similarly lettered, the name DE LA HARPE. The black marble slabs bear the message, in Afrikaans, that the gravestones are in loving memory of Valerie Wilcocks, born on 23 September 1910, and Johan Bestendig de la Harpe, born on 17 December 1911, killed by lightning on Mont-aux-Sources on 18 December 1932.

The dreaded lightning flash.

On Thursday, 15 December 1932, a party of 12 young people, most of them students, left the family farm Schaapplaas near the small town of Clarens for the Drakensberg. Among them were Valerie Wilcocks, daughter of the Administrator of the Free State, and Johan de la Harpe, son of Percy de la Harpe, owner of the farm, and Johan's sister Elodie, now Mrs Wiid, and today the only living surviving member of the party.

Valerie was born in Jagersfontein and was 22. She was a student at the then Grey University College in Bloemfontein. Not only was she a most promising student, but she also excelled at sport, playing in the first hockey teams at all three University Colleges she had attended.

A year previously, while holidaying near Knysna, she had dived fully clothed into a river to save the life of an African girl.

Johan, who was due to celebrate his 21st birthday in two days' time, was studying for a degree in agriculture at Pretoria University.

Clarens is only about 65 km from Mont-aux-Sources in a straight line, but to reach the peak one has to make a wide detour through Witsieshoek.

The young people were well equipped for the journey. All were mounted, and they had with them an oxwagon. On the sides of its tent a large tarpaulin had been tied. This could be let down so as to give the men sleeping quarters under the wagon. The girls slept in the wagon. The wagon was well stocked with provisions: quantities of biltong, "boere-beskuit", and so on.

They set off on Tuesday morning, 15 December, travelling through the

143

magnificent mountain country of the eastern Free State. That night they slept at Golden Gate, in those days only a simple farmstead. For the second night they camped just outside Witsieshoek and by Saturday evening, Johan's birthday, had reached Brand's store, in the foothills of the Drakensberg, underneath Sentinel Peak. Here they had to leave the wagon, and next morning, Sunday, they set off at first light on horseback for the Namahadi Pass (see map no. 1).

The Namahadi Pass, variously called Mopeli's Pass, Monontsa's Pass and the Gould-Adams Pass, lies two kilometres west of the present chain ladder. Up to about 1920 it was the generally accepted route to the summit, and between 1929 and 1933 was still often used by climbers eager to reach one of the most spectacular areas in the whole of South Africa. It is rarely used today as the new mountain road from Witsieshoek and the chain ladder have taken its place.

They stopped for lunch at the Eland River ford, and then commenced the long haul up the pass. It was, of course, too steep to ride up, and they had to dismount and lead their horses. The pace was slow, and it was 5.30 pm before they reached the top. Johan was first up, and then he went back to help the others with the horses.

Near the top Valerie spotted an old broken ladder. She picked it up and started to carry it, saying: "You never know: we may need this some time." When they arrived at the top the Basuto policeman stationed at the police post, since demolished, came to greet them and asked them to sign the visitors' book.

From here, of course, the actual summit of Mont-aux-Sources is another three kilometres away, to the south. To the east lay the Amphitheatre Wall, and

144

it was in this direction that the party headed, over a bleak, stony plain. They planned to sleep at Crow's Nest Cave.

But by this time heavy clouds were banking up, both in the east and the west. It looked as if two storms were heading for each other. The party left the police post in the direction of the Amphitheatre. Elodie, Johan, Valerie and Jimmy Krige were on foot. The rest of the party were mounted and slightly ahead. Elodie called to the others to hurry as the weather was worsening, and mounted her horse.

"Johan and Valerie were leading Johan's horse, Moscow," Mrs Wiid told us. "They were about five paces behind me, together with Jimmy Krige with his horse. Behind Jimmy was an African, Bombata. I had just turned my horse to follow the others when there was a terrific clap of thunder and a blinding flash of lightning. My horse jumped a ridge and he and I landed together on the other side. I knew immediately that Johan and Valerie had been hit. I hurried back. Valerie was lying, stretched out, nearer me, so I got to her first. I saw at once that she was dead. Johan was writhing in agony. Jimmy and his horse had been flung down and were dizzy, so was Bombata. One horse was dead and two of the others had bolted."

Mr E. M. de la Harpe (Johan's brother), well ahead, suddenly heard shouting and screaming behind him and two horses bolted past him. He made a grab for the horses, turned, and saw the dead horse and three or four of the climbers stretched out on the ground.

Fortunately they were still quite near the old Basutoland police post and two of the party ran down to the station for help. Meanwhile, Johan de la Harpe was the chief concern of the survivors.

He was unconscious, his body contorted, and he appeared to be grinding his teeth. E. M. de la Harpe and another student, Conradie, immediately began artificial respiration, and then gave him some brandy. He managed to swallow this, and recovered partially, but was obviously in great pain, and was unable to speak. Makeshift stretchers were quickly made up (they used the broken ladder Valerie had retrieved) and Johan and Valerie's body were carried down to the police station, but in spite of all their efforts Johan died there at midnight.

At first light next morning two of the students set off for Witsieshoek, 30 km away, with news of the tragedy, and the task of transferring the bodies of the two victims to the Witsieshoek Police Station commenced. The two students who had set off for Witsieshoek early that morning reached the village at midday, and the police immediately telephoned Percy de la Harpe at Fouriesburg. Mr de la Harpe contacted the authorities at Bloemfontein, and friends at Summerstrand, in the Cape, broke the news to Mr and Mrs Wilcocks, who were holidaying there. They immediately left for home by train.

At 4 pm on Wednesday, 21 December, the two students were laid to rest in the quietness of the hills they loved in what was to become the Golden Gate National Park. High up on that bleak and lonely plateau where they died there stands today a bronze plaque. It was carried up twelve years later by Carl Wilcocks, Valerie's brother, and erected at the spot where the tragedy happened. There it stands, a sombre reminder to the mountaineer of one of the hazards he faces in the mountains.

The magnificence and the tremendous impact of a storm in the Drakensberg has to be seen to be believed. First come the black clouds, enmeshed with billowing soft puff-balls of gleaming white. It grows ominously darker and the clouds are heavy as lead. There is a distant growl of thunder. And suddenly the storm is upon you. The cloud is split by a fiery javelin of white-hot light, a sharp crack which merges instantly with the mighty roll of thunder, and you know the dreaded thunderbolt has struck not far from you. And then they come, one after another, hammer-blows, and you stand appalled at the fury of the storm. Sometimes so rapid are the discharges that the whole sky and the boiling clouds seem to throb and glow with fire. Cataracts of flame pour down on the earth, glowing like molten iron, and the roar of the storm is an unending, deafening cacophony of sound.

No wonder the ancients thought they were witnessing the anger and black hatred of their gods. Modern science, of course, has explained much of the wonder of the storm, especially the mechanics of lightning, but still there is much that we do not know, much that is still unpredictable.

We know that as the thundercloud builds up it becomes a huge dynamo, generating millions of volts of electricity. Then a separation of electrical charges takes place, the positive charge streaming to the top of the cloud and the negative to the bottom.

Then, by a complicated interaction of electrical forces, the negative charge at the bottom of the cloud induces a positive charge in the earth below it. As the cloud passes slowly over the countryside, it draws the positive charge below on the ground after it, and the two drift together, down-wind.

It is, of course, a well-known fact that if a positive charge is brought into contact with a negative charge, electrons flow from one to the other. But the two charges do not necessarily have to touch. If they are brought close enough together, the electrons will jump the gap, causing a spark. The spark is nothing more than air intensely super-heated to 30 000 °C in a split second. No wonder you hear a crack (the air expanding with the heat) when you touch the two terminals of your car battery together. And no wonder you hear the mighty roar of thunder, and see the spear of light, when the lower terminal of the cloud (the dynamo) and the earth come close enough together.

One consequence of all this is that lightning, contrary to popular belief, does not strike down. Actually, three things happen almost simultaneously. First there is certainly a downward discharge of electricity, about one million volts in barely one hundredth of a second. But then there is a surge of high voltage

electricity flashing back up the original path (of stage one), again in a minute fraction of a second. It is this second, upward flash that does the killing. Lastly, there is a sustained and longer charge between the cloud and the earth, lasting for about one-tenth of a second. It is this charge that burns or melts the object struck. The total voltage, in a single flash of lightning, can reach 100 million volts. Of course, all this can also take place between one cloud and another, if they are differently charged. High-speed photography has proved all this.

Heat is the main killer. When a tree is struck by lightning it looks as if the bark has been split open. That is exactly what has happened. The intense heat, passing through the core of the tree, causes the sap to expand explosively, and to burst open the enclosing bark. The electric current runs up through the roots and trunk and out through the branches and leaves, raising the temperature in the flash of a second to millions of degrees centigrade.

Lightning is completely unpredictable. There are certain general rules, but the main rule appears to be that these are continually broken! For instance,

A thunderstorm over the Cathedral Range.

147

climbers are told to avoid high points during a storm, on the theory that lightning will always strike the highest point. But I have often sat on a hillside during a storm, and watched the lightning strike down in the valley below me. Even so, it is a wise precaution to choose low, flat ground (not a slope) as a place in which to sit out a storm.

What other precautions can one take? First of all, on no account shelter under an isolated tree. Clumps of trees, or forests, are safer, but it is better to avoid even these. Also, keep away from wire fences, posts, horses and cattle. If you are mounted, dismount and move away from your horse. Drop anything metal that you are carrying, and don't, whatever you do, run for shelter. Running seems to produce a magnetic field which can attract lightning.

A deep cave is safe, but avoid shallow caves and overhangs, and also cracks and chimneys, especially if water is flowing down them.

The safest place in a storm is a car or building. There is some evidence that in a dry storm the bodywork of a car can be damaged by lightning, but we know of no case where a person sitting in a car has been killed or even injured.

If you have no car or house in which to shelter, the best course is to sit down on some insulating material, such as a sleeping bag, draw your knees up, put your arms around them, and sit the storm out. It is a good idea to drape something like a cape around you. Don't lie down and don't stand up. Above all, don't panic. Remember that, statistically, it is extremely unlikely that you will be hit.

Actually, although African huts in the Drakensberg are often struck by lightning with fatal results (thatched huts are potentially very dangerous),* we know of only one other case of climbers being killed by lightning in the Drakensberg.** This was in 1979.

John Clarke, aged 27, was a Natal Parks Board game ranger. He was stationed at Injasuti Outpost, in the Solitude area of the Drakensberg.

He had recently become friendly with Carol Richter, 23, who had worked as a receptionist at various Berg hotels and at several game parks. On Wednesday, 19 December 1979, she decided to visit John Clarke at Solitude.

Both John and Carol were lovers of nature and of the outdoors. Together they had spent many happy hours, away from the noise and bustle of the towns, in the foothills of the Drakensberg, studying the shy creatures of the wild and the lovely flowers in the valleys of the Little Berg. John, especially, was essentially an outdoor man and loved animals. He was particularly fond of dogs and had a springer spaniel, Buck, his constant and much-loved companion.

Carol had recently been offered a new job at Ceres, in the Cape, and the two

John Clarke

---

* South Africa holds a world record in this respect. Some years ago a hut in which 64 Africans were holding a party was struck by lightning, and 61 were killed instantaneously.

** In January 1922 two young men were killed by lightning near the Ebusingati Trading Store, in the approaches to the Royal Natal National Park.

Carol Richter

had planned to motor down together early in the new year, John partly to help with the driving and partly as an opportunity to see his parents at Worcester.

The Injasuti Outpost (it used to be called Hewson's Cottage, after its first occupier) is on the summit of a spur of the Little Berg, overlooking the Solitude Mountain Resort (now called the Injasuti Hutted Camp – see map no. 4). It is a small cottage in one of the most isolated and lonely portions of the Drakensberg. Its only real link with civilisation is a jeep track along the summit of the Little Berg, linking it with Main Camp at Giant's Castle, some 30 kilometres away. The track is negotiable only by four-wheel-drive vehicles, and the journey takes at least one and a half hours. But there is a rough footpath leading down from the cottage at 1 952 m (6 400 ft) to the Solitude Mountain Resort far below, at an altitude of 1 464 m (4 800 ft).

On that Thursday Carol was not John's only visitor. He was also expecting two friends from his old Kruger National Park days, and was eagerly looking forward to seeing them again. The idea was that John should go down and meet them at the Solitude Mountain Resort, and that they would then climb the Little Berg together and spend the day at John's home, the Injasuti Outpost.

All four (together with Buck, of course) breakfasted with "Tiny" and Pat Harries (owners of the resort) that Thursday morning. Carol had brought with her a month's supply of provisions for John. After breakfast the four young people, with Buck at their heels, set out on the climb to the summit, a walk of about an hour for the young and fit.

The morning had dawned bright and clear, but as they reached the top of the climb, the clouds began to gather around the crests of Monk's Cowl and Cathkin Peak. Soon it was obvious that a storm was brewing.

Solomon, John Clarke's African cook, had prepared lunch for the four of them, but when John's two friends saw the storm they decided not to wait for lunch, but to return immediately to the resort below. John and Carol walked part of the way back with them, and then returned to the summit. At the edge of the plateau, about 60 m (200 ft) from the cottage,* with a sheer drop of about five metres (16 ft) down to the slopes below, they stopped beside a few protea trees to watch the approaching storm. In front lay one of the fairest views in all Africa. Far down below, the silver ribbon of the Injasuti River threaded the valley, the cottages of the resort, tiny white specks in that colossal sweep of mountains, hills, valleys, pinnacles and gorges, the side valley sweeping up to the towering spear of Monk's Cowl, the flat-topped Cathkin Peak, and the frightening cliffs of Champagne Castle. The sky was dark now with boiling thunderclouds, sweeping down on them from the high peaks. But it was still a long way off. They stood there, fascinated, watching one of nature's grandest spectacles, a developing thunderstorm in the mountains.

Then came a freak thunderbolt – one blinding flash of lightning, the simultaneous explosive crack and the mighty hammer-blow roar of thunder, and all three of them, John Clarke, Carol Richter and Buck, lay dead on the ground.

When they failed to turn up for lunch Solomon was not unduly concerned. He had watched the four of them commence the descent. They had obviously decided to go on and have lunch below. Even when night came and they were not back he did not worry. He assumed they had decided to spend the night with Mr and Mrs Harries, as John had often done before.

Next day being a Friday the labourers knocked off at 2.30 pm, and set off towards the edge of the escarpment on their way down the mountain to the

---

* The distance was paced off afterwards by Dr Lester King, who was staying at Solitude at the time – exactly 66 paces.

resort. There they found the three bodies, 24 hours after the tragedy. The protea trees were smashed to pieces.

They immediately returned to the cottage and told Solomon what they had found. Solomon tried to radio Main Camp at Giant's Castle, 30 kilometres away, but reception was bad and neither Eric Jensen, the ranger in charge, nor his son Carl, could hear Solomon clearly, so they got the Landrover out and set off for the Outpost.

The three bodies were lying close together among the shattered protea bushes. There were hardly any marks on them. One of Carol's socks had been burned and there was a small burn in John's beard on the side of his cheek. Otherwise they seemed untouched. John was lying in a perfectly relaxed position, with his hands in his trouser pockets.

They had died doing what they had always loved to do, watching Nature at work.

Sombre as these two tragedies are, there is at least one reassuring footnote to them for the mountaineer. In both cases the victims had failed to comply fully with the generally accepted safety precautions. Valerie Wilcocks and Johan de la Harpe were in the middle of a group of horses, and John Clarke and Carol Richter had been standing beside a protea tree in one of the most exposed positions one could imagine – the highest point on a bleak, remote and rock-scarred plateau.

Actually it is interesting to note that the scene of the Injasuti tragedy was notorious for bad lightning strikes. John Wyatt, the previous occupier of the Outpost, had reported to Natal Parks Board Headquarters, in Pietermaritzburg, that to his knowledge his house had been struck several times, but without damage to person or property. He even claimed that it had been struck five times in one night.

17 Fire!

Periodical fires are necessary in the Drakensberg to maintain the balance of ecology. But fire can be a killer.

3 September 1966 is a day that will long be remembered in the Royal Natal National Park (see map no. 1). The day had dawned with a strange stillness in the air, but by 9 o'clock a raging bergwind had roared down from the heights above Plowman's Kop, and the sun was only a pale disc in the dust-laden sky.

Jock Fraser, the warden, was sitting in his office on the banks of the lower Mahai, not far from the hotel, watching the trees bending to the wild fury of the wind and the branches and debris whirling high into the tormented air. This was no day to be out in the open. The patrol over to Castle Rocks could wait! He had a sizeable backlog of correspondence and bookwork to catch up on – this was a good excuse to get on with it.

Suddenly an African game guard burst through the door and shouted "umLilo!" ("Fire!") Fraser put down the letter he was reading, looked through the window, and saw the plume of smoke on the slopes of the Little Berg.★ He leapt to his feet and headed for the African compound.

Here he quickly gathered a team of six game guards, sacks, fire-pumps and extinguishers, and together they made their way rapidly up the slopes to the scene of the conflagration.

It was quite impossible to extinguish the blaze – the hungry flames were towering eight metres (26 ft) high into the air, and it was impossible to get near enough to use the fire-pumps. It looked as if the camp site, the Fisheries office and two staff houses would go, but Fraser and his men managed to put in a back burn, and these were saved.

★ It was established later that a small party from the hotel had set off that morning along the path up the Mahai valley. One of the party, a woman, had attempted to light a cigarette and had thrown the lighted match down on the grass, thinking it was out. The grass was tinder-dry after the long winter, and the wind was blowing great guns. In a split second there was a sheet of flame, and the fire was racing up the mountainside.

They then turned their attention to the main blaze, which was now roaring up the mountainside with the speed of an express train. Again, a break in front of the advancing flames was the answer, if only they could get ahead of the main fire. Together they raced up the mountain slopes, but suddenly the wind changed and the fire swept down upon them.

In one leap it cleared a gap of 100 m (330 ft). They were now in a patch of particularly long grass, the flames were ten metres high and licking the tops of the tallest trees with a menacing roar. There was only one hope, a large rock about 50 m (165 ft) away. Towards it the seven men raced, and had nearly reached it when one man panicked. Terrified, he flung down his pack and ran in the wrong direction. In a split second he disappeared in the hungry flames.

The other six managed to reach the rock, neck and neck with the fire. They leapt and scrambled desperately for the top. Three reached it and lay down flat on the summit, face down, the flames sweeping over them. But again, two of the guards panicked. One jumped off the rock. The warden leapt after him. He landed on top of him, and, fighting desperately, managed to hold him down. The flames were all around them. The second man, gravely burnt, managed to crawl into the lee of a rock, and survived.

At last the roar of the fire died away as it travelled swiftly up the slopes. The six survivors staggered to their feet, all gravely burnt. But first priority was to look for the first man who had panicked. They found him. He was, of course, dead. So fierce had been the flames that had engulfed him that he had taken only five steps before he fell.

Then, supporting each other, the six survivors staggered as best they could back to the camp. Here, at last, was help. All were given first-aid treatment. Three were pronounced reasonably safe, but the other three, including Jock Fraser, were rushed to Ladysmith Hospital, where they spent many months in intensive care. The warden has never fully recovered, a bitter price paid by a gallant man for saving the life of one of his team.

But the fire was still unappeased. It had grown in size and fury. With a thunderous roar it swept on, devouring everything in its path, heading now in the direction of Tendele Hutted Camp. On its way it caught another African.

Just outside Tendele a large party of more than 100 campers were climbing the mountainside. They were right in the path of the rapidly advancing wall of fire! And then, miraculously, the wind suddenly changed again, and the terrified climbers watched in horror as the flames swept past them.

The fire raged completely out of control until it finally spent itself against the cliffs of the escarpment.

Four years later it was the turn of the Cathkin area (see map no. 4).

Towering 730 m (2 400 ft) above the Monk's Cowl Forest Station is a spur of the Little Berg with a fire look-out on the summit. It also looks down on my own home, "Emkhizweni", in the Drakensberg. Early on the morning of

The alarm has sounded, and a helicopter ferries a team of fire fighters into the deep recesses of the Drakensberg.

Monday, 17 August 1970, a fire broke out about a kilometre away from the hut. Frans Visagie, the Forestry officer in charge of the Station, immediately sent up a team of African game guards to put out the blaze. They arrived about midday, and immediately set to work, but suddenly the light breeze that had been blowing since early that morning gusted into a howling gale, changed direction, and five of the team found themselves surrounded by a wall of flame. Three panicked and began to run in the wrong direction, where the flames were thickest.

It was Bomvana Mpinga who saved the situation.

Bomvana, 36 years of age and father of six, was an experienced fire fighter and a leader of men. Remaining perfectly calm, he grappled with the three fear-crazed men and forced them through a narrow gap in the flames into a fire-break he had burned. Then he calmed the others. But in spite of his courageous action all five were severely burnt and in agony, one so badly burnt that Bomvana did not think he could survive for very long.

The rest of the team managed to get the five injured men into the look-out hut, and then Bomvana set off at top speed, down the mountain slopes, to

Cathkin Park Hotel, the nearest hotel to the scene of the disaster. Exhausted, he staggered into the hotel at 5 pm.

It was winter, and almost dark, but Anton Zunckel, son of the legendary Gerald Zunckel, immediately took swift action. His first decision was to alert the South African Air Force 19 Squadron in Durban. Stretcher evacuation of the five men down the precipitous Little Berg would be far too dangerous, was his first reaction. He contacted Champagne Castle Hotel and the Emmaus Mission Hospital for medical help, and then set off immediately up the Makurumani Gorge for the summit. He had with him Frans Visagie, the Monk's Cowl forester, and Philip Boustead, officer in charge of the Cathedral Peak Forest Station. Soon no fewer than four relief parties were toiling up the mountainside from different directions, in the darkness of the night, with medical supplies and stretchers.*

Meanwhile, the fire was now completely out of control, and soon fire-fighting teams (30 men altogether) from Monk's Cowl Forest Station and the Cathedral Peak Forest Station were converging on the scene, together with the four relief parties.

Up at the look-out hut the five men – Willie Masengumu, Mqushela Mazibuko (who subsequently died), Mkhemazi Mbele, Mhlawuli Mpinga and Mkhumazo Dhladhla – were writhing in agony on the floor of the hut. The relief parties began to arrive, guided to the hut in the inky darkness by the moans of the injured. The first doctor arrived at 4 am, followed soon after by the second, and from then on they worked on the five men, in freezing cold and cramped quarters, dressing the deep burn wounds and administering life-saving intravenous plasma and pain-killing drugs.

At first light on the Tuesday morning a helicopter from 19 Squadron took off from Louis Botha Airport in Durban, piloted by Major James Sclanders. Sclanders knew the Drakensberg well. He arrived at 7 am, but light mist and smoke from the fire prevented an immediate take-off from Monk's Cowl Forest Station, and it was not until three hours later that the helicopter could take to the air.

The most seriously injured, Mqushela Mazibuko and Willy Masengumu, with 50 per cent to 60 per cent burns, were immediately airlifted to Estcourt, where ambulances took them to the Estcourt Hospital. They were later transferred to Edendale Hospital in Pietermaritzburg, which is better equipped for skin-graft operations. The other three were taken to Estcourt in a second trip.

---

* The relief parties were Anton Zunckel and two companions; a doctor from the Emmaus Mission Hospital accompanied by the Ladysmith Police Station Commander, Captain S. D. O'Reilly; John Tungay, founder of the Drakensberg Boys Choir together with one of his pupils, 14-year-old Hanna Botha; and a party from Champagne Castle Hotel, which included a Pietermaritzburg doctor holidaying at the hotel. Anton Zunckel's party carried blankets (it was bitterly cold) and a good supply of the pain-killing drug Pethidine, raided from the hotel's horse stable medicine chest. Captain O'Reilly had a walkie-talkie with him, to "talk down" the rescue helicopter when it arrived.

Rescuers carry the injured to the waiting helicopters after the disastrous fire on the summit of the Little Berg on 17 August 1970.

And the fire? It raged for days, completely out of control, eventually reaching the Cathedral Peak area and even penetrating into Lesotho. An estimated 4 050 hectares (10 000 acres) of valuable grassland were destroyed.

The smoke cleared, the rescue teams dispersed, the scarred veld regained its mantle of green, and four of the five men recovered. Three and a half months later a pleasant little ceremony was held at Cathedral Peak Hotel. Gathered there on the afternoon of 30 November were a number of Forestry Department labourers and officers. They were addressed by Mr M. G. Lotter, Under-Secretary of the Department of Forestry.

He had been sent, he said, by the Government in Pretoria to do honour to a very brave man, a man who had not thought of what might happen to him, but only of the safety of his fellows.

Mr A. Burgers, regional manager of the National Occupational Safety Association, presented the NOSA Award for Bravery in Industry to Mr Mpinga. Mr Mpinga was also presented with a watch, an inscribed transistor radio, and a cash gift.

Yes, fire, servant of man, can be a vicious killer. What precautions can we take against it?

First, remember carelessness can cost lives. One lighted match in the Royal Natal National Park, in 1966, cost the lives of two men, a further six injured, and incalculable damage. In winter, especially, the grass in the Drakensberg is tinder-dry, and a tiny spark can set off a huge conflagration. If you do light a fire in the Drakensberg (remember it is illegal to light a fire at any place except a designated picnic spot) make sure it is out before you continue your hike.

You are climbing the Little Berg, where the grass is usually thick and long. You suddenly see, far below you, a line of fire, out of control, advancing upon you. A fire burning uphill, in a gale-force wind, can move at a terrifying speed. What do you do?

Head for a grove of forest trees if there is one within range, perhaps in a mountain kloof. You are perfectly safe there. If there are no trees and you are standing out in open country, then set alight the grass where you are standing. Soon you will have a patch of burnt grass around you, into which you can step, and the fire will sweep past you. It is a wise precaution always to carry a box of matches with you in winter, even if you are only out for an afternoon stroll up the slopes of the Little Berg.

If you have no matches with you, and all else fails, run straight into, and through, the wall of fire. Remember, fires in a raging wind, burning uphill, can move with unbelievable speed. When you are through the flames, roll on the ground. Your clothes are almost certain to be on fire, but this will put the flames out. To try to outdistance a racing fire, especially uphill, is fatal. If you face it, and run through it, you at least have a sporting chance.

18 Snakes and Snakebite

Of all the hazards one is likely to encounter in the Drakensberg, the one that is least understood and perhaps the most feared is the possibility of snakebite. Snakes, in the case of most people, provoke a sense of horror and revulsion, and the supposed inevitability of certain death from snakebite has caused a feeling of morbid fear in the minds of most people.

The facts do not support this fear. To begin with, we know of only one case of death from snakebite of a climber in the Drakensberg, and even this is doubtful (see the next chapter). There have been deaths among Africans in the foothills. This is because Africans in the area almost always go barefoot, do not recognise the necessity for immediate medical attention, and often rely on worthless remedies.

But the danger to the climber does exist. What can we do about it? In this chapter we shall discuss snakes and snakebite generally, and in the following chapter give the stories of the only two cases of snakebite suffered by climbers in the Drakensberg that we know of.*

We suggest the most important thing is: know your enemy, assess the chances of being bitten, learn to identify the various species of snakes found in the Drakensberg, the harmless ones, the mildly venomous ones, and the ones to be really feared. Learn the habits of snakes, how they are likely to react in a given situation, and how to avoid them. And, of course, you must know what to do and what not to do in the unlikely event of your being bitten.

First of all, note that the vast majority of snakes in the Drakensberg, indeed in the whole of South Africa, are quite harmless. Of the 150 to 160 known species of snakes in South Africa, only 35 are considered dangerous, and fewer than 20 are potentially lethal. Of these 20 only three occur in the Drakensberg. Learn to recognise them.

---

* On going to press, we learnt of a third case. On Good Friday, 5 April 1985, Miss Ann Halley-Wright was bitten on the ankle while on the contour path in the Giant's Castle Game Reserve, by a Puff-adder. She survived the attack.

Hardly a dozen people a year die of snakebite in South Africa, and most of these are rural Africans for the reasons given above. In a seven-year period in Natal, there were 588 cases of snakebite reported, and of these only 21 died, most of them Africans from the country districts.

But the danger does, admittedly, exist, and it is wise to be prepared.

Altogether there are 21 different species of snakes in the Drakensberg (22 if the doubtful Rhombic Night Adder, *Causus rhombeatus*, is included). Of these, only three are potentially dangerous; five are mildly venomous and may be disregarded: no deaths have ever been recorded from their bites; and 13 are non-venomous.

The three venomous snakes are the Puff-adder (*Bitis arietans arietans*), the Rinkals (*Hemachatus haemachatus*) and the Berg or Mountain Adder (*Bitis atropos*). Of these only the first two are lethal. These two snakes are easily identified, and the third, the Berg Adder (the least dangerous of the three), fairly easily identified. (See the colour photographs of these three species opposite

All three species of highly venomous snake found in the Drakensberg may occur at this level.

159

p. 121.) The Berg Adder is the only venomous snake that is found at all levels in the Drakensberg. On the summit of the escarpment, at 3 000 m (10 000 ft), only two snakes are found, the Berg Adder and the mildly venomous Cape Many-Spotted or Reed Snake (*Amphlorhinus multimaculatus*). The Puff-adder and the Rinkals are found up to the summit of the Little Berg (2 000 m or 6 600 ft) and for a few hundred metres up the basalt slopes of the Main Berg, but not on the summit.

The Puff-adder is thick and squat, with a short tail. It has a broad, flattened, triangular-shaped head, quite distinct from the neck. The average length is from 60 cm to 90 cm (2 ft to 3 ft), but larger specimens are often encountered. The maximum for Southern Africa is about 1,25 m (4 ft).

Colour varies greatly, but usually it is light to dark brown, sometimes almost black, with yellow, white or brown chevrons over the body, pointing towards the tail. The belly is yellow to yellowish-white.

Puff-adders are sluggish, slow-moving snakes, and are often found lying on paths waiting for prey (mice or rodents) or among rubbish (stones and planks) in your back-yard. They are sometimes found basking on sunlit rocks or on top of low branches and bushes, especially after heavy rain, when the ground is too wet for their liking. They are among the best-known snakes in South Africa and are responsible for about 90 per cent of snake attacks, largely because of their wide distribution and large numbers.

Most snakes will slither out of your way long before you reach them, but the Puff-adder does not do this as it relies on cryptic coloration and immobility to escape detection. It is fatally easy to step on one, and then it will strike with lightning rapidity (it is the fastest-striking snake in South Africa, but it cannot strike backwards as some people think). Fortunately it will often give warning of its intentions by hissing noisily if too closely approached.

The fangs, often nearly 25 mm (an inch) in length, normally lie horizontally in a resting, inactive position, enclosed in a sheath, but when the snake is ready to strike, with the jaws open, the sheath is drawn back and the recurved fangs stand out starkly.

The venom is mainly haematoxic or cytotoxic, which means that it acts on the cell structure. It is highly toxic, but the results of a bite are seldom fatal, most victims surviving without serum treatment. There is usually plenty of time, at least four to six hours, before serious symptoms may appear. After a bite there is usually an intense, burning pain at the site of the bite, extending up the limb, with swelling and reddening.

The second highly venomous snake found in the Drakensberg is the Rinkals (*Hemachatus haemachatus*). It is sometimes called the Ring-necked Cobra, or the South African Spitting Cobra, but there are no true cobras (genus *Naja*) in the Drakensberg, and to avoid confusion these two names should not be used. The Rinkals is differentiated from the cobras by having keeled dorsal scales (cobras have smooth scales), by the absence of solid teeth on the maxilla, and by being ovo-viviparous (giving birth to live young) rather than oviparous (egg-laying).

The Rinkals is a fairly large snake, with an average length in South Africa of 1 m (3 ft). Colour is variable, and is usually dark brown to black, with two or three whitish-grey bands across the throat, the lower often broader than the others, hence the name Rinkals, Afrikaans for ring-necked. The head is broad and flattish, and not distinct from the neck. The body is a little thicker than is the case with most of the non-venomous snakes, though nothing like as thick as that of the Puff-adder.

But the best identifying feature is the Rinkals' habit of rearing up when disturbed, and expanding the hood.

This expanding of the hood (common also to the true cobras) has intrigued herpetologists. It is obviously partly intimidatory. Also, the thickened neck would make it difficult for a small carnivore to obtain an effective grip on the snake, while a bite at the edge of the hood would not be as disabling as a bite elsewhere. The raised head, of course, would give the snake a point of vantage over its enemies, especially in long grass.

Another distinguishing feature of the snake is its ability to spit. Actually "spit" is a misleading term. "Squirt" would be a better word to use. The venom, when ejected, is practically colourless, and of the consistency of glycerine. It comes out in a thin stream, which then breaks up into a fine spray, with a range from 1 m to 1,5 m (3 ft to 5 ft). The snake usually sprays, very accurately, for the head and chest area; the venom is neurotoxic and very potent, and unless treated very quickly (see later) can cause serious injury to eye tissue.

Another highly defensive mechanism which the snake has is its ability to feign death. It will suddenly go limp (especially after spitting) and turn on its back. The jaws will gape open and the tongue hang out, but if approached too closely, or handled, it will strike, again with lightning rapidity.

The Rinkals is not an aggressive snake, unless disturbed in the mating season, and it seldom bites with deliberation. But if it does bite, the consequences can be serious. Fortunately the snake receives good warning of your approach, and it is only very rarely that you come to close quarters with it (unlike the Puff-adder). The Rinkals is found throughout the Drakensberg to a height of 2 260 m (7 400 ft).

The only other venomous snake in the Drakensberg is the Berg or Mountain Adder (*Bitis atropos*). Not as easily identified as the Puff-adder and the Rinkals, it is yet quite distinctive. Again a little thicker than the slender non-toxic snakes, it is much smaller than either the Puff-adder or the Rinkals. Its average length is only 30 cm to 35 cm (12 in. to 14 in.) with a maximum of 60 cm (2 ft). Its colour varies from greyish-olive to black, sometimes with a tinge of brown, but dark grey is the prevailing colour. Its markings, coupled with its thickness and small size, are distinctive. These markings consist of a silvery white line halfway up the body on each side, from head to tail, against which are a number of dark squarish blotches, usually pale-edged. It is one of the commonest snakes in the Drakensberg.

View from the summit. Of the three species of venomous snake found in the Drakensberg, only the Berg Adder occurs at this height.

Like most adders, the Berg Adder reacts violently if annoyed. It is often found on the grassy slopes of the Little Berg, and even up to the summit at 3 000 m (10 000 ft). You might also find it lying on the path in the late afternoon as you return home from a day in the hills. It will strike aggressively and rapidly if molested.

The venom of the Berg Adder is unique and does not respond to the ordinary polyvalent serum supplied by the South African Institute for Medical Research. In any case it is now considered dangerous to apply this serum, especially by the amateur, and doctors rarely use it. Treatment should be symptomatic.

The reaction to a Berg Adder bite is unpredictable. The exact position regarding the venom is not known and will have to be determined by further research. What is known, is that the venom has both neurotoxic and haematoxic elements, but does not cause any respiratory distress.[1] It has a specific action on the optic and facial nerves. Symptoms following a bite may be a burning pain at the site, with slight swelling of the affected limb. In other cases there may be giddiness, loss of balance, difficulty in focusing the eyes, blurred and double vision, with the pupils dilated, and a distorted sense of taste (but not smell). The victim may become semi-conscious, but the results should not be fatal. There have been no recorded deaths from Berg Adder bites.[2] When the patient recovers, the effects of the venom on vision may last from four days to three months.[3]

These, then, are the only three species of snake you need worry about in the Drakensberg.

If your patient is the victim of a spitting Rinkals attack, all you need do is to clean the eyes as quickly as possible. Wipe the excess venom away from the eyes with a damp cloth, and wash the eyes out with clean water. (Any liquid within reason can be used. Even urine has been used on occasion.)

It is outside the scope of this book to discuss the ultimate methods of treating snakebite in a hospital, but it might be of interest to know that treatment is basically symptomatic. As we have already said, anti-snakebite serum is rarely administered today.

In dealing with snakebite, which is actually only a slight hazard in the Drakensberg, there are two things to be considered. The first is to take common-sense precautions to avoid being bitten, and the second is to know what to do in the unlikely event of being bitten.

It is wise to get into the habit of looking ahead and scanning the ground in front of you. You will often spot a snake before he sees you. Hardened mountaineers do this, automatically and unconsciously, all the time.

Remember that a snake cannot hear your approach. Snakes have no external ears or eardrums, nor do they have the auditory mechanisms that you and I have, but they can pick up contact vibrations, and most snakes (the Puff-adder excepted) will slither out of your way long before you reach them.

Always in open country wear socks and stout, strong boots, and preferably long trousers, though the latter are not essential. A bite on the ankle can be serious. Owing to the large complex of nerves and veins in the ankle, this is one of the most vulnerable parts of your body where snakebites are concerned.

Do not step over logs or large rocks, because a snake could easily be basking on the other side. Rather step on top of the obstruction first.

At night never go out without protective footwear and a torch. Many snakes are nocturnal.

---

1. This needs qualifying. Sometimes the muscles of the neck are affected and this can cause difficulty in breathing.
2. With the possible exception of Ian Muller. See the next chapter.
3. See Appendix 2 for a detailed case history of a Berg Adder bite.

Be wary of holes in the ground. Never put your unprotected hand down one. A snake could easily be hiding there.

What do you do if you are suddenly confronted by a snake? Don't panic and don't attempt to kill it. Stand perfectly still and then move slowly backwards. The distant vision of most snakes is poor. Close-up vision is fairly good, but a snake will always pick up a moving object rather than one that is motionless. Often a quick movement, made perhaps unconsciously near a snake, will precipitate an instinctive strike.

If you have to kill a snake, break its back with a stick first of all. Throwing stones and rocks at it can be dangerous, as it could easily attack you. But never kill a snake unless it is absolutely essential (e.g. a highly venomous snake in the vicinity of a dwelling house, where the lives of others, especially children, might be at stake). All snakes have their part to play in the complex balance of nature. They keep rodents and other vermin down. Recently I have noticed an alarming (and infuriating!) increase in the number of moles in our lawns. I am sure this is due to the indiscriminate killing of Mole Snakes by ignorant and uncaring amateur hikers. The Mole Snake is harmless and feeds on most rodents, including moles. We plead that even venomous snakes, remote from human habitation, should not be killed. They play their part in the complex ecology of the countryside and they have the mystic gift of life: why should you or I deprive them of it?

Then, of course, never play around with a seemingly dead snake. Many snakes have the ability to feign death, the Rinkals especially, as we have already noted. Adders will often remain completely immobile, despite provocation, and then suddenly strike like lightning.

And finally, when camping, be wary of clothing and gear left lying about, especially overnight. A snake will often seek the shelter and the warmth of such items, and give you a bad fright, if not worse, when you come to retrieve the items later on.

The treatment of snakebite has undergone considerable changes over the last few years, largely due to the painstaking research carried out by David S. Chapman. Permanganate of potash, tourniquets, cutting the wound and sucking, which used to be *de rigueur* in the old days, have now all been abandoned, or nearly so. Even the injection of anti-venom is now rarely resorted to, and it should never be administered by the amateur. Never take a snakebite outfit with you into the Berg. Leave it at home. Better still, destroy it. "Don't worry," says John Visser, South Africa's leading expert on snakebite, "if you've been taken to hospital after being bitten and your doctor does not give you an injection of serum. He knows what he's doing!" Anti-venom is administered by medical men these days only as a last resort.

What should we do then?

First of all, if you are bitten by a snake in the Drakensberg, do not automatically assume that you have been bitten by a venomous snake.

Remember, there are only three dangerously venomous snakes in the Drakensberg and you should be able to identify them. If you are unable to identify the snake the chances are that it is non-venomous. In one recent study in KwaZulu, notorious for the number of its snakes, it was found that of all the patients seeking medical help after having been bitten, only 14 per cent had been bitten by highly venomous snakes. In another study in the same part of the country, covering 1 067 cases, only 10 per cent of the patients were severely affected and only 2 per cent died.

Even if you are sure that you have been bitten by a venomous snake, do not conclude that your life is in immediate danger. Most Drakensberg bites from venomous snakes are inflicted by adders, and adder venom is extremely slow in its action. Up to ten hours can elapse before life-threatening symptoms appear, and these are usually respiratory in character and can be countered even by non-medics by basic life support action, such as the kiss of life. Tissue damage, however, can be severe with adder bites, and only an hour or two is necessary for permanent impairment or disfigurement. All Drakensberg hotels, caravan parks and camping sites are within an hour of medical help, often immediate if a doctor is among the guests. If one is back-packing, with tent and equipment for 10 days in the remote fastnesses of the Drakensberg, the position is a little more difficult, but even here by no means hopeless, as will be noted in the next chapter when we consider the case of Tony Maddison.

From all this it follows that if someone is bitten by a snake in the Drakensberg, the first and most important thing to do is to summon medical help immediately, or to get the victim to hospital as quickly as possible – preferably within six to ten hours.

In the meantime, keep him calm. Reassure him. There is no need to panic. Panic could be more harmful than the bite itself. Your patient is not going to die. Don't suck or squeeze the bitten area, and don't apply a tourniquet. A lightly bound tourniquet (a thick, padded bandage) to slow the poison is admissable in the case of a Rinkals bite if medical help is some distance away, but never in the case of an adder bite. Do not give alcohol in any form. In fact, it is better, especially in the case of a Rinkals bite, for the patient to have nothing to eat or drink. As far as the bite itself is concerned, clean the wound of any excessive venom and apply a clean dressing. It is advisable to avoid, if possible, any physical exertion or movement of the limb, as this speeds up the action of the venom, but if the victim is some distance from medical help, he may have to walk. He should not run. In other words, "make haste slowly". Your doctor will know that in all major hospitals in Natal there is a Poisons Centre at which expert advice is available by telephone. It is of vital importance for your doctor to know what species of snake has inflicted the bite, so if you are not sure, kill the snake and take the body in for identification. If, before the doctor arrives, respiratory difficulties set in, apply the kiss of life.

It is outside the scope of this book to discuss the ultimate methods of treating snakebite in a hospital, but it might be of interest to know that treatment is basically symptomatic. As we have already said, anti-snakebite serum is rarely administered today.

19 The Cases of Ian Muller and Tony Maddison

In April 1955 a young man, Ian Muller, died from snakebite in the Drakensberg mountains. Ever since, his death has been widely discussed by mountaineers, for he had been given the orthodox treatment of the time. Why did he die? A strange twist to the debate was added in January 1984, when another young man, Tony Maddison, also bitten by a venomous snake, survived. Why was this? We must investigate, and compare, the two cases.

The first news of what was to become a poignant tragedy in the Drakensberg appeared in the *Natal Mercury* of Tuesday, 12 April 1955:

RESCUERS RACE AGAINST TIME IN BERG DRAMA

In a desperate battle against time and weather, 24 people spent yesterday afternoon climbing the Drakensberg Mountains to find 22-year-old Ian Muller, of Cato Road, Durban, who is lying critically ill in a remote ravine.

The search party set out on foot and on horseback about 11.30 am yesterday when John Burrows stumbled into the Champagne Castle Hotel exhausted after a seven-hour struggle in driving rain to bring news that his companion had been bitten by a snake on Sunday night.

Tired and footsore after his nightmare journey through the mountains, 22-year-old John Burrows insisted on accompanying the search party.

In shivering cold with temperatures nearing freezing and hampered by a thick mist and persistent rain, the party continued the search throughout the afternoon for Ian Muller and his companion Peter Newman, who had remained behind with him.

Most of the searchers are experienced mountaineers and they carry with them a stretcher, modern pain-killing drugs, anti-snakebite serum, hot drinks and warm clothing.

Ian Muller, a brilliant Natal University student, set off from Champagne Castle Hotel late on Thursday afternoon, 7 April, into the mountains with two friends,

Peter Newman of the architectural staff, University of Natal, and his brother-in-law, John Burrows, son of Professor H. R. Burrows of the same university. Ian knew the area well, but for Peter Newman and John Burrows it was their first trip into the Drakensberg. They carried two tents with them, a small one-man tent which Ian used, and a two-man tent for Peter and John.

They followed the usual route up the Little Berg (see map no. 4), past the Sphinx, and an hour after leaving the hotel camped down for the night beside Breakfast Stream, on the summit of the Little Berg.

They were up early the following morning, had breakfast, packed up, and set off for Base Camp in the Mhlwazini valley. By 11.30 am they had reached Hlatikulu Nek and were gazing down into the beautiful Mhlwazini valley. By 4 pm they had reached Base Camp and their tents were pitched again. Around them towered the sheer cliffs of Cathkin Peak, the fang-like Monk's Cowl, Champagne Castle and the serrated spires of Dragon's Back.

They were now at the base of the final escarpment cliffs of Champagne Castle, and next day, Saturday, they set off on the long slog up to Grey's Pass, the rocky gully that leads through the final summit cliffs to the top. Soon after midday they were through the pass and a short walk across the Nkosezana valley brought them to Nkosezana Cave, where they spent Saturday night.

Sunday dawned bright and clear. They planned to head south and descend via Ship's Prow Pass, but instead of taking the direct route to the pass they followed the line of the escarpment past Monk's Cowl, with some of the grandest scenery in the Drakensberg.

Then came Ship's Prow Pass, a long and difficult descent down boulder-strewn slopes and heavy bush. Eventually, just on dusk, they reached the point where the contour path crosses Ship's Prow Pass stream, and here they decided to camp for the night.

Thankfully they offloaded their heavy packs and untied the tents. "Look," said Ian, "you chaps set up camp, will you. I'd like to have a look around." He grabbed his stick and started to cross the stream.

On the far side of the stream was a low bank, which Ian started to climb. And then, suddenly, disaster struck. In climbing up the bank he caught hold of the base of a small sapling growing out of a bush with his left hand, to haul himself up. It was then that the snake struck, sinking its fangs into his left wrist. Ian staggered back and called out "I've been bitten". The fangs had gone straight into one of the main arteries.

The two others rushed down to the stream, and with a shoulder under each of his arms, helped him up to the tent which was lying opened out on the ground. It turned out to be his last resting place. Neither of the two tents was erected. There was no point in doing this. The two-man tent would have been too small for three men to work in. All three spent the night in the open, on the spread-out tents.

168 Ian was given immediate first aid. Peter Newman applied a tourniquet to the

upper arm, incised the wound with two transverse cuts, then rubbed in Condy's crystals (permanganate of potash). John Burrows began to assemble the snakebite outfit, getting the syringe out and breaking open the serum ampoules. It took a little time to assemble the syringe, and John had trouble with the serum. It appeared to be thick and coagulated. But eventually Ian was given an injection in the upper arm.

Ian had the reputation, in mountaineering circles, of having a phobia where snakes were concerned. He always took every precaution to avoid being bitten, he had read up all about snakebite, and he knew exactly what symptoms to expect and how to treat them. Throughout the long night that lay ahead (until he became incoherent) he was able to give instructions to his two companions as to how his symptoms should be treated.

The first symptoms appeared within ten minutes – he became unsteady on his legs, though this may have been due to shock. About ten minutes later came the next symptom, loss of bowel control, as he had predicted. Then his breathing became laboured, and round about midnight he asked for artificial respiration. He was able to direct the other two on how to time this, how to wait until he had his lungs full, and then how to press down to enable him to exhale. Then his speech became incoherent, and he had to give directions with his arms. He would pound his chest with his fists to show he was not getting enough air.

Snake alert! Ian Muller on his way to the summit, the day before he died. Ian had a pathological fear of snakes. Here, suspecting a snake in the grass, he approaches cautiously, probing ahead with his stick, and with his hat in his left hand protecting his face in case of a spitting snake.

Three-quarters of an hour after the first injection Ian was given another, in his rump, and in the early hours of the morning, when he was obviously sinking, he was given a third, in the soft part of the stomach. This was a most painful operation, Peter Newman having to sit on him and hold him down as the needle went home.

In the meantime, to add to their troubles, conditions in the camp grew uncomfortable. It was bitterly cold. They covered Ian with the other tent and started a small fire. Then a steady drizzle set in. There was no point in erecting either of the tents: they just sat it out. The fire provided them with hot drinks throughout the night, but to get the water they had to go to the very spot where Ian had been bitten. They cut their visits to the stream to the minimum!

Slowly the long hours of the night ticked by, with the rain pouring relentlessly down and Ian growing weaker and weaker. Desperately, the other two battled grimly on, trying to save the life of the stricken man. He soon lost all power of speech, and all they could do was to continue with the endless artificial respiration. Eventually, as dawn was breaking, he slipped into a deep coma.

Now was the time for action. Up to now, in the darkness of the night, neither of the two young men could go for help. They were both new to the Berg, and did not have a clue as to where they were or how to find the hotel. Now, with the light breaking, there was a chance. It was decided that John Burrows should attempt to go for help. Equipped with a map of the area there was just a chance that he might get through in time, and find the hotel, 20 km away.

He set off at six o'clock. Two hours later Ian Muller died.

We should spare a thought here for Peter Newman. He was in a truly terrifying position. He was alone, in the depths of the Drakensberg, with no experience of mountaineering, without a clue to where he was or how he was to get home. He was hemmed in by heavy mist and the silence of great brooding peaks. There was no guarantee that John Burrows would ever find his way back to the hotel and return with help. Beside him lay the body of his friend, and the rain kept coming relentlessly down. He nearly panicked and lost his nerve. He confesses that he began to hallucinate. Eventually, in despair, he erected the little one-man tent, crept inside, and fell into an exhausted sleep.

He awoke at 5 pm to hear the sound of whistles. It was the relief party, he realised. John had got through, and they were trying to find him! Excitedly he hunted out his own whistle and gave an answering blast, and the next ten minutes heard a cacophony of sound as the searching whistles answered each other.

John Burrows had managed to find his way back to the hotel, through unknown country, arriving there at 11 am. Here he ran into Mike Barrett, a friend and fellow-student, who was also holidaying in the area. Mike immediately set about organising a rescue party, with the help of Mr and Mrs D. R. Wallace, proprietors of the hotel. Unfortunately, on the way back they lost a good deal of time trying to find the Ship's Prow Pass stream. At least six or seven other streams flow down the flanks of Cathkin Peak into the Delmhlwazini River, and John Burrows could not remember which valley they had come down. They lost several hours turning up incorrect valleys until they found the right one.

By now it was too late to return to the hotel, so rescuers and rescued decided to camp down for the night beside Ship's Prow Pass stream. Little did they realise that 25 years later their camp site was to be the scene of an even more horrifying tragedy (see p. 130).

And there was drama not only here in the mist-shrouded peaks of the Drakensberg, but also away down in Durban. Here two families sat out the night together in gnawing fear and anxiety.

A kindly reporter from one of the Durban newspapers had telephoned the Burrows and Newman families with the news that one of the three young men had been bitten by a snake and was in trouble, but the reporter didn't know which one it was! Who was the victim? Anxiously the two families huddled around the radio, waiting for news. In the case of the Professor, was it his son or his son-in-law, or his star honours pupil in the Department of Economics? In the case of his daughter Audrey, was it her husband or her brother, or Ian Muller whom she knew well? It was some hours before the answer came through to the two waiting families.

A few comments are necessary before we write finis to this moving story.

Since Ian Muller died there have been endless discussions as to just why he died even though he had been given the orthodox treatment of the time. Closely tied up in this discussion is another question: what type of snake was it that bit him?

It could only have been one of three snakes, a Puff-adder, a Rinkals or a Berg Adder. It is well known that Berg Adder bites do not respond to the anti-snakebite polyvalent serum supplied by the S.A. Institute for Medical Research, and many felt this was significant, pointing to the possibility that it was a Berg Adder. But, broadly speaking, Ian's symptoms were not those associated with Berg Adder bites, which are primarily dysfunction of the cranial nerves. It is also generally held that Berg Adder bites are never fatal. The snake must, therefore, have been either a Puff-adder or a Rinkals.

But again, Ian's symptoms were not completely synonymous with the bites of either of these two snakes. We put the whole question to Dr Graham Hukins: just why did Ian Muller die?

Dr Hukins has had fairly wide experience in the treatment of snakebites. After interviewing Peter Newman, Dr Hukins said:

"It is extremely difficult to answer this question with any certainty. Ian Muller's symptoms were those associated with a neurotoxic snakebite – that is, a gradual and progressive paralysis of the muscles. I do not think he suffered from a Puff-adder bite because there were no recorded symptoms of cytotoxicity – simply an area of swelling about the wound.

"Of the poisonous snakes found in the area we are left with one of two

171

alternatives, either a Rinkals or the Berg Adder. However, up to now medical opinion in South Africa has been that, though unpleasant and even painful, the effects of a Berg Adder bite are never fatal.*

"Could it have been a Rinkals? Certainly the symptoms he suffered from could have been caused by a Rinkals, but if we accept the Rinkals bite as being the cause of death we have to explain why there was no response to the orthodox treatment of injection of polyvalent serum.

"There are possibly two explanations for this. Firstly, it may be that insufficient serum was injected. Rinkals bites may require large quantities of serum. Secondly, the route of administration might have been ineffective in neutralising all the venom which the snake had injected with its bite. (For example, an intravenous injection might have been more effective than an intra-muscular one.) Partial neutralisation of the venom might also be the reason for the abnormally prolonged period between the bite and the time of death.

"Could this be the second recorded death from the bite of a Berg Adder? The site of the bite was most unusual. It was into one of the superficial veins on the medial aspect of the left wrist. This would have carried a high dose of the venom directly into the systemic circulation. This may have been responsible for a bulbar paralysis which would have led to a selective paralysis of the throat muscles, leading to obstruction of the air passages and eventual asphyxiation.

"It has been suggested that he died from anaphylactic shock, and such fatalities after the administration of polyvalent snakebite serum to susceptible individuals allergic to the serum are by no means unknown, but in these cases the patient starts to develop symptoms within ten minutes of the administration of the serum, and death follows rapidly. Ian Muller died as long as 14 hours after his first injection.

"It has also been suggested that he may have died from hysteria, and it is known that he was abnormally afraid of snakes and snakebite. I would not rule this out entirely. It may have been an ancillary cause of death, but I am fairly certain it was not the main cause.

"Beyond this I cannot go."

"Could there," we asked, "have been more than one factor responsible for the rather unusual clinical picture and the eventual death – perhaps hysteria plus the effects of the venom?"

"Yes," said Dr Hukins, "I certainly think this might be considered."

The story of Tony Maddison, though there are striking parallels, is completely different.

Only ten days before Tony Maddison was bitten by a Berg Adder I had

* In Walter Rose's book *The Reptiles and Amphibians of South Africa* there is a brief reference to a Berg Adder fatality from Riversdale, in the Cape, but no details are given.

written my first rough draft of the previous chapter (since amended). In it I had said: "If you are bitten by a poisonous snake in the Drakensberg, don't panic and assume that you are going to die. You are practically certain to recover. Let us imagine the worst that could happen to you. Let us imagine that you are bitten by a poisonous snake in the remotest possible portion of the Drakensberg, the furthest away from help, say the summit of the Mnweni area. You have about six or seven hours before fatal results set in. (You couldn't be bitten by a Rinkals, where the time limit is shorter, because the Rinkals is not found at that altitude. If you had been bitten by a Rinkals it could only be in the Little Berg, where help is much nearer.) Your nearest telephone would be either Cathedral Peak Hotel, four to five hours away (Martin Winter did it, you will remember, in three and three-quarter hours), or the Police Post in the Lower Mnweni, two and a half to three hours by a fast runner. A helicopter, with the necessary medical assistance, could be with you within an hour to an hour and a half after that, plenty of time to save your life."

Tony Maddison

By a remarkable coincidence, exactly ten days after I had written that paragraph, the very circumstances I had envisaged occurred, in the very area I had postulated.

Due west of the two Mnweni Pinnacles, in the Mnweni Cutback, are two minor pinnacles (see map no. 2). Though unnamed, they are pinpointed on the South Africa 1 : 50 000 map 2828 DD as spot heights, 9745 and 9555 (these figures refer to altitude heights, in feet). They stand at the head of a valley in which runs a stream flowing into the Mnweni River about 750 metres upstream from Shepherd's Cave. These pinnacles had been seen by two Transvaal mountaineers on a previous trip, Tony Maddison and Clive Ward. In January 1984 they decided to come down from Johannesburg, explore and photograph the two pinnacles.

Tony Maddison, 29 at the time, is a Johannesburg metallurgist. Although having been in this country for only two years (he comes from the UK) he has done a good deal of climbing in South Africa, and is a member of the Transvaal Section of the Mountain Club's Search and Rescue team.

Tony and Clive left Johannesburg on Wednesday, 18 January, and drove straight to the Police Post in the Lower Mnweni. Here they camped for the night.

Next morning, after signing the Mountain Register at the Post, they set off up the main Mnweni valley, crossing the Ntonjelana (running high) about an hour later. The hike up the Mnweni was long and tiring, but they made good time, and soon after lunch they reached Shepherd's Cave. From there they proceeded another three-quarters of a kilometre, and entered their valley, at the head of which stood the two pinnacles. Two to three hours from Shepherd's Cave they found another small cave, in which they spent the night.

Friday dawned with heavy mist blanketing the mountains. In spite of this they continued their climb, gaining height rapidly. They were now behind the

Black & Tan path, and had reached an altitude of about 2 500 m (8 200 ft). They then ascended a steep grassy buttress, an easy slope, and then up a second buttress. The mist began to lift from the peaks.

On the way up they had seen several Berg Adders, and they had spent about 45 minutes photographing them. They then realised that they had climbed a little too high, and that to reach the position they wanted they would have to descend a steep grassy bank. It was too steep to walk down, so they simply slid down on their buttocks, with Clive in the lead. It was just as Clive called up that he could see a small Berg Adder that Tony grabbed a tuft of grass to steady himself and felt a sharp prick on the ring finger of his right hand. He never gave it a second thought – it was probably only a sharp stone, he reckoned. The time was then 12.30 pm.

When they reached a suitable resting spot he had a look at his finger and saw a small spot of blood. Even then he did not associate it with a snakebite. After half an hour, however, the finger became painful, and then the gland under his arm began to swell. It was only then that he realised he had been bitten by a snake.

Within an hour his sense of taste was affected; then his vision became blurred and his sense of balance began to go. By then both men knew Tony had been bitten by a Berg Adder.

But there was no panic and no real alarm. Both men were experienced mountaineers; they "knew their enemy". They knew the Berg Adder bite is not fatal, and that only the cranial nerves would be affected. They calmly continued on their way. After two hours Tony began to have double vision.

They decided not to try to get off the mountain immediately, but to sit it out. Clive knew of another small rock shelter near by, and they spent Friday night there. By now Tony's sense of taste had gone completely haywire. Anything sweet or spicy, or slightly acid, like fruit, tasted dreadful. As the evening wore on his eyelids became heavy and he had slight pain in the throat. He tried eating, and drinking tea, but these only brought on waves of nausea. Any movement, like trying to move round camp, brought on nausea and dizziness.

When they woke on Saturday morning Tony found his neck muscles wouldn't support his head, and his vision was worse. He was also in a permanent state of nausea. They held a conference and decided to try and get down to Shepherd's Cave, which could easily be reached by a horse. They reckoned that if they could get as far as that Clive could go for a horse and Tony could be carried out that way.

They covered one eye with a bandage to overcome the problem of double vision, packed up camp and set off down the steep slope. Owing to the loss of his sense of balance Tony did most of the journey on the seat of his pants. After a couple of hours they found they were getting nowhere. They had been able to descend only about 230 m (750 ft). At that rate it would take days to reach Shepherd's Cave.

The only answer was a helicopter. But they were still in exceedingly difficult country, high up on the escarpment slopes, hemmed in by the ravines and rock spires so typical of the Mnweni Cutback. It was impossible country for a helicopter. They had to continue the descent somehow as best they could.

At last they reached a grassy, rocky knoll which they judged to be big enough for a helicopter to put at least one wheel down. Here they pitched the tent, and Clive made sure his friend had enough food and water to last a week. Then he sped off down the valley. The time was 1 pm.

It was downhill most of the way and Clive made good time. By 7.10 pm he was back at the Police Post and the mountain rescue squad had been contacted by telephone.

Sunday dawned another cloudy, misty day. The helicopter arrived about 8 am, but weather conditions made any further flying at that time impossible. However, the clouds soon began to disperse, and at 10 am Tony, sitting outside his tent, heard the comforting sound of the whirring blades.

Tony was taken first to Ladysmith Hospital and then on to Grey's Hospital in Pietermaritzburg. Five days after he had been bitten he was interviewed in hospital by James Byrom, and we were able to obtain a first-hand account, not only of the symptoms, but also of their time sequence. Tony was still suffering from double vision and his sense of balance was still impaired, although improving. His sense of taste also was still bad, though this too was improving. His eyelids drooped heavily over his eyes.

Tony was also visited in hospital by an ex-Rhodesian who had himself survived a Berg Adder bite. "He told me," said Tony, "that he had heard about me on the news, and felt he had to come along and reassure me. His symptoms and progress had been logged and his experience was later to become the first Berg Adder bite case to be officially recorded in medical journals. We discussed the symptoms and mine were exactly the same as his – bad taste, nausea, sore throat, weak neck muscles and heavy eyelids. In fact, he said his eyes closed completely and he couldn't open them. He recovered completely and there were no lasting after-effects."

Tony has now completely recovered from his ordeal. For medical research purposes the two men kept a meticulous record of the onset of symptoms and of subsequent treatment, and as this is of considerable interest to mountaineers, we are privileged to be able to reproduce it as Appendix 2.

20 Rock Friability: Dick Barry

One of the hazards of climbing in the Drakensberg is the friability of the rock. Fred Snell, one-time Rector of Michaelhouse, who had climbed in the Himalayas, would seldom climb in the Drakensberg. "I've too much respect for my neck," he used to say.

There are two types of rock in the Drakensberg, both fragile. The Little Berg is made up of sandstone, laid down by wind erosion millions of years ago. This is soft and crumbly, weathers easily, and little serious climbing is done here.

The Main Berg, or High Berg as it is sometimes called, is a different matter. Here the rock is basalt, volcanic in origin, and it is here that 99 per cent of serious climbing is done.

There are two main types of igneous rock, granite and basalt. Granite is a light-coloured, coarse-grained rock. It is formed from the slow cooling of magmatic material at great depths beneath the surface of the earth, hence under pressure. As a result these rocks acquire a very hard texture, consisting of well-formed crystals. Most of the rock in England, Scotland and Wales is granitic in origin.

Basalt is very different. Basalt is a fine-grained, dark igneous rock. Here the magmatic material has been hurled high into the air by tremendous volcanic forces. It is cooled rapidly, under minimum pressure, with the result that these rocks lack the well crystallised texture of granite, and are hence softer and more friable. It is basalt that makes up the main Drakensberg range.

So friable is Drakensberg rock that it is an accepted rule in Drakensberg climbing that only one man in a team moves at any one time, and he must be firmly belayed to at least one other team member.

Sometimes rock falls in the Drakensberg are of epic and frightening proportions. Leland Bybee, holder of the 1949 coveted Gold Badge of the Mountain Club of South Africa, tells of one fall he witnessed in the Ntonjelana area in 1938:

"With a thunderous roar some hundreds of tons of rock and earth broke away from the cliff on the opposite side of the kloof and tore down the

177

slope taking everything with it – a magnificent sight but not one to inspire confidence in a climber perched perilously on a razor edge."

At least two Drakensberg climbers have lost their lives owing to rock friability, both of them brilliant young students, Dick Barry and Ross Osborn.

The story of Dick Barry has often been told. His was the first fatal climbing accident in the Berg, and it has caught the imaginations of people, not only because it was the first, but also because of the peak itself where he died, Monk's Cowl. This is one of the grimmest peaks in the Drakensberg, dark and menacing, a spear-like fang held between the two clenched fists of Cathkin Peak and the fearful cliffs of Champagne Castle. Except for its tip, it is seldom seen. What has never been properly told, however, are Dick's amazing climbing exploits before he came to the Drakensberg, and secondly the epic attempts to bring down his body after he had fallen to his death. This and the next chapter are devoted to these two topics.

Dick Barry was born in Johannesburg in 1916. In 1932 he obtained a First Class Honours Matric at St Andrew's College, Grahamstown, and the following year went to England to study for a mining degree at Birmingham University. His university career was as brilliant as his school career had been.

He was blessed with a natural ability for climbing. He was light in build, and had a long reach and an amazing balance. On rock he "moved with a swiftness, a cool deliberation, a grace and strength that was a joy to watch". Above all, he had tremendous staying power and a boundless enthusiasm for the sport. When he died he had a library of nearly a hundred books on climbing. (These books are now housed in the library of the Transvaal Section of the Mountain Club of South Africa.) In 1938 the *Alpine Journal* said of him: "By 1936 there was scarcely a rock climb in Britain about which he did not know everything."

In 1935 he went to Yugoslavia to work in the mines there, but before leaving he decided on a final fling in England: to try and climb all of the major crags in the Lake District in one day – an almost impossible task.

He left the Robertson Lamb Hut at Langdale at 3.15 am, and first tackled Dow Crag at 7 am, using a route known as Jones's Route. From there he trekked over to Scafell and climbed Moss Ghyll. At Pillar Rock he met another climber, and together they ascended the Rib and Slab route. At the Wasdale Head Hotel he stopped for dinner, and then pushed on hard for Gavel Neese, which led to a climb up the Needle, and then the Naper, using the Needle Ridge route in the late evening. It was practically dark now, but he set off for the last climb, the Cimmer. But when he arrived there night had fallen, making the climb impossible. He had failed his record by one peak!

Shortly before this climbing epic Barry had achieved what at the time was recognised as almost certainly the most difficult and hazardous rock climb (in terms of steepness of rock and technical difficulty) in British climbing history: the attempt on Deer Bield Central Buttress. At the time only two routes on the

Richard Vincent Merriman (Dick) Barry

Buttress had been opened up: the Chimney and the Crack. Barry decided to attempt a direct route up the Buttress, which had so far defied all previous attempts to climb it. He set off with two companions, and after seven and a quarter hours of some of the most strenuous and terrifying climbing the three men had ever experienced, the assault came to an end and they had to call it off, with less than ten metres (33 ft) to go to the top. Barry was in the lead at the time, standing precariously on a small piece of rock jutting out from the sheer precipice, with the other two men below him, when the rock on which he was standing began to crumble. Barry shouted a warning to the two men below him that the rock might break away, and was then heard to mutter plaintively to himself, "It's a pity I ever came up here!" They decided to call off the attempt and managed to abseil safely down. It wasn't until 1951 that the route was finally conquered by Arthur Dolphin, to become the second hardest climb in the Lake District, but Barry's attempt in 1935, though unsuccessful, still stands as one of the epics in British climbing history.

In 1936 Barry turned his attention to the Alps. 1935 had been a spectacular year for him: 1936 proved even more brilliant. Among many others he climbed the Aiguille des Pelerins by the north-west face, the Aiguille de Glace face. (The final pitch of this climb is so severe and dangerous that there are few guides in the area who will attempt it without arranging beforehand for a colleague to provide a rope from above.) Barry climbed it without artificial aids.

Together with the famous guide Armand Charlet he made for the first time the double traverse of Mont Blanc from north to south in three days. They descended by the Innominata Buttress and reached the Gamba Hut in seven hours. From there they climbed the Peuteret Ridge to the summit of Mont Blanc in ten hours. Barry's pace was so blistering that Charlet nearly gave up.

In November 1936, after completing his university studies as a gold medallist at the head of his year, he sailed for South Africa and joined the Crown Mining Company. "Here I am," he said in a letter to a friend, "working at a depth of over 6 000 feet below the surface, with my thoughts more than twice that height above."

After joining the Transvaal Mountain Club, Barry soon clocked up a series of magnificent climbs in the Magaliesberg, many of them hitherto considered unclimbable – Hangklip Frontal, Zimbabwe, the Coffin (so called because it was climbed in a totally enclosed chimney in complete darkness). In six short months he opened up 11 new routes.

In January 1938 he decided to have a crack at the Drakensberg.

He and a friend Colin Gebhardt arrived at what is now known as the Cathkin Park Hotel (in Barry's day it was called the Cathkin Hostel) early on the morning of 28 January. They left immediately for the Mhlwazini valley and camped that night at the head of the valley, at Base Camp. Towering high above them were Cathkin Peak, the hitherto unclimbed Monk's Cowl (their objective), Champagne Castle and the saw-toothed ridge known as Dragon's Back.

Next morning they climbed the nek between Monk's Cowl and the cliffs of Champagne Castle, but here the weather held them up. It rained for a couple of hours, but by ten o'clock they were able to start their climb up the almost vertical precipices of the Cowl.

The going was hard, providing some of the most sensational rock work either man had ever experienced. Then it started to drizzle and the mist crept up. Round about 2 pm they were nearing the top. Dick was in the lead, with Colin Gebhardt close behind. Both men were roped together.

Suddenly a rock which Gebhardt was using to heave himself up broke loose and Gebhardt fell, pulling Barry off his stance. Both men went over a sheer drop of 18 m (60 ft), rolled down a slope, over another 6 m (20 ft) drop, down another almost sheer slope and came to rest at the bottom of another 9 m (30 ft) drop. Both were badly shocked, and Dick unconscious, with a deep cut in his skull. The time was about 3 pm.

Two hours later Dick regained consciousness, and was quite coherent. But the two were now in a dreadful predicament. They still had the major part of the mountain to descend. They had no spare rope, their rucksacks, pitons and other climbing gear had been left behind at the point where they had fallen, they were alone and badly shaken on the precipices of an unclimbed mountain, and darkness was upon them.

Gebhardt was in a better condition than Dick, and it was decided that he should lead. They came to a sheer drop of some 15 m (50 ft). It looked grim, but if they were to survive they had to attempt it.

They first tried belaying Dick down the pitch, but owing to his condition he could not make it. Dick then suggested that Gebhardt should go down: he would watch and see how it was done, and then follow Gebhardt. Gebhardt managed to make it, and he called up to Dick to come on down. Again Dick set his face to the climb down, but again he failed. Gebhardt was unable to retrace his climb, with the result that the men were now separated.

Dick then called down to Gebhardt saying he would try and find an easier way down. Gebhardt tried to dissuade him, but what else could they do? In the gathering darkness Dick moved off to the side, keeping in touch with Gebhardt by calling repeatedly to him. Then suddenly there was silence. "I knew immediately Dick was dead," said Colin Gebhardt later. "God knows how I did, but I knew."

Gebhardt spent a miserable night alone, at close on 3 000 m (10 000 ft), in a small cave he found. He had no food, and throughout the long hours the rain came pitilessly down. Around him stood the peaks in the silence of the night, remote, immutable, uncaring. But a man had died.

At first light Gebhardt was up. He knew where he would find his friend, and he was right. He found him where he had expected to. Dick was dead.

At first he tried to lift and carry him, but he was too exhausted. The only thing was to go for help. It was the start of one of the longest and most arduous operations the Drakensberg has ever known. It has never before been told in full. It deserves to be recorded.

21 The Recovery of Dick Barry's Body

The first act in the drama was Colin Gebhardt's dash for help. Alone, bruised, dazed and drenched, having had no food for 24 hours, he first had to get down and off the mountain. He had an injured leg, and he was in stockinged feet. Owing to the wetness of the rock they had discarded their boots in their climb and these had been left high up the peak at the point from which they had fallen, together with all their warm clothing. It was bitterly cold. Somehow he managed to climb down the remaining pitches, and then came the difficult, rock-strewn Cathkin Gully. He managed this, reached Base Camp where they had pitched their tent, and then came the long haul home, 20 kilometres of rough mountain paths, down streams filled with washed boulders and bush-choked gullies in stockinged feet. His route lay down the Mhlwazini River, up to Hlatikulu Nek, along the spine of the Little Berg past Ndanjane, down Jacob's Ladder and so home to Cathkin Park Hotel.

At midday he was found shocked, dazed and exhausted, wandering aimlessly around the hotel golf course, by a group of hotel guests. He was taken down to the hotel where he just managed to gasp out his story before he collapsed completely and was put to bed with a sleeping draught. It was Sunday, 30 January 1938.

Udo and Gerald Zunckel were the two sons of Otto Zunckel, doyen of Drakensberg hoteliers. At the time they were running Cathkin Hostel, as the Cathkin Park Hotel was then called. They immediately swung into action, and within half an hour were on their way with the relief party – Udo, Gerald, Mr J. van Heyningen, the local Forestry officer, and 11 Africans. The mist came down, dark and heavy, and in the silence of rain-drenched valleys they battled their way up to the high peaks. They arrived at Base Camp at dusk.

That night the rain came down, hard and heavy, and it was bitterly cold. Next morning heavy mist blanketed the area and it was still raining. Conditions in the camp grew steadily worse. They had only one small tent, 0,75 metres square, no blankets, and their food began to run out. That night all 14 in the party slept together – virtually piled on top of one another.

183

Tuesday dawned, and still the rain came down, but during the morning it eased off, and for a brief moment the mist lifted. It was then that Gerald spotted an eagle circling over the spot where it was thought Dick's body might be lying. Then the mist closed in again, and it was gone. By midday their provisions were down to less than 1,5 kg of potatoes, half a cup of rice, three loaves of bread and one small tin of sardines. It was decided to send Gerald and Thys Robertse, who had arrived at the camp that morning, down to the hotel for further supplies and to relieve the anxiety of the watchers down below.

Meanwhile, down at the hotel, the tension was mounting. No word had come through from the recovery party since they had left on the Sunday morning. Otto especially was worried about the safety of his two sons, high in that desolate wilderness of rock and stone in some of the most appalling weather any of them could remember. In spite of the mist and his age (he had just turned 60) he determined to set out for the mountains himself to find his two sons. He set off at 5 am, accompanied by Geoff Wolf, an hotel guest. They reached Base Camp at 8 am.

Later that morning Dick's father, Mr R. A. Barry, who had come down from Johannesburg on hearing the news, set out alone to try and reach the relief camp. He was found by Gerald and Thys Robertse on their way down, with only the clothes he stood in, and with no food. He was persuaded by the other two to return to the hotel with them. Later still that morning Colin Gebhardt also left the hotel. He had wanted to accompany Dick's father, determined, in spite of his shocked state, to join in the search for his friend. For his own safety his friends had locked him in his room, but he had managed to get out. He finally limped into Base Camp just on dark.

That evening Gerald and Thys Robertse, tired, worn out and unshaven, together with Mr Barry, stumbled into the hotel. Hurriedly they collected supplies of food and extra climbing equipment, and then had a brief sleep. They planned to leave again at 3 am the following morning.

With two additional men to cater for that night, conditions in the tent became impossible. An additional rough shelter out of shrubs and the branches of small trees was built.

Wednesday morning dawned clear, and the recovery party was at last able to commence the task of locating the body and bringing it down to the hotel. Gebhardt, after his second terrible journey, and in view of the fact that he still had to get back to the hotel, only went a short way, but he was able to point out to Udo and the others the spot where he believed the body lay, high up on the face of those terrible cliffs. Accompanied by the 11 Africans Udo, his father and Geoff Wolf continued their climb up Cathkin Gully in a determined bid to recover the body.

Halfway up the gully the old man's strength began to fail, and Udo persuaded his father to stay behind and watch the proceedings through a pair of field-glasses. Udo and Wolf went on alone with the Africans.

They reached the top of the gully, and then commenced the arduous climb up the steep cliffs of the Monk. The going became steadily more difficult, and then Udo decided to go on alone with the best climber from among the 11 Africans.

High up on those impossible cliffs they found the body, wedged face upwards between two huge rocks, the eyes open towards the peak. The face appeared to have escaped serious injury, but the sight was sickening: the body appeared to have been smashed to pieces, almost every bone broken. Dick's climbing rope lay spread out around him.

Quickly Udo untied the ropes around the body and with the assistance of the African placed the remains in a sack. From here it was let down a steep slope and then over a sheer cliff by means of a rope. From there it was taken by the waiting party down below and placed on a rough stretcher made from poles and sacking.

Then started the long march home, down the treacherous Cathkin Gully, along the stream bed of the Mhlwazini, and over Hlatikulu Nek, with relays of bearers. Soon the mists closed in again and the party had to grope their way through the wet grass and over rocks and boulders. Suddenly they heard voices ahead of them. It was Gerald Zunckel and Thys Robertse, on their way back with food and further equipment, together with a *Mercury* reporter. Gerald took over the leadership, relieving his brother and taking charge of the carrying party until it reached Champagne Castle Hotel. Here a lorry from Cathkin Park Hotel was waiting for them, and finally, as night was closing in, they reached Cathkin Hotel.

Top: Monk's Cowl with Cathkin Peak on the left and the cliffs of Champagne Castle on the right.
Bottom: A peaceful stream in the Mnweni area, with the Rockeries in the background.

Dick Barry's grave.

Meanwhile, on the Tuesday (the previous day), a group of Transvaal mountaineers, consisting of Harry Barker, Gordon Potter and Ken Lewis, had come down to help in the recovery operation. All three were Dick Barry's friends and had climbed with him on many occasions. On that Wednesday morning they had set off on their climb up the Little Berg to the scene of the accident. Halfway up, however, they came across Colin Gebhardt on his way back with the news that the body had been recovered. They turned and went back with him to the hotel.

On Thursday, at ten o'clock in the morning, Dick Barry was laid to rest in the mountains he loved. The chosen spot was a gentle grassy slope about six kilometres away from the hotel, overlooking the Ndema valley. In front were Cathkin Peak, Champagne Castle and just the tip of Monk's Cowl.

Today the grave is still well cared for. From down below comes the ripple of the Nkwakwa stream, but otherwise all is silent. Very rarely the occasional hiker or climber comes by. Perhaps he pauses awhile and wonders, or, if he is of the older generation, remembers. And then he goes on his way.

22 Ross Osborn

After a brilliant career at Hilton College, Ross Osborn enrolled at Natal University in Durban, first of all for an architectural degree, but later switching to B.A. and LL. B. He was a first-class athlete, a prominent member of the Students' Representative Council, and a potential Rhodes Scholar.

On Tuesday, 24 November 1953, Ross and a fellow student, Stewart Ferguson, arrived at the Royal Natal National Park, intent on a few days' climbing after the end of year examinations. The following morning they set out for the summit of the Amphitheatre (see map no. 1).

They followed the usual route, up the Mahai valley to Basuto Gate, and then up the long zigzag to the base of the Sentinel, the chain ladder and so to the top. They reached the summit about noon.

After lunch they decided to descend via Inner Tower Gully.

Ross Osborn

Inner Tower Gully is formed by Inner Tower as it abuts on the main escarpment. It is a difficult route even for experienced climbers. Neither Ross nor Ferguson were experts. This was their first visit to the Drakensberg, but they elected to climb down one of the several lateral gullies that lead into the main gully. These are even worse than the main gully, and even experienced climbers would think twice before attempting such a route.

They set off soon after midday, Ross wearing only a pair of shorts, but carrying a jersey with him.

About 300 m (1 000 ft) from the top the side gully enters the main gully, and they then proceeded down this main gully. Soon after entering it, however, they encountered a vertical rock face next to a waterfall which plunged down the escarpment. Ross was leading, but he soon found it impossible to proceed any further. He called up to Ferguson, "Go back – we can't make it." The two men started to climb back up the gully, and it was soon after this that the accident happened. Ferguson was leading with Ross close behind. He reached a ledge and stopped for a brief rest. He saw Ross's hand come up, feeling for a hold. Suddenly the rock crumbled and gave way, and Ross plunged out of sight. It was now 4 pm.

187

Horrified and badly shaken, Ferguson struggled back alone, up the almost vertical rock face, to the summit, electing to climb the main gully rather than the more difficult side gully. He reached the summit and then raced for the Mountain Club Hut where he found two young married couples. One of them, a Mr de Wit of Pretoria, immediately offered to go down to the hotel with news of the disaster.

The rescue operation, carried out by three young Natal mountaineers, Martin Winter, Bill Barnes (Natal Parks Board Fisheries officer in the Park) and Pip Adelson in a gruelling seven-hour race against time, is regarded today as one of the epics of Natal mountaineering. On this occasion we shall open these pages to one of the participants, Bill Barnes, and let him tell the story in his own words, a story which has never been told properly before.

"Well, I suppose that for me the whole thing started on the night of Wednesday, 25 November 1953. I was in bed at the time. In fact, I had been in bed all day with a dose of 'flu. It was 10.15 pm when there came a knock at the door. (At the time I was occupying the house at the National Park trout hatchery.) I jumped out of bed and ran to the door. Outside stood a rather tired and jaded looking man who greeted me with the news of an accident in the Amphitheatre. I gave the poor guy, who had come down from the Sentinel hut at great speed, a drink to calm his nerves. He was exhausted and in a state of shock.

"I then took him down to Peter Pope-Ellis, the warden, who had just turned in for the night; but like all good Parks Board wardens, he quickly rose and was all set for the job.

"We listened to the chap's story, and then phoned Martin Winter, farming at Frere, who at the time was convenor of the Mountain Club rescue team. Martin said he would come immediately.

"Peter and I then started to get things organised. Game guards had to be roused and horses found and made ready for an early start. Here the hotel was extremely helpful. George Harkness was running the place at the time. While at the hotel we met up with a young man who was still up and about and who offered his help immediately. His name was Pip Adelson, an old Hilton College boy and only just out of school attending university. Pip's job was to collect the sandwiches and other odds and ends that the hotel was preparing and then come down to Peter's house where we would await the arrival of Martin Winter.

"One important job we had to do was to inform the S.A. Police at Oliviershoek. In view of the fact that the victim of the accident was almost certainly dead, the police said they would come along with us. Unfortunately I cannot remember the policeman's surname, but his Christian name was Chris, a very pleasant Afrikaans-speaking man in his early twenties, but carrying, perhaps, a little excess weight.

"Slowly the party assembled. Martin Winter arrived about 3 am, Chris, the

188

policeman, about the same time. We decided to make up two rescue parties, one under Martin Winter to proceed up the summit via the chain ladder, and the other, under Peter Pope-Ellis, to proceed up the Gorge and thence to the bottom of Inner Tower Gully. I was alotted to the first party.

"At 5.10 am our summit party left on horseback, making good speed up the Mahai valley. It consisted of Martin Winter, Pip Adelson, Chris the policeman, two black constables and myself. We left our horses at the foot of the chain ladder with a couple of game guards and arrived at the hut at 8.15 am. A cup of coffee while Stewart Ferguson, Osborn's companion, told us what had happened, and then we were off, together with Stewart, for the top of the gully down which the two men had gone.

"However, when we reached the head of Inner Tower Gully, Stewart could not remember which gully they had gone down. As you know, there are dozens of gullies that run down the Amphitheatre wall, and several which actually run into the main Inner Tower Gully. This made things a little difficult, for it could have taken us days, if not weeks, to look into them all. The only thing Stewart was certain of was that it was not the main gully they had gone down. Then, to make matters worse, Stewart said he was not feeling too well and that he would like to go back down to the hotel. So he left us.

"We wandered around, looking into each gully, wondering what was the best thing to do, and eventually we had a rest on the edge of the escarpment, with our feet virtually hanging over the edge.

"We were about to move on when Martin's eagle eye focused on what looked like a footprint, some 20 ft below us, leading into the very gully we were looking into. We descended, and sure enough, a footprint, and a few feet further on, another, leading directly into the gully. The gully itself looked terrifying, but it was a possible route. We decided to go down.

"Martin suggested that for the sake of safety and speed we should abseil down. The ropes were prepared – two of 120 ft each, one of which belonged to Pip (brand new, a recent birthday gift) and the other to Martin Winter.

"Chris the cop, on seeing the preparations, took one look down the gully and said: 'Got, man, are you chaps going down there?'

"'Yes,' we replied. 'Come along down with us.'

"'Nee, dankie, I cannot stand heights and will never make it. I'm sure you chaps will be better off without me. Just give me a report when you get back.' With that Chris departed as fast as he could for the hut and safety.

"Then, as the three of us started the descent of the steep gully, we found a fresh sweet wrapper, conclusive proof that this was the gully Ross and Stewart had gone down. We abseiled some 600 ft, and then found that lower down this side gully led directly into the main Inner Tower Gully. Here we found more footprints and more sweet wrappers, confirming that we were on the right track.

"However, after another couple of abseils, we struck trouble – an abyss in

190

front of us, a vertical drop of some 250 ft, and there at the bottom lay the body we were looking for.

"We realised then that this was the spot the two men had reached. We recalled Ferguson's words back there at the hut. Ross had been in the lead, he said, a few feet below him, at that fatal moment. Suddenly Ross had called up to him, 'Go back, we cannot get down here'.

"Stewart had continued: 'I climbed a few feet, and then was about to turn. I saw Ross's hand come up and seize a rock. It gave way, and Ross fell like a stone. I got myself into a position where I could see him at the bottom. I watched for some time to see if there was any movement, but Ross lay motionless. There was little doubt that he was dead. Once convinced of this I realised that the only thing I could do was to climb back, make for the hut, and get help. I did not return up the side gully we had descended, but made for the main gully, which was easier.'

Bill Barnes

"To return to the predicament we now found ourselves in. Our job was to reach that body, 250 ft below us. We scouted around for a way down. Ross and Stewart had looked for a route on the left-hand side of the gully. We found a route on the right-hand side, down which we abseiled. Martin descended first as leader of the group. Unfortunately the rope was some two to three feet short of the small grass ledge he was making for, and there was no alternative for him but to drop free the last three feet, with the hope that he would be able to keep his balance when he landed on the ledge – unbeknown to the two of us on top. I saw Pip into the abseil position, and on the word from Martin Pip descended. Then it was my turn, to be told, just before I reached the ledge, that the last few feet would be a free fall. Thank God Martin and Pip were there to hold me as I landed. The ledge was just big enough to hold the three of us in a huddle.

"From this cramped position Martin drove in another piton to enable us to abseil another two rope lengths, which brought us to the bottom of the abyss. From here it was only another few minutes to where the body lay on the rocks. After such a fall there could be no reprieve, and death must have been instantaneous. The body had lost both shoes, and the clothes – a pair of shorts and a jersey – had been ripped to pieces.

"By now it was well after midday. We were now faced with the task of getting the body down to the bottom. We roped it up, using a short extra rope that Martin fortunately had brought with him. With two of us in front and one in the rear we started off, carrying the body as best we could. It wasn't easy.

"We had gone only about 165 ft or so when the first problem presented itself – a waterfall. It wasn't very high, only about 40 ft to 50 ft, but Ross was a big man, and lowering his dead weight down the drop sapped a lot of energy out of three already tired people.

"We carried on, down the gully, slipping and stumbling. Abseiling, of course, was out of the question, as we were encumbered with the body. Then came another waterfall, some 80 ft high.

191

"We held a brief discussion. It seemed heartless, but to lower the body as we had done down the first waterfall was beyond our failing strength. We felt sure, too, that Ross himself would have understood. So when the body was a couple of feet over the edge we simply let go. We followed by abseiling down.

"A few feet further down was yet a third waterfall. This was a fearful looking place, a drop of many hundreds of feet down black, glistening rock, and way beyond the climbing equipment we had with us.

"At this point we decided to leave the gully and traverse out to our left, on to the wall of the Amphitheatre. At this spot the Amphitheatre wall is particularly steep, but it was better than the gully. But those terrible, almost vertical grass slopes! We literally inched our way across this section, hardly daring to breathe, the body pulling heavily against us all the time. Our left hand would hold the grass whilst the right would try to support the body. It was a slow, laborious, energy-sapping business, and time was advancing. The sun had already set, darkness was almost upon us, and we dared not spend the night on those terrifying slopes. To make matters worse, heavy black clouds began to gather around the peaks, and far off we heard the growl of distant thunder.

"We proceeded as swiftly as safety permitted, and at last we came to a vertical drop of only 100 ft, and beyond that we would be back in the gully, with easier slopes. And, best of all, a shout from down below! It was two game guards, well ahead of the rest of help – the main party from the Gorge under Peter Pope-Ellis.

"But that last abseil is one I shall never forget. We placed the body some six feet from the edge of the drop, where a stone prevented it from rolling any further. Martin put in a grass piton. The soil was soft, but before the piton was right home it hit solid rock, leaving an inch or so out above the ground, and thus unable to take any great weight.

"'I hope to hell it holds,' said Martin, as he went down.

"I attached the rope to Ross and coiled the rest of it at my feet. Then I moved the body to the edge of the drop. Over it went, only to become snagged in a small scrubby bush a little more than three feet below the edge of the vertical drop. I was unroped, but I had to get that body moving. Slowly I inched down the side until my foot just touched the body. A slight shove, and suddenly it took off, the coiled rope uncoiling at an alarming rate. And then it happened. The last few coils whipped around my foot, and I thought my last day had come.

"But it was not to be. At that precise moment the body landed, and another Berg tragedy was averted!

"Eventually I got my breath back, the thudding of my heart slowed, and I sat gazing at those fearful slopes opposite me.

"'Why the hell have I got myself into this position?' I thought. 'Why the blazes do people want to climb these bloody slopes? Never again!' I vowed. 'This is my last Berg trip.'

"Little did I know that my mountaineering days were only just beginning.

"Then came Martin's shout: 'Come on!' I got into the abseil position, but the sight of that waving piton was unnerving in the extreme. But it had held Martin, so it would surely hold me, and, hopefully, Pip as well.

"At this stage Pip was sitting a few feet above me but out of sight, and holding on with his teeth. He kept muttering to himself that he had had enough, and that he wanted to get the abseil over with, and that he couldn't hold his position for very much longer. I must get going so that he could move to my position. I bade him good luck and dropped over the edge, the insides of my legs burning with the chafing of the rope as I worked at the task of lowering myself for the last time.

"At the bottom Martin was waiting. The piton held. Could it hold three men? Pip started his descent while we stood gazing upwards in the gathering darkness. Martin shouted 'Don't jerk! Come smoothly. Never mind how much it hurts.' You must remember that in those days abseiling was done in the old classical way, with the rope passing between your legs and over the shoulder, very different from today's more sophisticated methods. After more than 900 ft of abseiling we all had pretty burnt bottoms that day!

"But now our troubles were nearly over. Albert Madonsela and Siquokquo Miya, two of our most faithful game guards, were there waiting for us. Others were still coming up the gully, including Peter Pope-Ellis, who was in charge of the relief force."*

"By now it was 6.30 pm. Thankfully we handed over our burden and headed for Tunnel Cave, where we spent the night. An army of helpers was on its way and we reckoned that we had done our share and could leave it now to others. Mission accomplished!"

They had no food that night, and slept on the bare ground in their clothes. That didn't matter: they couldn't care less. They slept the sleep of the just – twelve solid hours.**

---

* Actually Peter Pope-Ellis's relief party was late. Toiling up to Tunnel Cave and the Gorge that morning Peter saw four figures on the summit returning to the hut from Inner Tower Gully. He assumed – wrongly – that they were Barnes, Winter, Adelson and Osborn who had recovered. They were in fact Ferguson, the Oliviershoek policeman, and two game guards. Peter therefore raced the stretcher and his relief party back to the hotel and up Sentinel Path, and only when he met Ferguson on his way back down did he realise his mistake. Whereupon he dashed back to the Gorge and Inner Tower Gully.

** Martin Winter still farms at Frere with his wife Pam. Bill Barnes has recently retired from the post of Chief Warden of the Drakensberg, and he and his wife Leila have a beautiful mountain home and trout farm at Giant's Castle. But tragedy overtook Pip Adelson. Two years after his epic climb he went to America and died in New York of polio.

Part V

CLIMBER EXTRAORDINARY

Fain would I climb

Line written on a windowpane
by **Sir Walter Raleigh**

No book on the Drakensberg would be complete without at least a reference to George Thomson, one of the most remarkable climbers this mountain region has ever known. Today, after nearly 40 years, his name is legendary, and, as is the case with most legendary figures, innacuracies, and sometimes wild exaggerations, have begun to cluster around his name. We have attempted in this chapter to correct wherever possible these inaccuracies, and we have tried to give a clear and balanced picture of the man whose exploits thrilled all mountain lovers in the middle forties.

23 The Story of George Thomson

George Thomson was a New Zealander who came to South Africa in 1943. He was then about 40. After a period of ill health the doctors had told him that his heart was in a bad way and that he had only six months to live. At the same time his marriage had broken up, and it is probable that these two circumstances were at least partly responsible for his decision to seek pastures new. 1943 saw him at Cathedral Peak Hotel, and soon he was being employed by Albert van der Riet in the building of his hotel.

There came a day in late 1943 when Stan Rose happened to be staying at the hotel on recuperative leave from the Army. Stan was a well-known Cape climber, and a most versatile man. He was, for many years, the holder of the Western Province half-mile record, and the runner-up in the welter-weight boxing championship. He was also a first-class hockey player. In 1935 he was in the parties that made the first ascents of the Little Saddle, Windsor Castle and the Litter, while in the following year he, together with Brian Godbold and Ken Howes-Howell, conquered for the first time that most formidable peak in the Cathedral area, the Pyramid.

At the hotel Stan met up with George, and suggested that he should join a party Stan was forming to climb the Pyramid again. So formidable is this peak that in the seven years since it had first been climbed, in 1936, it had only been climbed once again. This would be the third ascent.

George had never climbed a mountain in his life before, and knew practically nothing of mountaineering, but he said yes, he would give it a go.

They toiled up the lower slopes, managed to surmount the first few pitches, and eventually came to the crux pitch, the hardest of all. The whole party stopped and appeared to be uncertain as to how to tackle this pitch. Suddenly George, the novice, piped up and asked if the others would mind if he took over. They agreed, and to the astonishment of them all, George took the lead and went through to the top like a veteran, first on the rope. For ever afterwards George was hooked!

Most cragsmen learn their art the slow way, by meeting fellow climbers or attending climbing meets. But some men are "naturals", men who clock up difficult climbs right from the very beginning. They still have much to learn from their fellows, but they do this rapidly. George was a "natural", but he was also a loner. He preferred to learn the hard way, from his own mistakes. He loved nothing better than to climb alone, but he also enjoyed climbing with small groups. At the time of his first climb he had had no mountaineering background whatever, although as a young man in New Zealand he had often climbed down difficult rocks to good fishing spots, and climbed back afterwards with the catch. Now he started rock-climbing in earnest, with boundless enthusiasm.

Following on his success with the Pyramid, he made the third ascent of the Bell, in the Cathedral area. This is also a formidable peak, considered unclimbable by the Natal Mountain Club for many years, but it had been climbed by Hans and Else Wong a few months previously. It became his

Gay, debonair, it was the heights that drew him! George Thomson.

favourite climb and he tackled it many times from then on. He loved to introduce others to the climb, experts or totally inexperienced people. Soon after his first attempt at the peak Robin Forsyth asked him if he would take him up, and George agreed.

Staying at the hotel at the time was a young girl, Joy Surgeon (later Mrs Halliday), and George suggested that she come too. Joy was a complete novice, and expressed her apprehension, but George reassured her. "Don't worry," he said, "I'll be holding the other end of the rope." Joy agreed, and enjoyed the greatest thrill of her life, an experience she says she will never forget.

On one occasion the famous Zulu guide, John Mtateni Xosa, was in the party. When they reached the top, George remarked to John that he was the first Zulu to climb the Bell. "Yes," replied John wryly, "and the last!"

John (Mtateni Xosa), famous mountain guide.

It took George some time to learn the value of a rope, especially for the descent. In his early days he climbed peak after peak, alone, and without rope. We think it was probably his sensational ascent of the Column, on 9 December 1945, that taught him his lesson. This must surely rank as one of the finest mountaineering feats of all time.

The Column, 2 929 m (9 610 ft), is in the Cathedral area, a great fearsome-looking fang that towers up a sheer 610 m (2 000 ft) above the foothills. It had long since been written off by mountaineers as completely unclimbable.

But in December 1945 George decided to have a crack at it. He persuaded two other young fellows to come up with him, and on the 9th, a glorious morning, they set off from the hotel.

Arrived at the foot of the peak the first young fellow took one look at the giddy precipices towering above them, and said "Not on your life! You can break your neck if you want to, but not me." So the other two went on alone. After following George up the first easy pitch, the second fellow also opted out. "It was sheer madness," he said afterwards. But that didn't worry George. His climbing party had broken up: he would go on alone! He first saw his companion safely down the rock face, threw the rope down after him, and set his face to the climb. (He was wrong here. Especially in solo climbing a coil of rope is a tremendous help when descending.)

Down below his two companions watched breathlessly as George fought his way, inch by inch, up those terrifying precipices, up and over an impossible overhang, until eventually, a tiny speck against the blue sky, he reached the top.

Anyone who has since climbed the Column, with all the climbing equipment in the world, and with a strong party, will agree that it is a climbing experience to be remembered. That the first ascent had been made solo, by a relatively inexperienced mountaineer, without rope, is almost unbelievable.

The ascent, by any standards, had been difficult. The descent, alone and without rope, must have been a nightmare. Soon after he left the top he found himself on a narrow ledge, with nothing but empty space below him, and unable to reverse his movement. He was alone, on top of a remote, exposed, detached

199

peak, without a rope, and unable to move up or down. He must have realised then the value of a rope to a solo climber. All he would have had to do then would have been to curl the rope over a projecting spur of rock, slide down the double rope to a secure stance, and then retrieve the rope. But he had no rope.

The Column, first climbed by George Thomson, solo and without rope, in 1945.

There are two slightly different stories of what happened. John Poppleton, who often climbed with George, tells how George examined the rock face below him, and then decided there was just a chance he might be able to climb down it. He knew that the almost inevitable would happen, and that he would come off, but 12 m (40 ft) below him was a small bush. He reckoned that there was just a chance that he might grab it as he hurtled down, and so save himself. And that is exactly what happened. He launched himself on the descent, came off as he expected, but managed to steer himself towards the bush. The bush held. He had sustained a nasty gash on the leg, and took a little time to recover, but ten minutes later he was on his way again. If he had missed the bush he would have plunged at least 214 m (700 ft) to his death.

George told me the story rather differently, and I do not think my memory is at fault, even after 40 years.

"Soon after I left the top," he told me, "I found myself on a narrow ledge about three feet wide. I could climb neither up nor down. But about twelve feet below this ledge was another ledge also about three feet wide. I knew I would have to jump it, and I didn't like the look of it, but I said to myself: 'George, my boy, the longer you look at it the worse it gets, so . . . just-you-jump!' I jumped, failed to keep my balance, and fell straight into a vertical chimney. Hurtling down, I managed to slow my descent by pressing my arms and legs against the sides of the chimney, and suddenly, miraculously, I found myself caught in the branches of a small bush. I was a bit shocked, and had a nasty gash on my leg, but," he said with a grin, "I'd made it."

It must have been shortly after his Column climb that the Cathkin episode occurred. Few events in George's climbing career have been more badly misrepresented than this one. Fortunately we have Mike Kruger, veteran climber, who was with George at the time, to give us the correct facts.

Cathkin, at 3 149 m (10 330 ft), is one of the major Drakensberg peaks. It is a free-standing mountain, ringed by tremendous, sheer precipices, but the southern flank is breached by an almost vertical rock gully, and it is up this gully that the usual ascent is made. It is, however, a difficult climb, only to be attempted by experts.

The climbing party, consisting of George Thomson, Emil Perlstein, Joyce Cromhout and Mike Kruger, made good time after leaving Base Camp about 8 am. They were all fit and the weather was good, a clear summer's day after rain. They first climbed Cowl Gully, between Cathkin and Monk's Cowl, and then down the other side for ten minutes before traversing into South Gully (or Cathkin Gully as it is sometimes called). The climb up South Gully also went well, pitch after pitch, but on the second to last pitch Joyce forgot to bring up

201

South Gully, Cathkin Peak, attempted by the Stockers in 1888. It was while climbing in this gully that Thomson fell and broke his ankle in 1945.

the extra rope. George climbed down for it, with Mike Kruger belaying him. Mike then pulled up the extra rope and was coiling it up ready to send down for George when George called up: "Don't worry about the rope. I'm on my way."

Mike shouted down: "Don't be silly, George. Take the rope."

But George replied: "I'm almost up."

And he was. "I could see his blond head just below me," remembers Mike. "To his right there was a crack in which hung a sling, which George took to be one left by Des Watkins' party the previous day. George, to save time, grabbed the sling and, instead of using the rock as he had done the first time, started to use it. It broke, and George shot outwards. I remember him turning in the air, and his first contact as he landed on his shoulder. This shot him out again, and, still tumbling, he next landed on his foot, which was badly hurt. Even this did not stop his descent. He was still tumbling, and next landed on his stomach on a small grass ledge just big enough for his body. Here he stopped and lay still."

It had been a bad fall, 25 m (80 ft), measured by the rope they had. If he had missed this, the next ledge was about 122 m (400 ft) down. He was lucky. Total injuries: slight concussion, badly winded, broken ankle and very painful shoulder.

But amazingly he recovered before any of them could get down to him. He sat up, and called out: "I'm all right. Let me have the rope." He climbed up to them, where they taped his foot but could do nothing for his shoulder. Then up he went, determined to finish the climb, taking the lead again.

At the top, however, the weather changed. It suddenly turned bleak and cold. The clouds came racing up, and within minutes huge hailstones were raining down on them from a black sky. "I have never had such punishment," said Mike Kruger. "You can bet your bottom dollar we were off that summit in double quick time."

Their main concern now was for George, but his main concern was for Joyce. He concentrated on her, and had her securely on the rope all the way. Pitch after pitch down those almost vertical rocks they slowly made their way, with the hail turned now to rain. Off the rock, they had steep grass to negotiate. This George managed by sliding and pushing himself along on his bottom. Then came the climb up to Cowl Nek, which George accomplished on his hands and knees.

But he was obviously in a very bad way, and it was already five o'clock, with the promise of more rain. It was decided that Emil and Joyce should go for help while Mike stayed behind with George.

Emil and Joyce set off immediately, down Cowl Gully to Base Camp in pouring rain, and then along the Mhlwazini River. Fortunately the rain eased off, but it must have been a nightmare journey. They reached Champagne Castle Hotel just before midnight.

But worse was in store for George and Mike. Halfway down Cowl Gully the darkness closed in, and the rain was still pelting down. Mike tried to carry George, but found this impossible. It was too painful for his shoulder, as well as for his knee, which had also been damaged. George leaned on Mike and took short hops on his good foot, but this too had to be abandoned. For one thing it was painfully slow.

Three-quarters of the way down the gully, under an overhang on the Cowl, they sheltered from the rain and took stock of their position. They knew that at Base Camp, more than a hundred metres below them, there was an old tent left there by the Cathkin Hotel people, and which had given shelter to mountaineers for a decade or more prior to the erection of the Keith Bush Hut. If they could reach that they could at least look forward to a comfortable night. In one of their rucksacks they found a small army groundsheet, and they decided to try and use this as a sled. George sat on it, and Mike managed to slide him down the slope, but there were too many rocks and the going again was painfully slow.

By now it was quite dark, but the rain had stopped. Mike found a small tree from which he cut a branch, and George tried using this as a crutch. Progress was now a little better.

About 11 o'clock Mike estimated they must be near the tent, but where was it? For two hours he searched the river banks while George tried to get a fire going. At 1 am Mike gave up the search and returned to George, and then they began to look for food. All they could find was two slices of dried bread and six raisins. They ate the raisins and toasted the bread so they could have something hot to eat.

Meanwhile down at the hotel an uproarious party was in progress. It was Des Watkins' birthday. Suddenly, at midnight, the door burst open and in stumbled Joyce and Emil, on the point of collapse, with their news. The party came to an abrupt end, with all the guests grabbing rucksacks and climbing boots and streaming out into the night for the rescue. Mr van Heyningen, the proprietor, quickly saddled two horses, assembled a mountain stretcher, and soon caught up with them.

Back at Base Camp the fire slowly flickered out, the two men slept, and then came the grey dawn – and the tent only a few metres away from them! Better still, a shout from down in the valley. Emil and Joyce had done their job.

Des Watkins and Van Heyningen were the first to arrive, Charles Gloster much later. He had fallen down a gully and hurt his knee. (Dare one ask whether it was the champagne?) Yet others of the rescue party had themselves to be rescued, but by 1 pm all were back safely at the hotel. Mike fell asleep in his bath, but that night George gave all his rescuers another magnificent party – 36 bottles of champagne among 18 people!

George had had two narrow shaves within a few weeks, Column and Cathkin. He decided this wasn't good enough. He would have to learn roping techniques in a big way. During the next few months he taught himself all there was to learn about the art. He mastered no fewer than 50 different knots. One of these was a trick knot which enabled the climber to abseil on a single rope and still retrieve the rope. The usual procedure is to abseil on a double rope, threaded through a snap link at the top so that it can be retrieved and used again. If you abseil on a single rope, the top is fixed and the rope cannot be retrieved. George mastered a knot which ensured that the top of the rope was firmly fixed. When you were at the bottom, and off the rope, all you had to do to retrieve it was to release the tension on it, give the rope a flick, and it would come tumbling down.*

Then came Mponjwane.

Mponjwane is one of the mightiest peaks in the Drakensberg. It stands near the head of Rockeries Pass in the Mnweni area, a huge, solid block of mountain soaring up into the clouds. It is a free-standing peak, separated from the escarpment by a tremendous chasm, less than 75 m (250 ft) across, but 450 m (1 480 ft) deep. To climb the peak you first have to descend into this chasm, and only then can you start your climb. The peak had been investigated by Bassett-Smith in 1922 and had promptly been written off by this veteran climber. "The peak is perhaps the grandest to be seen anywhere," said Bassett-Smith. "It is a huge pillar of smooth rock, rounded on the top, fully two thousand feet in height, and seemingly inaccessible from all sides. It is too severe a climbing proposition even for baboons."

But this was nothing less than a challenge to a man of George's calibre. He was the last man to accept a statement such as this. His subsequent conquest of the peak in April 1946 established his reputation as a sound, magnificent cragsman, experienced and reliable, and as perhaps the finest mountaineer of his day. Here he was able to test, to his own satisfaction, his newly acquired knowledge of rope-work.

George teamed up with Kenneth Snelson, a young naval officer who was holidaying in South Africa at the time. Snelson was a member of the Cambridge University Mountaineering Club, and had had Alpine experience.

They left Cathedral Peak Hotel before sunrise on the morning of 8 April 1946, with food for four days, and made their way up Umlambonja Pass to the summit (see map no. 3). It was a long, hard slog, their packs were heavy (30 kg or 66 lb), and near the top, which they reached at 2 pm, the altitude began to tell, and their progress was slow. They pitched their tent that night beside a small stream near the Saddle, in Lesotho. It was bitterly cold, and the stars sparkled, clean and bright in a cloudless sky.

Next morning they were up early, continuing their trek northwards along the summit over ice-encrusted grass, which crunched crisply under their feet. By 10 am they had reached Mponjwane Cave (see map no. 2).

This cave is one of the best known in the Drakensberg. Situated in a small lateral gully, it faces directly across to mighty Mponjwane, and is an admirable

---

* This was not George's invention, as stated in *Barrier of Spears*. It was known well before his time to fishermen.

*Mponjwane, south-
west face, showing
Thomson's route to
the summit.
1. Route out of sight.
2. Around shoulder.*

jumping-off place for an assault on the peak. It was the cave in which Derek Schaeffer spent three of the last few days of his life in 1953 (see p. 41).

After making themselves comfortable in the cave, they went out to the edge of the escarpment to examine the peak, only 75 metres away. At first their hearts failed them. Snelson was frankly appalled. George himself wondered whether the peak would ever be climbed. "Grimly," he said afterwards, "I determined to go through with it, though I never at any time overlooked the fact that the mountain would be a supreme test of human ability."

After a preliminary inspection of the mighty face, they descended the 450 metres to the nek between the escarpment and the peak to examine more carefully the quality of the rock. Then, disconsolately, they returned to the cave for a quick meal. They had not found even a vestige of a route on the sheer, appalling face of the giant.

In the afternoon they continued their survey. Snelson went south, in the direction of Rockeries Pass, and George climbed to some higher ground behind the cave. Here, sitting on a rock, he vainly searched the great face in front of him for a starting-point for their climb. Suddenly he saw three wild pigeons flying across four water-worn grooves running up from the base about 450 metres below him. "Concentrating on these grooves," said Thomson later, "I concluded that it might be possible to ascend one of them and make a traverse out to another. At a point where this latter groove looked unclimbable, I saw the possibilities of another traverse on to the sheer face. From then on, for 500 feet or so, the angle seemed fairly easy. That was enough for me. I rushed back to Ken, whom I found waiting at the head of the pass, half an hour's walk away. 'I have found a route,' I exclaimed enthusiastically. 'How about returning to the cave, having a good night's rest, and tackling the monster tomorrow?'"

That night, lying in their sleeping bags, they watched the mists playing around the mighty face of Mponjwane in the moonlight, and listened to the wind in the crags. They thought of the morrow, and wondered what it would hold for them.

Next morning they were again up early. After a quick breakfast, they left the cave at 8 am, climbed down to the nek, and by 8.30 am were ready to start their way up the 550 m (1 800 ft) of precipice that towered above them. After climbing up the two water-worn grooves that the pigeons had shown them, they were confronted by several pitches of "E" standard, almost vertical. The last of these led into a chimney, and then followed two more chimneys, one of which was very narrow, and the other with a deadly overhang. They surmounted this, and then came several slabs of sheer rock, necessitating some extremely difficult traverses. The worst of these was a very steeply sloping slab, but fortunately they managed to find some small, undercut fingerholds in the overhanging face, at about the level of their knees, and this gave them the necessary support.

By this time they had reached the south-east shoulder of the mountain, and were only 100 m (330 ft) from the summit. But the most terrifying part of the

climb still remained. At this point their way seemed blocked. George attempted a slanting traverse to the left, failed, and returned to where he had left Snelson. The only answer was to go straight up. This was, perhaps, the most hair-raising part of the climb, for the rock was vertical, loose and dangerous, but they surmounted it successfully, and the summit could be seen, not far off.

Now they were confronted, however, by a terrific chimney, only five metres (16 ft) high, but with a most dangerous overhang at the top. George took it. In order to surmount the overhang, he had first to find a firm handgrip on the top of the overhang, and then put his full weight on his arms, his legs dangling uselessly into space. Feeling round for his handgrip, he dislodged a number of stones, which cascaded down on top of them and nearly put an end to the climb. All he could find was a loose boulder, but it might just hold. If it didn't, there was nothing to stop him hurtling down 500 m (1 640 ft) to the bottom. Then, with the boulder firmly in his grip, and his whole weight on his arms, he launched himself desperately on to the upper part of the overhang, and just made it. The boulder had held. Another minute, and Ken had joined him. Now the worst was over and the rest easy – a steep grassy slope and one final rock pitch, and they were on top. It was half-past twelve.

They built the traditional cairn, wrote their names on a sheet of paper with the crest of Ken's ship, H.M.S. Glasgow, on it, and placed it in a cigarette tin. This they stowed carefully away in the heart of the cairn. Each man collected a piece of rock crystal as a souvenir, and at one o'clock they commenced the descent. George had by now learnt to abseil, and they abseiled down almost the entire length of the climb. By 5 pm they were back in the cave, the billy was boiling, and the soup ready. By the time supper was over, darkness had fallen, and the moon was shining. They packed up, descended Rockeries Pass by moonlight, and camped for the night at the bottom.

One of the most amazing things about George Thomson was his tremendous vitality and stamina. Remember, he had been given six months to live because of his serious heart ailment. I have known him set out from the hotel at first light with three or four companions. They would climb peak after peak all day and reach the hotel at dusk, his companions almost on the point of collapse. George would shower, tuck into a four-course dinner, and then, spruced up and superbly fit, be ready for the evening's entertainment.

This tremendous stamina is vividly illustrated on the occasion when he took a party up to the top of the Cockade (see map no. 3). This is an easy escarpment peak, just beyond Cleft Peak, looking north-west. When they reached the summit a storm suddenly blew up, with heavy, driving snow. A woman member of the party began to tire rapidly on the descent, and it soon became clear that there was little hope of reaching the hotel before dark. With the weather steadily worsening, George decided to head for Twins Cave where they could spend the night. But conditions soon grew too much for the woman, so George simply heaved her on to his shoulders (he was already carrying a hefty

Mponjwane, south-east face, showing the completion of Thomson's route.

pack) and then carried her right to the cave, at least a couple of hours away. Arrived there the rest of the party sank down, finished, on the floor of the cave. Not George. Despite his own tremendous effort, in sub-zero temperatures, he was soon bustling around the cave preparing a fire and making the best arrangements he could for the night which lay ahead of them.

Another occasion, of course, was his two attempts to recover the body of Tom Pinkney, which we have told on pages 87 to 91.

I shall always remember my first meeting with George. I had heard many stories of this legendary figure, but, though I had done a good deal of climbing in the Drakensberg, our paths had never crossed. In 1945 Albert van der Riet asked me to map (by plane table) the Cathedral area. In 1946 I pitched up late one afternoon at Twins Cave. I was about to make coffee when a wiry-looking man of about 40, with a tremendous pack, strode into the cave. We greeted each other – he was on his way, he said, to the Rockeries area. He shared my coffee, and after supper we sat around our tiny fire, I with my pipe. "Done much climbing in this area?" I asked. "Oh, just a bit," he said, "nothing much." He was far more interested in what I had been doing. Next morning after breakfast we went our respective ways, and it wasn't until a week later, when I returned to the hotel, that I found that my companion of that night had been the celebrated George Thomson.

Stories, of course, of George Thomson abound. We cannot vouch for the truth of this one, but the story goes that at the start of a four-day escarpment trip from Cathedral to Cathkin, one of the ladies in the party insisted on taking along two enormous dogs with prodigious appetites. This meant a large quantity of dog food, and there was simply no room for it in any of the packs. But George was quite equal to the occasion. He grabbed two extra large billy cans, stuffed all the dog food into them, and set off without further ado, carrying one in each hand. He kept this up for the whole trip, in addition to the heavy pack on his back.

What are we to say about George as a climber? He has been accused of recklessness, of taking unjustifiable risks. He was certainly an unorthodox climber. He was also a loner. He never joined the Natal Mountain Club, though he often climbed with individual members of the club. In fact, at one time he was *persona non grata* with the club. They frowned on his unorthodox methods. But was there, perhaps, not a hint of sour grapes? George had shown that peaks hitherto listed by the club as unclimbable could be climbed, and even climbed solo – that the impossible was possible.

Let us admit that when he was climbing alone he did take unjustifiable risks, that he was impetuous. The Column was proof enough of this. We have often wondered whether the sentence of death the doctors had pronounced on him had not something to do with this. If he had to die, he might as well get the most out of life before the blow fell – go out in a blaze of glory. This is possible. But two things are unchallengeable: he can never be accused of lack of courage, and he never took risks when climbing with others, especially with the inexperienced. Here, as a leader, he was superb, with endless patience, care and understanding for the novice.

Harold Corbett, who, it will be remembered, accompanied George in his epic attempt to recover the body of Tom Pinkney, said of George: "You must disregard those who say he was reckless. As a leader he was most cautious, and I had supreme confidence and faith in his ability to lead us safely. If I hadn't had that confidence I would never have climbed with him."

One of his greatest delights was to introduce others to the joys of mountaineering. Strolling around the hotel grounds he would spot a likely "victim". "I'm going to climb the Bell tomorrow," he would say. "Like to come along?"

"Well, I've never done any climbing before, you know."

"Don't worry. I'll show you."

And when the climbing really did begin to get tough: "Now, don't get scared. I'll be holding the rope."

Mrs Joy Halliday (née Surgeon), one of those who, as a novice, climbed the Bell with him, remembers her first meeting with George.

"My first experience of George as a leader," she told us, "was probably about September 1944, when he arranged a trip up to Cleft Peak for two university students, Ken Taylor of Cape Town, another girl and myself. I shall never forget our six o'clock start on a perfect morning, or the breakfast stop when he made a fire (those were the days!), put on the pan and cooked us bacon and eggs. I remember his quiet and humorous encouragement to the other girl when she found the endless slog hard going, and his firm insistence that the two students stick it out and not turn back, though they were near to tears at times with fatigue. I remember the light-hearted fun we had playing in some old snow on the summit, and George falling through into water when he tried to ski. He was a grand companion."

There is no doubt whatever that George's solo ascent of the Column introduced a new era. The impossible could be done. The old days of cautious climbing were over. The young tigers took over. The climbing scene prior to 1945 was completely different to that of subsequent decades. And George was largely responsible for this revolution.

George's last major climb, his last first ascent, was in December 1948. On the 20th of that month he set out with Des Watkins, Barry Anderson and Charles Gloster to climb the Outer Mnweni Pinnacle. All were good climbers, Thomson, Watkins and Gloster in the front rank.

The two Mnweni Pinnacles (pictured on p. 174), not to be confused with the two Mnweni Needles, are free-standing peaks almost due west of the Mnweni Pass. The Inner Pinnacle, a remarkably symmetrical peak, spears the sky like an enormous church spire. Immediately to the east is the Outer Pinnacle, much broader and larger, in effect a long curved ridge of a mountain with only one edge climbable. Neither Pinnacle had been climbed (the Inner was to be conquered the following year), and the Outer was far the more difficult of the two. They decided to climb this more difficult peak.

They set off from the summit of the escarpment at 7.30 am, down an easy gully between the main escarpment and the Inner Pinnacle, descending something like 458 m (1 500 ft). They then contoured round the base of the Inner Pinnacle into the gully between the two Pinnacles. 214 m (700 ft) up this gully (they had roped up by now) they were on the face of the Outer Pinnacle.

After some sensational climbing, which included a 6 m (20 ft) high, narrow chimney, they reached a small ledge and took a breather: it seemed impossible to go any further. But Thomson and Gloster took the lead and went on over a huge boulder like an enormous bird's beak, and then up a terrifying face which necessitated obtaining a hold by putting your hand into a hole and clenching your fist. This was too much for Anderson and Watkins (in any case time was running out on them, and two always climb faster than four) and they decided to remain behind. Thomson and Gloster went on alone.

Some of the most dangerous and severe climbing George had ever experienced lay ahead of them. Chimney followed chimney and on one or two of the sheer knife-edges they were almost blown off the mountain by the wind. Steadily they gained height, and suddenly, one final heave and they were on top.

The mountain has been climbed many times since, but by a different route. As far as we know, this particular route, the Thomson Route, has never been repeated.

Early in 1949 George Thomson emigrated to Rhodesia (now Zimbabwe), where he married Ethel Pole, an old friend of some 20 years' standing.

Late in 1960 George's health began to fail, and he contracted hepatitis. This persisted, affecting his liver, and he died in a Salisbury (now Harare) hospital on 5 May 1961.*

---

* George had four children. Nick, born of his first marriage, became a missionary doctor in Papua New Guinea. A few years ago he left Papua New Guinea and bought a practice in Hunterville, New Zealand, where he still practises as a doctor. He is married and has two sons and two daughters. Nick's sister, Julia, qualified as a nurse and then married a Pastor in Switzerland. They live in Genoa and have four sons. Andrew, born of George Thomson's second marriage, went to Cape Town University to study civil engineering, but after two and a half years he abandoned the course and went to the London Bible College, where he took a degree in theology. He then joined the Overseas Mission Fellowship and was sent to Thailand, where he has spent the last nine years. He is married, and he and his wife work together among the Lisu tribes in North Thailand. Marjorie, George Thomson's youngest daughter, trained as a teacher and taught in what was then Rhodesia until her marriage to Robert Bresler of the Rhodesian Police. They left Zimbabwe in 1980 and are now living in Stanger, Natal. They have two sons.

Part VI

SAFETY IN THE DRAKENSBERG

Out of this nettle danger
We pluck this flower, safety.

Shakespeare, *Henry IV Part 1*

The Drakensberg has rich gifts to offer all who come to its soaring peaks and quiet valleys, but all too often the bright anticipation of the morning has ended in needless sorrow and regret.

We have, in various chapters of this book, touched on some of the hazards and dangers of hiking and climbing in the Drakensberg. We attempt, in this final section, to draw all the threads together and offer to the reader a balanced picture of these hazards, neither exaggerating them nor minimising them. We offer here what we hope will be useful advice to the aspirant hiker and climber in avoiding these dangers.

24 Safety Precautions

The Drakensberg is becoming more and more popular as a place for healthy recreation, as a place of escape from the tensions and turmoil of modern life, and as a place for spiritual refreshment. More and more people are coming to the Berg. And of course, because of this, more and more accidents happen.

Ninety per cent of these accidents should never occur. They are caused by sheer carelessness and ignorance. The Drakensberg is a place of matchless beauty and grandeur. It has rich gifts for the suppliant who comes with humility and respect. But for the casual tripper who could not care less, for the man who goes blithely but mindlessly on his way, heedless of the advice of those who know, it is a killer. We need to create a greater awareness of the possible hazards, and how to cope with them.

What can we do to avoid these totally unnecessary accidents?

First of all, plan your journey well beforehand. Get hold of one of the many excellent maps that are available today. The Directorate of Forestry has issued a first-class series of highly detailed maps of the whole Natal Drakensberg from Mont-aux-Sources to Bushman's Nek. And there are the 1 : 50 000 trigono-metrical survey maps issued by the Government Printer, Pretoria. Study your map well before your trip and plan your route carefully.

Secondly, make sure you are equipped adequately for the trip you have planned. Clothing and food supplies are largely a matter of personal taste, but there are certain essentials that must never be forgotten. Remember at all times to have plenty of warm clothing with you. Even on the hottest summer day blizzard conditions can blow up with startling suddenness. If you are on a summit trip take two sleeping bags with you, even in summer. Wind in cold weather can be a killer: make sure you have a windbreaker jacket with you. Today there are excellent down-filled anoraks (duvet jackets) on the market. You will often get wet while on the march. Make sure you have a change of dry clothing for when you reach your night's camping spot. Shorts are better for climbing than longs, but you must have something to change into at night. Track-suits are excellent for this purpose. Strong leather boots are better than

Some of the equipment necessary for safe camping on the summit in mid-winter.

shoes and "takkies" (and better than high heels!). To avoid blisters wear two pairs of socks, the inner thin, well soaped on the inside with soft shaving soap, and the outer thick knitted, with some talc powder between the two pairs.

Food, even more than clothing, is a matter of personal choice, but make sure that what you select is light in weight. Today there are so many dehydrated foods on the market that this should prove no problem. There is no point in carrying heavy tins of meat when a few packs of soup powder will do the job just as well.

One very important point: always carry more food than you actually require. This need not be anything elaborate: a few extra slabs of chocolate, extra oatmeal – enough to keep body and soul together for a few days in an emergency.

Always remember to fill in a Mountain Rescue Register at your point of entry into the Drakensberg, and to sign off when you return. THIS IS ESSENTIAL. These registers are available at all hotels, caravan parks, camping sites, Forestry offices and Natal Parks Board offices. They require you to give your name, your home address, telephone number of next of kin, colour of your rucksack, your car licence number, how many days' food you carry, what first-aid kit you have with you, and the exact route you intend to take. This information is essential for the rescue team in case you have an accident or get lost. Much valuable time and effort can be wasted as a result of insufficient or incorrect information. The party, for instance, who died in Ship's Prow Pass in 1981 (see Chapter 15) had filled in their route simply as "walk up Cathkin", which was both incorrect and meaningless. If there is a likelihood of your deviating from your planned route, you should say so. Even if you are going for only a short walk in the Little Berg, an afternoon's stroll, always tell someone where you are going.

Summit trips to the inexperienced are particularly hazardous. It is wise to embark on these gradually. Don't make your first trip to the summit a ten-day hike! Make your first trip a single-day one, and learn what the summit is like. At Royal Natal National Park, Cathedral Peak and Giant's Castle it is possible to reach the summit and return in a day. (At Champagne Castle it has been done in a day, but this is a hard, 14-hour slog.) Then go up and spend one night on the summit. See how you like sleeping out at 3 050 m (10 000 ft). It may not be your piece of cake! After that is the time to plan for longer trips.

It is wise to familiarise yourself with the various passes leading up to, and down from, the summit. The main escarpment is nothing less than a gigantic sheer wall of rock, sometimes 305 m (1 000 ft) high. But in the 100 kilometres from Mont-aux-Sources to Giant's Castle there are only 12 to 15 well-known passes breaching this rock wall, and it is wise to know where they are. If you are caught in heavy snow on the summit you may want to get down quickly, and your only hope will be one of these passes.

This brings us to our next point. If you are on the summit and the weather (especially in winter) does show signs of breaking, it is best to get down as quickly as possible, especially if you have had little experience of snow conditions. Sometimes, after days of snow, the passes become choked with snow and ice and it is impossible to get down.

You are out in the Drakensberg, the mist comes down, and you are lost. What do you do?

On no account start stumbling around blindly in the mist. You will soon lose all sense of direction and could easily be lost for days. It is best to stay put until the mist rises.

Sometimes, however, the mist can last for days, especially on the summit. Your food is running out: what do you do? If you are in the Little Berg, there should be no problem, especially if you are on a path. Keep to this path. Mist rarely lasts for long in the Little Berg, and in any case you are usually never very far from an hotel, caravan park or Forest Station. But if you are really caught out, away from a path, and the mist persists, simply follow the nearest stream downwards. All streams in the Little Berg flow roughly from west to east, and will lead eventually either to below the mist belt or to a habitation of some sort.

If you are caught on the summit in the mist, it is a little more difficult, for here there are no paths and the mist can persist for many days, especially in summer. It is still best to stay put, to sit it out, for it can be dangerous to start walking about in mist near the edge of the escarpment.

But if the mist lasts too long, your food is giving out, and you must seek help, the answer is this. Lesotho streams rising on the escarpment flow west into either the Khubedu or the Orange, both of which flow roughly south. If you follow any of these westerly streams you will, almost certainly, reach help within a day or so. Remember that human beings must have water, and that the Basutos always build their huts near streams. In addition to this, there is today a rough but well-defined motor road running north to south (parallel to the Berg) from Butha-Buthe to Mokhotlong, at an average distance of 25 kilometres from the Drakensberg escarpment. Sooner or later (within a day or so) you are bound to intersect this road. And, of course, the mist will disperse at the lower altitudes.

A few general points. Never go into the Drakensberg alone. You are asking for trouble. I will admit that I have sometimes broken this rule, but I was lucky. I managed to avoid trouble. You may not be so lucky! A party should ideally consist of three (or four), one to remain behind with the victim if an accident occurs, and one (or two) to go for help.

Too many people can ruin a party. The pace is always (or should be) that of the slowest, but more important, there have been many cases of one man being missed in a large group, and his disappearance only noted on the return home that night. If you must hike in a large group, insist on the most experienced person being the last man, and the next most experienced person (providing he knows the route) taking the lead. He must never let anyone get ahead of him, and he must also ensure that he is always within hailing distance of the last man. It is a wise precaution for both leaders to be equipped with whistles.

A number of accidents and fatalities have been recorded in the Drakensberg through unstable rocks. The cases of Sally Walker, Doyle Liebenberg, Bernard Shuttleworth and Dick Barry come to mind. There is little one can do to avoid this sort of thing, but experience does help develop a sort of sixth sense within you. If you have a feeling that a particular rock formation is unstable, avoid it.

Never stand on a rock (on the edge of a declivity, or crossing a stream) until you are quite sure it is firm. In climbing, never put your whole weight on a rock until you have first tested it thoroughly. Be particularly careful in climbing not to dislodge a rock if there are others below you. Remember, Drakensberg basalt is friable.

Make a special study of Drakensberg weather. Learn to interpret the cloud formations, the winds, and the signs that accompany a change in the weather. Remember that Drakensberg weather can change dramatically within a few minutes.

We have discussed on pages 147-8 what precautions to take against lightning, and on pages 156-7 what to do in case of fire.

Carry your passport with you if you venture on to the summit. One further word of warning: there have been a number of cases recently of climbers losing equipment to Basuto thieves. They will even filch your boots from your tent while you are asleep! Worse still, there have recently been cases of confrontation between climbers and Basuto herdsmen. On summit trips always have at least one man in your party, which should never consist of fewer than three members.

Never camp for the night in a stream bed. Flash floods can be killers. Remember what happened to the party that camped at the foot of Ship's Prow Pass in 1981 (Chapter 15).

Hypothermia (extreme cold) is another killer. Remember that it is not so much the cold that kills, but cold plus wind plus wetness plus fatigue. Cold alone is seldom the cause of hypothermia. Warmly clad, a person can be quite comfortable at an outside temperature of 0 °C on a windless day. But let the wind speed rise to only 10 km/h and the result would be the same as if the temperature had dropped to –40 °C without wind! The same applies to wetness. Water conducts heat away 240 times faster than air!

It is, therefore, essential to keep warm, dry and out of the wind. We have already stressed the importance of carrying plenty of warm clothing on a trip. In addition to warm woollies, a windproof, waterproof outer garment is absolutely essential.

Remember, too, that body heat is lost much more rapidly from the head than from any other part of the body. There is an old climber's saying: "If your feet are cold, cover your head."

The signs of incipient hypothermia are shivering and footstamping. The victim becomes withdrawn and anti-social. Memory is affected. These signs are followed by mental confusion and loss of co-ordination. As the temperature drops to below 32 °C (normal body temperature is 37 °C) the patient becomes lethargic and sleepy, with a marked slowing of the pulse, until, if conditions are not corrected, coma and death supervene at 27 °C to 26 °C.

To treat hypothermia the patient must be moved out of the wind, all wet clothing stripped from him and replaced with warm, dry clothing. He must then be placed if possible in a pre-warmed double sleeping bag. Putting him into a sleeping bag with someone else is an excellent idea. Hot drinks (but not alcohol) should be given. Extreme cases may need skilled medical assistance.

Finally, don't forget the precautions to be taken against snakebite, outlined in Chapter 18.

We have stressed here the necessity for caution and experience in tackling the wonder-world of the Natal Drakensberg. But we would not like to be mis-understood. There is another side to the coin.

Man has a deep-seated, built-in urge to test himself against the hazards of life, to pit himself against the elements, and we believe that it would be a sad day if the Drakensberg were ever made totally safe. It is this very element of danger that gives mountaineering its peculiar mystique. Man needs to know that deep satisfaction of discovering the limits of his abilities, of being able to stare, unblinking, into the face of danger, and to know that it was good. There is a risk that overemphasis of the hazards of mountaineering may become counter-productive, and may frighten off people who would become better men and women through having had to face danger and still remain unshaken.

"It must be a poor life that achieves freedom from fear," said Aldo Leopold, the great American conservationist. To which we might add the words of Henry David Thoreau: "But it is a characteristic of wisdom not to do desperate things."

Perhaps that is just it. What is needed, we suggest, is a balanced viewpoint. Let us take all due precautions, but at the same time recognise that our young people especially need the challenge of high and perilous adventure. They will find it in the Drakensberg.

The wonder-world of the Drakensberg.

Appendix 1
Statistics of Drakensberg Accidents

According to the records we have been able to compile, there have been 52 fatalities in the Drakensberg and Little Berg over the years. These have resulted from falls, rockfalls, lightning, floods, illnesses, snakebite, blizzards and fire.

In our research we found that many incidents reported in the Press as "Berg dramas" were minor incidents. In deciding whether such an incident should be recorded, we looked at the rescue. If the victim was brought in by helicopter, the Mountain Club's rescue team, on a stretcher, or had to receive hospital treatment, we included it.

These incidents provide so many variations that to draw statistical conclusions from the figures is almost impossible. The highest number of deaths – 29 – have resulted from the nearly 50 falls we have recorded. But what is a fall? Some deaths have been of trained mountaineers falling from the high peaks because of rock friability or equipment failure. Some deaths have been through hikers simply tripping while walking along paths as wide as central city sidewalks. Nine of those killed were climbing alone or had strayed from parties. Two killed were roped together on a climb. One man fell 30 m (100 ft) but a post mortem investigation showed he had suffered a heart attack. How did he die?

The 11 rockfalls have resulted in three deaths. Rockfalls high in the mountains have injured climbers. On the other hand, a woman hiker stood on a rock which rolled. She pitched forward and the rock rolled onto her, causing her injuries from which she died.

Two people have drowned trying to cross flooded rivers. Three others died in a flood – either drowned or crushed by the grinding boulders swept along by the floodwaters. Nine people have become seriously ill in the Drakensberg; three of them died of pneumonia or heart attacks. Some of the seriously ill improved as their rescuers brought them down to lower altitudes – a sure sign of mountain sickness. The survival rate for the ill has improved since helicopters have been able to lift them to medical help.

Missing persons number three. A minister of religion and an entomologist went walking and were never seen again. A third person was reported found – but not missing! A skeleton with leather shorts and a pocketful of gold sovereigns was found on the side of a mountain. Who was this rich man?

Where and when accidents occurred is proportional to area and seasonal patronage. Most falls have taken place in the Cathedral Peak area (18), followed by Royal Natal National Park and vicinity (11). They are followed by the Champagne/Cathkin area, the southern Berg, and Giant's Castle.

The months in which most rescues have taken place are October and December (the October and Christmas holidays). They are followed by April (the Easter holidays). A breakdown of 83 incidents involving 127 people (52 fatalities) shows the following frequency: January 9, February 0, March 5, April 11, May 5, June 6, July 9, August 1, September 8, October 12, November 5 and December 12.

The incidents reported in these statistics have taken place since 1906. The very few accidents up to the early 1940s were almost exclusively among mountaineers, that limited band of people prepared to travel over dreadful roads to the mountains for recreational purposes. From the 1940s patronage increased enormously, with the paths and trails of the Little Berg also becoming popular with inexperienced hikers. In spite of this, it is still safe to say that, statistically, the Drakensberg is a safer place than Johannesburg, Durban or Cape Town.

Appendix 2

Case History of a Berg Adder Bite

The following is a case history of the Berg Adder bite sustained by A. M. Maddison on 20 January 1984 (see Chapter 19).

A. M. Maddison . . . Date of birth 28/12/54

FRIDAY, 20 JANUARY 1984

12h30 — Bitten on right hand, 3rd finger, between knuckle and first joint. Snake not seen. Single puncture wound visible.

12h45 — Slight swelling of affected finger noted around site of wound.

13h00 — Finger swollen considerably. Painful to touch finger or palm of hand.

13h15 — Disagreeable, bitter taste noticed in mouth. Sense of taste impaired. Snake identified from symptoms as Berg Adder.

13h30 — Slight swelling and pain noted in lymph gland in right armpit.

14h00 — Slight blurring of distant vision noted.

14h15 — Blurred vision more pronounced and double vision of distant peaks. Near vision OK. Slight dizziness noted.

14h45 — Vision markedly impaired. Unable to focus on objects more than a few metres away. Unable to stand unaided. Arm muscles painful to touch. Lymph gland painful. Slight feeling of nausea. Taste badly impaired. Tingling sensation in lips. Sense of smell OK.

15h00 — Had a cup of tea and a sandwich. Tea was palatable although tasting strange. Sandwich tasted awful. Felt nauseous.

16h00 — Only able to move on all fours. Vision very poor. Sense of smell still OK.

18h30 — Ate some chicken stew and immediately vomited.

20h00 — Went to bed.

SATURDAY, 21 JANUARY 1984

07h30 — Slept reasonably well. Just able to focus on watch with one eye closed. Pain in throat noticed, similar to a bad sore throat. Swelling in finger reduced but slight swelling in back of hand and 2nd and 4th fingers noted. Lymph gland less painful. Unable to raise eyelids fully. Unable to support head upright for more than a few seconds. Ability to grasp objects with right hand not impaired, apart from some pain. Applied anti-histamine drops to eyes (Corvosan): no effect.

08h30 — Drank a cup of milky tea (no sugar): still nauseous. Lips numb. Inserted right-hand contact lens only and bandaged left eye to prevent double vision.

09h30 — Began descent (approximate altitude 2 700 m). Unable to stand. Unable to focus properly. Most progress made by sliding on my backside and probing possible footholds with a stout stick to check whether or not they were usable and how far away they were. Progress slow. Vomited. No evidence of tea having been digested after nearly three hours. Continually felt drowsy.

11h30 — Partner descended to fetch help leaving me alone with enough food and water for a few days, at an approximate altitude of 2 400 m. Slept most of the time.

224

SUNDAY, 22 JANUARY 1984

07h30 — Awoke. Just able to fill and light petrol stove with difficulty. Eyesight slightly worse: very difficult to make out figures on my digital watch. Still unable to stand unaided. Throat and neck muscles recovered. Swelling in hand virtually gone. Drank some instant chicken soup.

09h30 — Picked up by helicopter.

10h00 — Saline + 5% dextrose drip installed by paramedic at Lower Mnweni Police Station *en route* to Ladysmith Hospital.

11h00 — Arrived at Ladysmith Hospital. Pulse, blood pressure and temperature checked. Examined by Dr J. G. Feberwee. Tested my reflexes very enthusiastically (which made the opposite leg move). Diagnosed crossed reflexes. Questioned me as to whether I had been bitten by a scorpion or a spider, to which I replied I did not see what bit me, but from the symptoms I thought it to be a Berg Adder.

15h00 — Transferred by helicopter to Grey's Hospital, Pietermaritzburg. Admitted to Intensive Care Unit. Examined by Dr Brett Mackenzie who diagnosed classical symptoms of a Berg Adder bite. Drip changed to E2 5 mg Valium administered ND. Food. Connected to ECG. Blood pressure 120/90 (normal). Temperature 36,1 °C. Unable to move eyes at all. Pupils widely dilated. No reaction whatever to light. Very difficult to open eyelids fully. Taste and balance badly impaired. Sense of smell OK. Throat muscles OK. No visible damage to hand apart from small, almost invisible, single puncture wound. ECG, blood pressure and temperature monitored periodically throughout the night.

MONDAY, 23 JANUARY 1984

No significant change in symptoms. In the afternoon, after enquiring whether I was allowed to eat, I was disconnected from the ECG and the drip and transferred to Ward A. Ate some rice and drank milky, unsweetened tea.

TUESDAY, 24 JANUARY 1984

Still no eye movement. Balance slightly improved. No improvement in sense of taste. Still on 5 mg Valium eight-hourly.

WEDNESDAY, 25 JANUARY 1984

Able to move eyes slightly. No reaction to light. No improvement in taste. Just able to read by covering left eye and squinting. No improvement in distant vision. Managed to walk unaided. Taken off Valium.

THURSDAY, 26 JANUARY 1984

Very slight reaction of right pupil only to strong light. Able to move eyes more freely. Vision still blurred and double. Sense of taste slightly improved. Balance OK. Went for a walk outside alone. Difficulty experienced due to double vision. OK when one eye covered. Strength OK. No problem with 30 press-ups. Just able to read a newspaper with both eyes.

FRIDAY, 27 JANUARY 1984

Slight reaction of left pupil to light. Also able to move eyes reasonably freely. Vision still double. Taste improved. A little more able to eat bland fruits without a disagreeable taste. Persuaded Dr Mackenzie to allow me to leave hospital. Able to read and write with some discomfort.

SATURDAY, 28 JANUARY 1984

Vision and taste improved slightly. Double vision very pronounced when travelling in a car.

SUNDAY, 29 JANUARY 1984

Slight improvements again in vision and taste. Able to control double vision. Eyes slow to focus when moving from near objects to distant objects (up to four seconds). Left pupil noticeably more dilated than right pupil. Coloration normal. Second and fourth fingers numb on sides adjacent to bitten finger. Vision improved after dark since both pupils dilated to equal size.

MONDAY, 30 JANUARY 1984

Double vision almost entirely gone. Near vision satisfactory. Distant vision (over 10 m) blurred and distorted. Still slow to focus.

TUESDAY, 31 JANUARY 1984

Slight improvement all round. Visited local doctor. Left pupil still more dilated than right.

WEDNESDAY, 1 FEBRUARY 1984

Distance vision now reasonable. Drove car with sun-glasses to equalise pupil sizes. Double vision gone.

THURSDAY, 2 FEBRUARY 1984

Again slight improvement. Left pupil still enlarged.

FRIDAY, 3 FEBRUARY 1984

As for 2nd February.

SATURDAY, 4 FEBRUARY 1984

As for 3rd February.

SUNDAY, 5 FEBRUARY 1984

Vision and sense of taste now virtually normal.

MONDAY, 6 FEBRUARY 1984

Returned to work. Finger still numb.

TUESDAY, 6 MARCH 1984

Third finger still numb. Tips of 2nd and 4th fingers still slightly numb.

TUESDAY, 1 MAY 1984

Sensation fully returned to all fingers.

Index

Note: Figures in **bold** refer to pictures or captions.

229

Eastern Buttress

Devil's Tooth

Inner Tower

Three Witches

Zigzags

Car Park